THE
LILY NURSE

Rebooted/Re-birthed and
Finding a New Path

JULIA EVANS

BIG MOOSE
PUBLISHING

Copyright © 2020 Julia Evans
Cover Design: @romy
Edited by: Tiffany Wolf @HeliumCommunications
Author Photo Credit: Wyatt Heiberg @TandemXVisuals

Published by: Big Moose Publishing
PO Box 127 Site 601 RR#6 Saskatoon, SK CANADA S7K3J9
www.bigmoosepublishing.com

All rights reserved. No part of this book may be used or reproduced by any means, graphic, electronic, or mechanical, including photocopying, recording, taping or by any information storage retrieval system without the written permission of the author except in the case of brief quotations embodied in critical articles and reviews.

Because of the dynamic nature of the Internet, any web addresses or links contained in this book may have changed since publication and may no longer be valid. The views expressed in this work are solely those of the author(s) and do not necessarily reflect the views of the publisher, and the publisher hereby disclaims any responsibility for them.

The author(s) of this book does not dispense medical advice or prescribe the use of any technique as a form of treatment for physical, emotional, or medical problems without the advice of a physician, either directly or indirectly. The intent of the author is only to offer information of a general nature to help you in your quest for emotional and spiritual well-being.
In the event you use any of the information in this book for yourself, which is your constitutional right, the author and the publisher assume no responsibility for your actions.

ISBN: 978-1-989840-05-4 (paperback)
ISBN: 978-1-989840-06-1 (electronic book)

Big Moose Publishing 03/2020

Thank you to all of those who have been on this journey with me.
It may be that you stumbled on my path for a short time, or you have
been there through it all. I thank you from the depths of my heart. I feel
so blessed and grateful for every soul that enters my life. You are all a part
of my story; even if you weren't mentioned by name, you are still a very
significant part of my journey of enlightenment and self-discovery.

Blessed Be. We're all here for a Reason.

Contents

Acknowledgements..ix
Writing the Book..xi
Prelude...xv
Chapter 1: I Am Ready...1
Chapter 2: Waking Up..3
Chapter 3: Life Couldn't Be Sweeter......................................9
Chapter 4: This Is My Reality...17
Chapter 5: Our Children..19
Chapter 6: Happiness Is...25
Chapter 7: Ladies' Night 31
Chapter 8: This Is Really Happening..................................38
Chapter 9: Okay, Honey - Let's Ride..................................49
Chapter 10: Both Sides of the Vitals Machine....................56
Chapter 11: Debriefing 66
Chapter 12: Lessons From My Father 76
Chapter 13: The Depths of My Abyss.................................80
Chapter 14: DNR (Do Not Resuscitate)..............................90
Chapter 15: Bathroom Priveleges 108
Chapter 16: Something Bigger Than Us Is Always Listening..........120
Chapter 17: Here Is My Story 122
Chapter 18: What Is Happening To My Body?................134
Chapter 19: Where There Is Darkness, There Is Light 136
Chapter 20: Rebooted and Re-birthed 143
Chapter 21: Through My Family's Eyes 157
Chapter 22: Too Much Epi..165
Chapter 23: Is It True? 173
Chapter 24: Good Night and I Love You 176
Chapter 25: Can This Be? 186
Chapter 26: Walking Around the Unit.............................192
Chapter 27: Broken Heart 199

Chapter 28: My First Full Breath of My New Life 203
Chapter 29: Strength and Baseball..213
Chapter 30: The Great Outdoors 219
Chapter 31: Back to Work..230
Chapter 32: Everything Happens For A Reason 243
Chapter 33: One Month Later 246
Chapter 34: Aha Revelation 253
Chapter 35: Till Death Do Us Part 256
Chapter 36: What Happened To Your Heart? 260
Chapter 37: The Quest to Finding My Path 265
Chapter 38: Six Months Later 269
Chapter 39: Leaving It All Behind 273
Chapter 40: One Year Later 279
Chapter 41: Cheryl 281
Chapter 42: I Have Been Heard..295
About the Author 297

ACKNOWLEDGEMENTS

To my husband, Greg, my Light, my Love, my Everything — I love you so much! Thank you for always being by my side, in my corner, and for sticking with me through all of the obstacles, showing me the light within my darkest times.

To my children, Titus and Jayda — I came back for you. Thank you for always showing me the light and love that exudes from you both. You fill my heart with love and make me feel full and complete. You are a gentle reminder of how beautiful life is and how much the love within us needs to be shared with the world. I will always be here, with you both, no matter which plane or dimension I am in.

To my mother — even though you are dead and gone, you will always be in my heart. Thank you for illuminating the way to the existence I was always meant to be in: one full of love and light, joy and bliss.

Thank you to those of you who labelled me The Lily Nurse — in a weird and twisted way, it helped me view this story in a different light, view, and perspective. As I accepted the name, owning it at so many levels, an incredible energy grew around it, which gave me the strength to show the world the person behind that name, to share my side of the story, while helping me find my voice to heal from all of this.

Thank you to all of those who brought me back to life — the staff for physically saving me, and those, like you, the reader, and the ones who cared to listen, who helped me speak my truth, for mentally and spiritually saving me. It's a leap of faith and courage to view these words and to listen to all the details. Thank you for opening your heart, this book, your ears, and your eyes as you view my version, and to really see me for me.

Thank you to Shannon — you provided a safe and protected space to start and finish my book. You supplied me with the energy and love I needed to get my story out to the world; it no longer resides stuck in my heart and in a dark abyss for me to hide from. Thank you for listening to me — listening to me without judgment or your spin on the whole situation. You reminded me to ground myself and look at the bigger picture, which helped me find myself more ways than one.

Thank you to my editor, Tiffany for never judging me or the words I put down in writing. You showed such care in helping me grow my book to what it is today. Thank you for being the first to view the written inner depths of my heart and soul. I appreciate everything you did for me.

And last, but not least, very special thank you to those who have been named within my book, I hope that through me finding my voice, I have also helped you find yours. I recognize that you have your own experience of this crazy ordeal and have suffered in silence along side me. May you find peace, and thank you for helping me on this journey and path I was always meant to be on.

Writing the Book

"Why am I doing this?" I wail to myself, and to you, the readers. "Why am I writing this book?"

As I find these words and write them down in this book, I am reliving it all over again. Every time I write a new chapter, it is a huge shift and realization of what actually transpired....

This actually happened to me!

There's no denying it. No hiding from it. I lived through this! I'm living... this. I'm living through the pain, living the life, living the experience—every moment of every day. It is a blessing and a curse. Constantly being flipped: upside down, right side up, in the dark, in the light, happy, sad.

In this realm, this life that I am experiencing, it's so hurtful and I am so broken by what they did to me. I trusted and gave all of my heart, and they destroyed it (with no consequences).

I just carry on....

I try, with everything in my being, to wrap my head around it. I don't even have to try to relive that memory; it just plays over and over in my thoughts. I try to disassociate from it, try to make it a passive memory, not one that owns me.

So, I created this book to let it all go. To be free from that moment of pain and suffering. To look at it from a different view, a different perception, a different perspective.

I died and came back!

I got to see and experience something beyond anything that anyone could imagine, and to put it into words is bliss! I get little tastes, little snippets of it, here in this realm.

There's good and bad in everything we do. There is dark and light in everything we do. It's yin and yang. I am on this path, this journey, that no one understands. No one gets it, because no one else has ever experienced it. No one can even begin to understand my journey. I could write books upon books.

I'm giving you a little taste of what I go through, what I've been through. Maybe that's why I'm writing it? Maybe I'm writing it to have a voice?

I'm looking for my voice; I'm trying to find that word, the missing link or missing piece. It's so that I can wrap my head around it, so tht I can write it down and read it, as if it is not my story. Because what I have experienced, what I have been through—you can't even make this shit up!

This is just beyond!

Time does not exist, as I write this book. It moves so incredibly fast. As I write each word, each sentence, each paragraph, it's as though I am back in time. Now I'm trying to conceptualize it all in a different light, a different angle, and looking at it with a different view, a different perspective. I become more aware and awakened as I write and see these words written before me. I can ponder and come to new revelations of what this all means, and what I am, and have gone through.

It feels like it has taken years or decades to write down this story. It feels like ages for me to be able to find the right word, or to put it down into words. I try not to be consumed with all of the emotions, the feelings, as I am regurgitating it onto the computer, and onto paper.

And still, as I tell my story and write it down for others to see, I think of how others are going to perceive it. I try to break it up so that it is not too raw, not too emotional. I cushion it for the reader. Why? Why am I doing that? It sure as hell wasn't cushioned for me. I need to write how it happened, how it all felt, and how I perceived it. It's like looking through my eyes as you read my journey and my experiences through all of this.

I want people to understand and feel for a moment how I felt. Get a glimpse at what I went through in hopes that it may help them cope through things they have gone through. It may help them find the things they need to find in order to heal, which may help them find their own voice.

I write to be heard. I don't want to be ignored and put into the shadows anymore. I want people to get a sense of how I felt, what I have gone through. I want to have someone, anyone, listen and perhaps understand. I have all of this pain inside and I just want to transfer that pain somewhere else. Not so that someone else can absorb it...but so that someone else can understand it. So I know that I am not alone and dealing with it single-handedly in the shadows anymore. I want to be heard – that in itself has a power to heal.

It feels so good to get my story out, to have it written on paper for others to see, to finally be heard, to find my voice! It's been a true healing journey for me to relive this experience in a different light and learn from it.

It is absolutely fascinating which portions I remember, which ones were significant to me, and why I hang on to those memories. I'm putting them onto the computer, onto paper, to highlight the significance for others, so that they can grasp it, relate to it.

Some days I feel like I write for months. Then I look at the clock and it's only been a few hours and a few paragraphs. I think this story is never going to end—really, it's not, if you think about it. This is just a taste of what I have actually gone through. It's a sample. I don't know what people are going to get from this. I don't even know all of what I am going to get from this. I just know within my heart that I have to get it out. Maybe it's the belief that the pain in my heart will go away once I finish and get that last word, that I'll truly start healing from it. I don't know.

My heart broke on every level. Now it is healing at every level. This is very powerful! It's a powerful realization: We can break within a split second, but it takes a hell of a lot longer to heal, to become whole again. Maybe that is a fear in itself? That I'll become whole again, only to break again... it's a vicious twisted cycle. Every time we heal and break, we learn.... It's all part of the journey, all part of our path, our journey in this life.

The trick is to find balance, right in the middle: not too much of a good thing, not too much of the bad. Be Centred.

It's as though I am writing a weird kind of journal, not a properly written memoir.

I'm so excited to get it out, and to talk about it. I am excited to be free! Free to be me! It is time to spread my wings, and just to be... who I was always intended to be—*me!*

Prelude

~  ~

For many years, my focus was western medicine. Ever since I was three years old, after my mother died, I wanted to help heal people: to make them better, to help them not suffer, not feel so much pain, not be sick—in essence, help ease their pain and suffering. I believed the only way to achieve this was to become a nurse!

I clearly recall, at that tender age, determining my purpose in life.

>What I needed to be.
>What I was meant to be.

"I want to be a nurse when I grow up," my three-year-old self announced. She was very convincing, and very determined.

Ever since that moment in my life, I strongly believed in my heart, mind, and soul that this was the ultimate path for me—my calling and my purpose. I was utterly convinced that to help heal people, I would have to do it through western medicine and become an incredibly caring, strong and knowledgeable nurse. I wholeheartedly believed that this was the only way.

Or so I thought, until the Universe had another plan for me!

And so begins the story of…

THE
LILY NURSE

Rebooted/Re-birthed and Finding a New Path

Chapter 1

I Am Ready

~  ~

I have been struggling with everything that's happened. I've been consumed with trying to find my new path. I have seen so many signs that the Universe provided, yet I still feel lost, alone, and afraid.

It's very difficult for me to let go of my past. My former self. The person I thought I was meant to be. The path I set forth on at the ripe old age of three.

Who am I?

I loved the old me. I had become the incredibly caring, strong and knowledgeable nurse. And now it's a thing of the past. A former life. A memory. Something I feel I need to let go of. To grow from. To grieve.

I'm trying to put puzzle pieces together. And trying to figure out what I need to do, what direction I need to take.

It's grueling to try to look back at what happened. And to think of what is going to happen. I have to realize no one can tell me what the future will hold for me. No one can tell me the correct path I should take, or which path will lead me to the place where I am meant to be.

I am standing here with open arms, pleading for help. Here is my cry:

I ask the Universe to further guide me to the path I am destined to follow. I fully believe within my purest soul that I am ready for what is on my horizon. I ask upon the moon, sun and the stars to light my path to what is meant to be.

I am grateful for my new life! Blessed Be...
I call upon you to lead me.
I am Awake! I am Alive!
I am ready for my new journey...

Chapter 2

Waking Up

As I open my eyes and look around the room, I am astounded that I, Julia Evans, in fact, woke up.

I survived the night!
I am awake!
I am alive!

Thank God I'm here to live another day. I'm flooded with emotion. This was not a dream or a nightmare. This was happening…

I awake in the morning lying in a hospital bed. *My* hospital bed! I am so weak. I just lie there for a moment with my eyes open. I am still. Very, very still…

I take several long blinks as I try to absorb my surroundings. I'm imprisoned in a hospital bed. All the side rails are up, and I just lie there in an unnatural semi-upright position. I slowly turn my head to the right and notice my hospital room door is closed. I'm closed off from the world. I'm all alone in this room, isolated, and trying to figure out this new reality. It's so eerie and cold, yet it has a beautiful peacefulness. It's as though all five of my senses are waking up for the first time. As if this is the first day of a new life.

I take in a long deep inhale through my nose. I smell plastic. There's oxygen tubing up my nose, bringing oxygen to my nostrils, to my lungs, to my exhausted, drained, depleted, decrepit body. I'm breathing. Struggling, but I'm breathing. I rest my eyes and take in another deep inhale, followed by a quick exhale.

I look down at my chest. It feels so heavy. So sore. As if someone jumped on it, repeatedly. My lungs struggle with each inhalation and exhalation. And my heart...well my heart hurts! It feels like every beat is a struggle for my heart to keep beating. Fighting to keep me alive. It's slow. Really slow. I'm connected to all sorts of wires (leads) upon my chest. These wires extend from my chest to a monitor that watches my every heartbeat. And the monitor lays so nicely in a strategically sewn pocket in the front of my hospital gown.

I have no clothes on except for this oversized hospital gown which is draped over my frail little body. I am covered with a synthetic fleece hospital blanket. It's scratchy and has obviously been through the wash several times, but at least I'm covered. Still, I feel very exposed and vulnerable. I'm overwhelmed by this reality.

I cannot believe this is happening! That all of this actually happened! *To me!*

I question myself, *Is this really my world, my existence right now?!*

Am I really alive?

THE LILY NURSE

I cannot fathom the circumstances I've been presented with. The emotions I am feeling are literally suffocating. Debilitating. I want to scream, cry, swear.

FUCK!

My eyes are overrun with tears and they spill down my face, over my cheeks, onto my lips. I can taste the saltiness of my tears. I feel my eyes swelling from the abundance of fluid expelling from my tear ducts. I hold my hands to my face and cover my eyes to escape for a moment. To hide from this reality. To close off at least one of my senses, just for a moment. This new world is so surreal. I can't wrap my head around it.

The last thing I remember before falling asleep, before the medication knocked me out, was an old nursing school friend sitting beside me. She was assigned to be my nurse that evening during her night shift. I remember her going above and beyond for me. This is truly her nature; most of us nurses have this nature. But what she did for me, meant more to me than anyone could have ever imagined. She just sat beside me. Validated me. Acknowledged all of what I was feeling and went through.

"I'm scared to close my eyes!" I voiced my fear, looking up at her from my hospital bed. It was as if she could read my inner soul, seeing and sensing all my pain, anguish and fear.

"I am watching you and monitoring your heartbeats," she said in a soft, confident, reassuring voice. "It's on my monitor at the nursing station too and I will be close by all night. You have had quite a day. Take the Lorazepam and get some sleep. I will sit beside you as you drift off to sleep."

She sat down beside my bed, in the oversized cream-colored pleather chair placed in the corner of my room, slightly above the right side of my head. There she sat, in the darkness, supporting and comforting me. We talked at first, but after a few minutes of chatter we both became silent. It had been quite a day. For all of us.

Her presence, just her being there, gave me a feeling of relief, a sense of comfort, and a stillness. It provided me with a much-needed sense of safety. This allowed me to give my mind permission to close my eyes and fall into a deep restful sleep. I started to have longer blinks as the medication took effect. And there she sat, honouring her promise.

Now, after a night of rest, a night of turning off from the real world, I am faced with the morning and this new reality. This new beginning.

I take another breath, this time really emphasizing my exhalation. I remove my hands from my face and place them on my chest, over my heart. I open my eyes and look up. I take another long deep breath. And I smile!

I Am Alive!

The door swings open and there is my friend, my nurse, finishing up her shift. Routinely doing her morning rounds.

"Good morning, love." She greets me with the most beautiful angelic smile.

"I woke up!" I announce in awe, trying to fight back my tears. I can feel my eyes welling with tears again.

"Yes, you did!" she reassures me as she continues smiling, walking towards me, fighting back her own tears as well. "Now let's get you up to the bathroom." She approaches my bed and drops the side rails—what a sense of freedom!

I remove the oxygen tubing from my nose and tuck it under my pillow for later use and to keep it from falling on the floor. I try to sit up quickly but am unable to achieve this task. Something so simple, something most us can do with ease and without thought, is now methodically done with assistance. I'm slowly positioned to sit at the edge of my bed. I am dumbfounded that I am so weak. I take a moment to adjust to this new awareness of my body. I take a few more deep breaths. I gaze towards the bathroom in my room, which is only a few feet away, and I dread the thought of having to walk all the way there.

Another nurse enters my room and together they help me up and to the bathroom, one on either side, supporting me in case I can't make it. Like two angel wings helping me to fly—or in this case, walk 10 feet to the restroom. And it will be a well-deserved rest on the toilet for a moment after the exertion of getting there. This is truly a display of dependence. Weakness. Having to depend on not one, but two people to assist you to the toilet to expel your stored bodily fluids. At this time yesterday I was running on the treadmill at the gym.

We made it. Wow, what an accomplishment! The two nurses slowly lower me onto the toilet seat. I readjust the front pocket that contains my heart monitor, so it lays more comfortably between my breasts. As I'm doing this, one nurse lowers the side rails attached to the wall and places them on either side of me. I am exhausted. I sit upon the toilet and release a loud exhale, hunch my shoulders, and lower my head, like a sad, defeated soldier.

"Who would have thought that getting to and sitting on a toilet could be so draining?!" I laughed out loud, breathing quite heavily at this point, as if I just completed a 10-mile run.

My friend/nurse is laughing too as I cut the tension with my giggles and disbelief of this situation. I sat there on the toilet, my throne, my trophy for my strenuous 10-foot walk. I rest there with her hovering over me like a worried mother hen watching her frail new chick.

"I'm not leaving your side," she announces. "You're too weak."

"Well good thing I don't have to poop; that would be awkward," I sheepishly chuckle. "And I know from experience that it could cause a vasovagal reaction and you'd probably have to pick me up off the floor. And besides, I'm too scared to take that risk." We both muse at the awkwardness and thought of that image.

After I complete my morning task of expelling my urine, one of the other nurses helps me into a pair of oversized hospital drawstring pants. Now that is a sense of empowerment, having all your bits covered and not feeling so exposed and vulnerable! We then conquer the assisted walk back to my hospital bed.

I am so drained. I place my oxygen tubing back into my nose, partake in several inhales of the oxygen, and fall back to sleep.

Chapter 3

Life Couldn't Be Sweeter

"Mom! Bike faster! Try to race us home."

Titus and Jayda are clearly beating me to the driveway of our house as they call to me with excitement.

Jayda is first to reach the garage, already punching in the code to raise the door. She's panting from the exhilaration of winning the bike race around the block. Of course this competitive and energetic nine-year-old girl would be the first at the door. With her drive and motivation, she could be the CEO of a large corporation, and still have the energy to compete in a race around the world. She has a lean, athletic physique and always wants to improve her performance in everything she does. She has no interest in fitting into the mold society has for how she is meant to be, or how she should be presented. Never conforming. Never stopping. Always moving.

She's: Just Jayda!

Titus is merely seconds behind his sister on the driveway. He's got an old soul for a thirteen-year-old boy, so gentle and kind—a real teddy bear! He wears his heart on his sleeve, so pure and full of love. His genuine caring nature has him always checking on his loved ones, making sure that they are okay, that they feel loved and cared for. He's chill and laid-back, but has an instinct to protect those in need, objecting wrongs and standing up for what's right. His broad shoulders and stocky stature remind you of a strong soldier with wisdom beyond his years, but he's still young enough to be squishy and snugly. He likes to sit back and observe, watching the world with cautious, protective and loving eyes.

He's: The Boy!

Now they are both celebrating in the driveway, teasing and taunting me with their victory. They are both gleaming with the pure satisfaction of their triumph. Once again, they won a race against their mother. Even though I wasn't trying. I could have beat them hands down, if I wanted to.

I gracefully glide onto the driveway without a care in the world, smiling from ear to ear. I'm taking my sweet-ass time to get up to the garage. The sound of my retro 90s dance music from a tiny speaker in my bicycle basket announces my presence. The kids laugh at my laissez-faire speed and persona.

"I didn't want to show you guys up," I banter, as they laugh hysterically at my loss. "Besides, I was digging the song that was playing." I snicker at my not-so-cool portrayal of myself.

"Let's have a quick snack before baseball; we'll leave in 15 minutes," I shout up the driveway, hoping they hear me. They've already put their bikes away in the garage and are racing each other to get into the house.

It's always a race with these two, a fun competition to display who is the fastest, the strongest, the top dog. They are pushing and laughing, doing whatever they can to beat the other to the door. I laugh and shake my head at their playfulness.

I take a moment for myself before entering the garage. I just stand there with my bicycle in the middle of the driveway and take a mental picture of this beautiful moment.

My ears fill with the joyful sound of my children laughing as they enter the house. The music brings me back to my youth and my smile widens. I'm intrigued at this tiny little contraption with just enough sound to radiate in a 10-foot circumference around me. It's the only thing in the dark brown wicker basket hanging on the oversized handlebars of my beautiful "old-lady cruiser" with its extremely large cushioned seat.

I love this bike. It gives me such a sense of freedom to be able to glide through my town with such ease, not putting any pressure or strain onto my body. Mobility freedom! This freedom allows me to partake in our family fun outings. Our family unit loves to have fun! We always say: Live life to the fullest. Consider every moment a blessing, and never take anything for granted. Life is just too short, and too important to be taken too seriously. So, enjoy it!

I hold that motto within my head and my heart, with the image of all of us living life the way we know how, through laughter and playfulness. I visualize all of us being in a playful moment—enjoying every second.

I feel the warmth of the sun beaming down on me. It kisses the top of my head, starting at the roots of my long, flowing, dark brown hair and trickling down the rest of my body. It's like I'm being cradled in a giant loving hug that's wrapped around my entire body, from head to toe, soothing me from this outside environment to my inner core. My outer and inner being are filling with warmth, love and light.

The children's hustle, bustle and laughter have moved inside, and

I can acknowledge the stillness of our neighborhood. Our quiet little community is tranquil and peaceful. It's so warm, loving and inviting, just like the sun beaming down on me. I close my eyes for a moment, feeling the caress of a soft breeze through my hair. I'm absorbing it all in, totally lost in my thoughts…

"Mom!" Jayda calls, interrupting my Zen moment. "Titus says I have to come to the baseball practice."

I snap back to the present but am a bit shocked at how far I'd drifted into a reflective state of mind. *Wow, that's not like me to go so deep into my thoughts. Oh man, I was really in another space.*

I shake my head to awaken myself from my meditative state and to fully come back to my awareness of the task at hand.

"Yes, Jayda, you have to come to practice" I say. "It's going to be fun! Make sure you grab a snack. Sounds like you are getting hangry."

I have to laugh at the fact that they are already at each other, bugging and pushing each other's buttons. And that my little reflection had been abruptly interrupted. I figured this was good timing on Jayda's part. I did have to get my butt in gear; I still have to get dressed in my baseball attire. Since I am helping with the team this year, I should look the part. In my son's 13 years of sports, this is my first opportunity to assist with coaching or managing. I'm so excited and quite nervous. I really know nothing about baseball aside from the basics: Throw the ball. Hit the ball. Catch the ball. And there's some running. Oh yeah, and the bases. So, I figure I should at least look the part!

I quickly put my bike away and run through the house to the stairs, passing the children devouring their food at the island in the kitchen, quietly enjoying their snacks. Oh, how I love that they have the knowledge and ability to be so independent and make their own food. It's sure a time saver.

Once I reach my closet upstairs, I realize I don't have any idea what to wear. I slightly panic at the thought of what a manager is supposed to wear for baseball practice. That's my thing: always look the part, portray confidence, and the rest will follow. *Seriously, what am I going to wear?* I think to myself, feeling quite flustered. I can't find anything in this closet that characterizes a confident, go-getter, team-spirited manager. I'm putting myself into a tizzy.

"Calm down," I imagine my husband saying to me, as he has done in the past, "Relax! No one really cares what you're wearing. Just throw something on."

Then inspiration hits. "Hah, knickers!" I quietly say to myself with excitement. That would work! I lean over the railing and call downstairs, "Titus, do you know where your old baseball knickers are?"

"Dad washed them," he calls back up. "I don't know where he put them."

Darn. I guess it really isn't necessary to wear the white baseball knickers to practice. Besides, I'm just managing the team and as long as I'm involved and engaged, it will all work out. I look up at the clothes hanging in my closet and spot a royal blue Broncos baseball shirt. Perfect! I'll have the right team name and colour on.

"Mom, you almost ready?" Titus calls from the bottom of the stairs. I can sense his excitement to get moving and arrive at the field.

"Just need to put on pants!" I call back.

Shit! Pants! I frantically think. *What the hell am I going to wear for pants?* From the corner of my eye I see my black ringette sweats. "Perfect!" I slip them on over my Lululemon shorts, tuck in my blue Broncos shirt and fly down the stairs, just in time to gather both my kids back into the garage and set forth to another journey, this time to the baseball field.

"Looking good, Mom," Titus says with the biggest smile on his face as he puts his arm around me, embracing me into his side, making us pause our world for a brief moment. He's a lot like his father; he always seems to sense exactly what I need to hear and feel within this crazy world. He's my protector, my calmer, the one who takes it upon himself to help ground me. He has always done this with me, ever since he was a wee little boy. He encourages me to breathe and free myself from the self-inflicted stress.

"Thanks, handsome!" I grin back at him, as my heart fills with pure joy and warmth. "You're looking great yourself."

"Thanks, Mom," he says, giving me a squeeze before releasing his embrace.

"Got all your stuff?" I question.

"Sure do," he reassures me, before going through a verbal check list. "Bat, glove, hat, water, Spitz! Got it all Mom, and I brought water for you and Jayda too."

"Thank you. Okay, let's go!" I say, excited to start this season of baseball.

As we separate from our embrace, I notice Jayda sitting quietly in the backseat of the car. Her head is down and she's pouting about having to come to practice. I recognize her need for attention and softly say to her, "Jayda, are you okay?"

"I don't really want to go to the baseball diamond," she mopes. "All of your attention is going to be on Titus, and I'll have nothing to do." She lowers her head further, looking at the water bottle in her lap and avoiding eye contact.

"Jayda," I say, "I understand that you want all of my attention, but sometimes we have to share me with your brother. Think of all the times I helped your ringette team. I was the manager a few times, and I helped with coaching. It's Titus' turn now. He has never had me help out with any of his teams." I'm trying to illustrate the bigger picture for her to understand.

"Besides," I continue, "I need you there. I know nothing about baseball." I gesture with head and hand signals to express my hidden truth and expose a tiny bit of my inner fear of not being good enough to do this task at hand. "Maybe you can help me. You can be my sidekick, my assistant, or better yet, you could help the whole team by being our mascot!"

She looks up at me with the biggest smile on her face. "What do I have to do as the mascot?" she inquires eagerly.

"You would be a big part of the team," I say. "Bring the team up! Cheer them on and help make this season fun!" I use jazz hands to really emphasize the fun.

Jayda's aura lightens and now her voice exudes a spark and passion to be there. "Okay, that sounds good, Mom. I'll help you!" She sits straight with shoulders up and back. Her head is held high, signaling her pride and yearning to be part of the team.

Titus is clearly annoyed with the delay, but he swiftly jumps out of the car. Jayda and I look at each other with bewilderment. He rustles around in a bin at the back of the garage and pulls out a small baseball glove which he hands to Jayda. "Here, so you really feel like you're part of the team. Now let's go," he casually says. "I don't want to be late." Then he jumps back into the front seat of the car, as if nothing happened. Jayda's and my eyes connect in the rear-view mirror and we smile at each other, silently noting this small but grand gesture from Titus to boost his little sister's spirit.

We back out of the garage, with music blaring, wind blowing through our hair and the anticipation of our new adventure.

We set forth down the street towards the next town to our first baseball practice.

I yell out with excitement, "Here we go! This is going to be fun!"

CHAPTER 4

THIS IS MY REALITY

"Julia."

I can hear someone softly saying my name. I slowly open my eyes and begin to focus on a room full of visitors, spectators who hover over me, staring down at me in bed. My confining, uncomfortable hospital bed. I try to quickly adapt to the foreign unpleasant surroundings I am woken to. My thoughts are surging through my brain like a freight train. *What is happening? Why are these people hovering over me?*

"Julia. you're alive!" one spectator says, attempting to reassure me and emphasize the craziness of this reality. "You gave us one hell of a scare!"

"Oh, Julia, thank God you are here!" another one says through her tears, bringing her hands to her face in a prayer-like position.

Another just stands there in shock, crying silently in the back of the group. Tears saturate her face.

Yet another slowly approaches me with arms open. She leans over my side rails to embrace me, tears pouring from her eyes. She can't bring herself to say anything other than my name, as if her words are struggling to come, not wanting to be spoken for all of us to hear. As though what she wants to say is too heartbreaking and too surreal to put into words.

They surround my bed, staring down at me as though a mystical creature lays before them. None of them veer their gaze away from me; they just stare in awe at me, with an uneasy stillness. None of us want to take in a full breath of this situation. There's a sense that if we did, we would all have to accept the reality of what actually happened, and face the reality of the person, me, who lays upon this hospital bed, broken, but alive.

At this point, my brain cannot even begin to compute what is happening. It tries to turn off and separate from this reality—tune it all out!

Escape this reality and create a world that is comprehensible!

I am aware of my surroundings now, but do not accept them. I am aware that I lay before these people in a cold and unsettling hospital bed. I can hear myself talking to them. I am aware that I am making jokes to try to make light of this situation. I can hear them trying to converse with me, telling me their perceptions, their reality. But I still am not truly comprehending it. I tune it all out and close off my mind, not wanting to acknowledge this reality.

But the blatant and brutal fact is
This *is* my reality!

Chapter 5

Our Children

"Mom, I love you." Jayda whispers in my ear as we snuggle up on the couch to watch a movie.

"I love you too, Jayda." I respond with a smile. Her beautiful soft-spoken words make my heart sing and fill with joy. Her loving nature is so pure and heartfelt. I hold her tightly in my arms, giving her a loving squeeze and kissing the very top of her little head, then the middle of her forehead.

"Can I join in, too?" Titus inquires, hovering over us. He asks permission to join in even though he already knows the answer, standing there wanting to snuggle up with us like a litter of kittens. I love it when our kids want to do this. We tend to do this when we need to feel more connected, loved and protected in this world, to just be with each other and let our troubles melt away.

"Of course you can," I respond with a huge smile, making room for him to join in. He lays beside me and nuzzles into my side. I wrap my right arm around him like a protective wing and kiss him on the middle of his forehead too.

"I love you, Titus," I say to him in my nurturing mothering voice.

In that moment, all I want is to hang on to my two babies, our arms entangled around each other to create a comforting and protective little nest on the couch for the three of us. Time stands still, for just a moment, so we have time to breathe and *be*. We hold on as if we are completely inseparable—one completely connected, loving and protected entity.

"I love you too, Mom," Titus says as he squeezes me back.

The three of us watch an entire movie snuggled up like this, no wiggling or squiggling, no bickering or horseplay between the children. No one really moves except to give the occasional loving little squeeze. With our arms wrapped around each other we just lay together like nothing else in this world matters but the love between a mother and her children. The feeling of safety, belonging, protection and unconditional love is what we all need and crave.

Life can't get any sweeter!

As the movie credits began to play, Titus looks up at me and asks, "Mom, can I read my speech to you? I have to read it in front of my class, but I want you to hear it first."

"Yes, of course you can," I say enthusiastically. "I would love to hear it. What is it about?" I'm a bit surprised and intrigued by his request.

"It's a speech we had to write about optimism," he reports.

"Well, I am very excited and honoured to have you read it to me," I say, grinning from ear to ear. "Let me sit up in the chair, and you can have my undivided attention."

THE LILY NURSE

I sit up straight in one of the bistro chairs in front of our bay window, as if it's a front row-seat to an award-winning performance. Jayda perches herself upon my lap, wanting to be included. Titus' sudden need to share this with me is really intriguing. He's never really been eager to share any of his homework with me before. Actually, I haven't really seen him excited about any homework before—especially not a speech he had to read in front of his class.

My heart is fluttering with excitement.

"Okay, Boy," I say. "We're all ears; begin when you're ready." I nod and give him a beaming smile. Jayda and I give him a thumbs up, our eyes fixed on him like glue, ready and eager to hear his unexpected, independently written speech.

He raises a paper copy of his speech to chest level, looks down and hesitates for a moment before he begins to read it aloud. He changes posture, stands up tall and proud, looks at Jayda and me, then calmly and assertively recites his speech.

> "My speech is about optimism. What is optimism? According to my research on Google, the definition of optimism is, 'hopefulness and confidence about the future or the successful outcome of something.' The most optimistic person I know is my Mom. So, I based my speech on her."

My ears perk up, and I listen even more intently, sitting at the edge of my seat in awe. *Did I hear that right? Did Titus really write a speech about me? Yes, I really did hear this. Titus really did write a speech about me. His mom! And he's reading it out loud before me, right here, right now!*

> "My Mom was diagnosed with Multiple Sclerosis (MS), just over two years ago. At first, she felt like nothing would go her way. Then she became optimistic. She always looks at things that will get

her up, never down. Even now when nothing goes her way she still looks at it positively and never with a negative thought.

What is MS? MS is a disease that eats away at the myelin. That is the protective layer of the nerve. This causes the brain's messages to the body to be interrupted. My Mom has many interrupted messages to her body, also known as symptoms, like numbness, pain and optic neuritis. Some nights in the past, when my Mom was really weak and unable to walk, I had to carry her up the stairs. It was scary! But even though it was scary, we all still managed to laugh, be silly and make it a positive experience. My Mom has taught me to be optimistic, even when things get scary. She always makes everyone around her happy.

Since my Mom has found out she has MS, she has been fundraising to find a cure; and is always optimistic that they will find a cure. That is the reason she does fundraising: to hopefully find a cure. When there's people like her everything feels good even when times are rough. If everyone was optimistic like my Mom, the world would feel greater and everything would turn out better. If everyone was optimistic the world would be better because everybody would build each other up and not down. What the world gains from optimism is a happier world. As my Mom always says, 'Everything is a blessing, if you just look at it positively.' My Mom builds people up by trying to help them find their strengths. If we would just find each other's strengths, be positive and build each other up, the world would be a happier place."

(Written March 16, 2017 by Titus Evans, Grade 6.)

As he finishes reading his speech, I'm completely speechless. I sit there stunned, proud and honoured, with a slight tear trickling down my cheek. This blew me away! It was so well written, so expressive, with such a profound message. And he wrote it about me!

Oh my God, he based his optimism speech on me! My perspectives, my beliefs. He truly sees and understands the positive attributes I try to demonstrate and facilitate through my struggles. I'm always trying to reiterate to my children that life goes on; it doesn't stop. It keeps going and so should we. No matter what we are faced with, there will be good that comes out of it.

Live life to the fullest!

I believe we are only given what we can handle, and there are always two paths for what we must endure:

> 1) Allowing whatever we are faced with to completely consume us and finding all the negativity within the situation and within our life—complete misery and unhappiness.

> Or…

> 2) Taking a breath and finding new perspectives to the thing we face. Put a positive spin to it. If we are faced with a challenge, create a new outlook, problem solve. How can we work around this so we can thrive?

And here was proof that he understood that attitude.

"Titus!" I cry. "That was unbelievable!" I stand and embrace him, holding and squeezing him tightly. My heart melts with the utmost sensation of pride and honor.

Jayda runs over and joins in our embrace, wrapping her little arms around Titus and me. Now we are all back in this beautiful loving entanglement, mirroring the embrace we had created on the couch.

"How did I get so lucky to have you both in my life?" I ask them, highlighting and emphasizing the blessing I was feeling towards them—at that very moment, and always.

"Titus...' I say in shock and disbelief. "I can't believe you wrote a speech about me. I am absolutely honoured, and so incredibly proud of you! Thank you for reading this to us." I give him yet another squeeze.

"Thanks, Mom." Titus sheepishly looks down and soaks up all the praise he was receiving.

"Titus, that was really good," Jayda compliments her brother.

"Thanks," he says with a smile.

I lean back a bit so they both can see me, and I can see them. "I know it's really scary sometimes for you both, especially when Mommy is really weak and sick. Know that Mommy will do whatever she can to never give up!" I reassure them. "I will keep trying every single day to stay positive and strong. I won't let this disease take me over, and when things get really scary remember I will always love you and we will always try to adapt to the challenges and obstacles that are in our way. We'll keep going!"

As a parent, your goal and purpose is to create a wonderful, nurturing life for your children, for them to feel safe and loved, to have a sense of belonging within this crazy world. But there are times when their world gets scrambled and fear kicks in, so as a parent you just have to show them the way to the light, to the silver lining. Reassure them that everything happens for a reason, good and bad. We just need to view things differently, to find the positives and the blessings in disguise!

Chapter 6

Happiness Is...

~  ~

"Okay, beautiful, I'm going help you get up the stairs and up to bed," Greg reassures me in a take-charge tone.

He can see that the day has taken its toll on me; my legs are not functioning as they should. I struggle to stand up from the couch and can't take any steps without assistance. My body and the messages from my brain are not allowing me to move any further. I stand in the middle of the living room, feeling frustrated and defeated. My legs are like lead weight—not wanting to move, fighting against my brain like a toddler having a temper tantrum. This is common if I allow myself to get to the point of exhaustion. I try not to get to this point, but sometimes it's hard to accept that I am sick and disabled. I don't want to miss out on life! And so, I push it. I push my body to see what it can or cannot handle.

"I guess I should go to bed; the pain and my vision are getting worse too," I admit to Greg. It's difficult to submit to this challenge my body has provoked.

Greg walks over to me, entering my terrified space. He leans down and greets me with a passionate kiss, holding me at my waist. I wrap my arms around his neck, and we anchor each other's fear, grounding one another though this intimate moment. We hug and hold each other in a reassuring, tight, loving embrace.

He lifts my legs at my thighs, and wraps them around his waist. We are chest to chest, heart to heart, his strong arms locked under my bottom. I gently rest my head upon his shoulder, nuzzling into the crook of his neck, hiding my face and tears from the rest of the room, from our children, so they don't see the extent of my defeat, my fear, and my weakness.

"Good thing you're so light," he chuckles to lighten the mood.

I laugh, switching back to the positive, fun, look-for-the-silver-lining attitude I like to preserve. The kids laugh at his comment too.

"I'm just taking Mommy to bed," Greg tells them. "I'll be back down in a bit, once Mommy is settled, and we'll play a board game."

"Good night," I call out to both of them. "I love you!"

"Love you too, Mom!" they both call back.

Greg carries me up the stairs and down the hallway to our bedroom, careful to avoid hitting the walls with my body. I hold on to him tightly, but we keep the mood light, me by giggling and nibbling his neck, him by pinching my bum as we enter our room. Making light of all these crazy obstacles we face seems to help us manage. We always remember to love, to be silly and to be there for one another, to giggle and smile through the pain and fear, to stay positive and strong! He gets me changed and comfortable in bed.

"It's just a little blip, Julia," he reassures me and himself again.

"Another challenge that we are faced with. Besides, I like carrying you to bed!"

He looks at me with bedroom eyes. "And you can't run away from me," he snickers and starts to seductively crawl over me, kissing my neck and leading his lips up to mine. "Get some rest, love; you're back at the hospital for more steroid treatment in the morning." He leans in for another passionate kiss.

"Good night, Greg. I love you," I say as I close my eyes to fall asleep.

***

When I finally wake in the morning and begin to emerge from bed, Greg is not beside me. Unusual, for I almost always wake before him. I must have needed the sleep. I slowly get out of bed; my legs are still heavy and weak. I use my cane to assist me down the hall to the bonus room. Greg is working in there—and had been all night. I thought I was dreaming the commotion I had heard throughout my slumber.

He transformed our bonus room into a pole studio just for me! He took all the kids' toys and debris out, and created a stunningly beautiful, open-concept dance space for me. It's breath-taking. There is so much love and thoughtful detail, with a 12-foot by eight-foot framed mirror attached to the wall and surrounded by sparkly white lights, and some of my personal favorite dance pictures taken of me framed and scattered through this space. I stand in the hallway frozen in awe.

"Oh my God, Greg! What is this?" I inquire with an excited and puzzled tone and expression.

"Happy birthday, Julia," he says. "I give you hope! You will dance again, and you will walk again!" He presents this space to me with a beaming smile and encouraging emphasis on the notion of hope.

I begin to cry overwhelmed by happiness, joy and love! I drop my cane, and he rushes over to me and picks me up into a ginormous, compassionate, loving hug.

"Greg," I whisper through my tears, "it's beautiful. Thank you!"

The kids come running up the stairs, beyond excited by the surprise. "Do you like it? Do you like?" they both yell with enthusiasm.

"I love it!" I yell, unable to contain my excitement. "Thank you so much!"

Greg carries me to the middle of the studio to the pole that is attached to the floor and the ceiling. I hold the pole and gaze into the mirror at myself, studying my reflection, viewing this form of a woman who looks back at me. This beautiful, extremely blessed and supported, spirited woman is not defeated, weak, or ready to give up. This woman has the strength to go on, keep pushing, keep living! I've got this!

I then pivot towards the pole and start climbing it using only my upper body—my weak legs dangle and point to the floor. I slowly lower myself to the ground. Jayda runs over to the stereo in the corner of the studio and starts the song "Unsteady" by X Ambassadors. The melody and lyrics of the song resonate and spark a little light inside of me. I've had it on my playlist since I heard it on the radio; only now does it create a whole new message and meaning for me. Hold on to me, don't let go, even though I'm a little unsteady.

The love from my family is endless and I am never alone in this. They will continue to help me fight, especially when I'm a little unsteady. They are here to support me and are never giving up on me, never letting go, therefore I should never give up on myself.

> Don't let go Julia, be strong.
> Be you and dance.

> Free the music through your body
> Embrace it!

I look over to my family. They are all watching me, beaming and smiling, knowing what I am about to do next. I close my eyes and breathe it all in. I begin to move and flow my body around the pole in a fluid motion, always hanging onto the pole to support my movements and providing my upper body the ability to demonstrate my strength. My grip on the pole helps me to feel confident with my movements as the music flows from the stereo to my body and soul, and allowing this freedom to come over me. I feel empowered, strong and so incredibly supported by my family! Our love for each other gets us through our most difficult times.

> **"The love of a family is life's greatest blessing!"**

This quote is displayed throughout our home on several store-bought pictures. I'm unsure from whom it was originally quoted. All I know is that this quote is so incredibly true, and it resides within our hearts. We live by this quote; it has become one of our mantras, for the essence of it is so true. Our love for each other is our greatest blessing in our lives.

> The name of our studio is:
>
> **Happiness is…**
> **Empowerment, Confidence, Strength & Support**
>
> Our entire family utilizes this space.
> Especially when emotions are dragging us down.
> Someone will run upstairs and blare the music.
>
> **Dance it out!**
>
> Flow through the pain,
> the joy,
> the stress,

and really all of the emotions.

We utilize this space not only
to dance,
but to have a real sense of togetherness
to have fun.
Be in the moment.
Build strength
physically and emotionally
Free ourselves from life's troubles and burdens.

Laughing and embracing the little blessings life has to offer us.

**Experiencing the Joy of Life -
Hope, Happiness
and Love.**

Chapter 7

Ladies' Night

I'm back at the hospital yet again. I'm getting pulse therapy, another five-day stint of extremely high doses of intravenous Methyprednisolone. It is a steroid treatment for an incredibly sudden and intense flare up of MS symptoms. This treatment, in theory, helps relieve MS flare ups by reducing nerve inflammation, easing symptoms more quickly than not doing anything at all. Recovery from the flare up is gradual even with this medication/therapy, but it seems worthy to do. It does have many risks and side effects, often outweighed by the intensity and suffering endured by the MS patient.

This time my symptoms are well beyond what I normally endure and I don't question doing this therapy once again. My legs are barely working. They keep giving out, and I'm using a cane when my legs allow me to take small struggling steps with a very unsteady gait. That isn't even the worst of it; this time my newest symptom is my swallowing difficulties. My esophagus spasms and any solid food gets stuck. I have to purée my food, and massage the exterior portion of my throat to gently remind my body to swallow. My body is deteriorating at a rapid speed. This is by far my scariest relapse.

I have no idea what the future has in store for me. What further obstacles will I be forced to face? I don't know how much more I can take of this, or how much more my family can handle. I am struggling day in and day out, trying to stay positive and strong, to keep going, and face whatever life has to throw at me.

I sit in this "treatment chair," like that name helps this situation; it's just an oversized recliner that I get to sit in for a few hours to rest while a hefty dose of steroids are pumped through my veins. I'm here, and I hope and pray that this will work. I am so weak right now. My legs feel like lead, glued to the floor. My brain sends messages to them to move, to function, but all they do is feel heavy and sore. And on top of this, I have the awful sensation of intense pins and needles throughout both of my legs. I'm basically locked into this chair by the intravenous pump that's administering this drug into me.

"Awesome!" I amuse myself by saying the word aloud, for this is not awesome. But I am thankful for this drug and treatment; in the past, it has helped to shorten the duration of my intense flare ups.

It does, however, have side effects. I can handle them, but they are nonetheless crazy side effects. One that is the most substantial to me and the one I favor most is the feeling of Hulk-like strength (you feel stronger than ever), and the mind-racing energy it enhances. I completely understand how people can get hooked on this false feeling of reality. You feel unstoppable, revved up and ready to go!

The problem is that I can't move around; my legs limit me from expelling physical energy. So, it leaves my mind to go haywire with its thoughts, a thousand thoughts a minute. That's when I get the idea: I'm going to host a ladies' night!

The ideas start forming for an epic evening of fun and laughter. A night to forget the pain, fear and just be me! It will be like a last hurrah, just in case the MS gets any worse. I can do this as a fundraiser for the MS Society for research to help find a cure.

That's it; I'm going to do it! I encourage my thoughts to keep rapidly firing fantastic ideas.

I ring for a nurse to gather a clipboard, paper and pen for me. I start frantically writing down ideas, googling and putting these ideas into action. By the time my treatment is finished and Greg is there to take me home, I have decided on a date, a venue, the entertainment and a draft of the ticket design. I am now officially hosting an epic evening of fun and entertainment. Thank you, steroids; I may not be able to move, but I can plan one hell of a party!

***

The doors are about to open for my epic event—a ladies' night to remember! We've sold 220 tickets, collected donations, and made the place look flawless: decorations, lights, raffle tables, swag bags, food, drinks and taboo entertainment. This is going to be a night to remember. I can't believe I pulled this off. I actually did it.

I breathe in this moment, and all the excitement of this epic event. I feel extremely blessed, and I think to myself, *Ahhhh thank you friends and family for all your help, support, and for truly believing in me and supporting my cause. Because of that I am able to put this all together.*

As the ladies start to enter the building, I take a step back and look at what I have created and what I have accomplished. This is all because of the difficult place I have been put into, being faced with my biggest challenge—the declining state of my disease. But I keep going, and with Greg's help and determination to stay positive and strong, I'm able to conquer this fun task. I can keep my head up high and keep looking for that silver lining, despite my challenges. I can look at my MS as a blessing! I am able to look at the world differently. I'm able to view life in a positive manner, to eat right, exercise and take excellent care of myself. I can get rid of the negativity and stressors within my life, and I surround myself with people I love and who love me. Instead of taking life for granted, I'm living every day to the fullest, even when I don't want to.

When I get up on stage, I share why I am hosting this event, why this is so significant. Being diagnosed with MS was a huge life-changing moment—not only for me, but for everyone in my life. I have had many challenges with this disease, but through this journey I have learned to love myself—to live life to the absolute fullest—because I never know what tomorrow will bring.

Then I thank my husband, my biggest support. He is the love of my life, because without him I wouldn't be able to face my challenges every single day. He keeps me positive and strong, and never lets me feel sorry for myself. He helps me create the most amazing memories and life experiences. So, as a tribute and dedication to him, I played the chorus of Salt-N-Pepa's "Whatta Man" from the 1993 album <u>Very Necessary</u>—because he *is* a mighty, mighty good man. Yes he is.

I blow a kiss across the room to my husband. He gives me the most beautiful smile and blows a kiss back to me. We both hold our hands over our own hearts to signify our admiration and love for one another.

I turn my attention back to the crowd to share my vision for the night.

I wanted an epic night out with friends. A night to remember fun with ladies, having the power of sisterhood unite with the roaring sound of laughter from experiencing something fun and exciting. A night to forget pain, fear, and suffering. I wanted to just be me! And in doing so, bring awareness to MS and raise money to help others that are struggling with this life-changing disease. I know the struggles, and if I can help others with their challenges through sharing my story and experiences, it was all worth it. I added a (slightly paraphrased) quote from Maya Angelou that ignited something within me, a thirst to live. I say to the crowd:

> "My mission in life is not to merely survive,
> But to thrive,
> And to do so with,
> Some passion
> Some compassion
> Some humor
> And, fuck yeah, some style!
>
> Live life as Mark Twain says:
> Life is short.
> Break the rules.
> Forgive quickly.
> Kiss slowly.
> Love truly.
> Laugh uncontrollably.
> And never regret *anything* that made you smile."

I then announce that I am going to perform a pole routine choreographed to demonstrate my physical and emotional strength. I reiterate my message with a lyric from the song I am about to perform to – Rachel Platten's, "Fight Song:" Know that I still have a lot of fight left in me!

I am not willing or ready to give up. I try to fight each and every single day to keep going — to keep finding that silver lining. I have a fire inside of me and an intense drive to keep going — to stay positive and strong. It seems as though it's a never-ending battle that I am made to face, but this girl, Julia May Evans, has a lot of passion, drive and fight within to keep going, to keep living!

> Never give up!

The DJ starts the song and I dance my heart out. I showcase my love of dance, and the strength it provides me—especially at my weakest times and when I'm at my most vulnerable state. I show this group that through the love and support of my family, I was given a chance to see hope to keep going! Hope to walk again and to dance; not to give up, to stay strong and positive. This hope drives me to really live for another day. Live through the challenges, pain, fear and suffering!

I was gifted a sanctuary—my pole studio—and now I am able to demonstrate to this room what that studio represented for me: a place of hopes and dreams, a place that my husband built for me, to remind me of where I came from, where I am meant to be. To dance, flow, and to be free. Free to be me! Free of my struggles and pain, allowing my soul to breathe and to live beyond fear! I'm stepping out of the shadows that surround me. The shadows of darkness that suppress and confine my soul to a place of misery and the darkness of the abyss I endure.

Through dance and the endless love of my family, I am able to briefly step away from that darkness and flow to the music, permitting my soul to expand its wings and be free to float through the space I am dancing in. I am free to express my deepest, darkest internal emotions through the music's frequencies and not having to say a word, but finding strength and my voice through my expressive fluid movements. I feel the vibrations penetrate every cell in my body to shake things up a bit.

It's my own kind of therapy
Happiness is...
Being free to express oneself.
Dancing like everyone is watching.
Showing the world
Your inner Strength and Pain.

Dance it out!
Spread your wings

And Fly
Like a Butterfly.

For the butterfly often signifies endurance, transformation, hope, joy, and life!

Don't be afraid to live.

Chapter 8

This Is Really Happening

I'm lying in my hospital bed, scanning my environment. I still don't have enough strength or energy to really do anything other than stop, rest, heal, and be. I lay here alone, in my bed, gazing out of my window. I hear the hustle and bustle of the unit, and it rings throughout my ears. I'm helpless, and alone with only my thoughts to keep me occupied within the stillness and despair of this room. I'm too exhausted and blindsided by this entire experience. It has been one hell of a ride! I am not ready to comprehend, or even think about the complexity of it all. I can't even begin to fathom what really transpired today and all the events that brought me to this state of being.

I am physiologically broken

My mind and body,
Gave up
Completely Shut Down
Everything stopped

THE LILY NURSE

My heart literally broke
And the rest of my body struggles because of its ill effects.

I have been stopped in my tracks
Only to be given a second chance.

The world around me keeps going. It doesn't stop or skip a beat in its own chaos. As I lay here, I feel like everything on my path has stopped, and been rerouted. Everything is different for me and the world around me inevitably keeps going, no matter what is happening within it.

Here I am, stunned, numb, and bewildered in my own little world. No one else can see or understand what I am going through. My own little world is merely a fragment of this entire world, and my world is not even being considered by those around me. Others put their own spin on what is happening, not allowing for my truth to be told, shared, or seen. So, I stay quiet.

I am the only one experiencing all of this firsthand. I am the one in this realm who knows exactly what I went through, what I saw, and what I experienced. I contain an insight that I am puzzled by. I am unsure of how I can communicate all of this to others. How do I share what I'm going through, when I don't even comprehend any of this? It's very disconcerting to me. Everything is not as it seems, and I lay here in my hospital bed, trying to conclude that this is not serious, just a blip in the road. I try convincing my conscious mind that this is just another hurdle to face, a temporary challenge, a small detour.

I am alive,
So how can this all possibly be?
How is this really my world?
And what do I do with all of this now?

My thoughts get even more philosophical: *Can this really be happening, or am I dreaming? Did all of this really happen? Did I really experience this? All of this? Am I really back to this body, back in this world, this realm? Why is everything so different and yet so recognizably the same?*

From what I can see out my window, it's a beautiful spring day, with a brilliant, clear blue sky. The calming, endless blue stills my mind and silences my thoughts. I have become completely mesmerized by its purity and beauty.

I try to sit up to see more of the outside world, but alas, the view is obstructed by another side of this hospital building. I am trapped—in this bed, in this hospital, in this broken body. I'm trying to accept that this is my reality, and I'm desperately trying to make light of everything. I'm not allowing myself to really absorb the magnitude of all of this. I don't want to accept this fate. I want to close my eyes and my mind from this world. Right now, I wish things would go back to where they were, back to the world that I was familiar with—the world I had grown accustomed to.

Why is this happening?
I just want things to be normal again!

My phone lights up. It's a message from my friend Kim, the manager of our baseball team. She took over the entire role when I stepped up to coach the boys.

> Did you find someone to bring the kids to you?

> Yes.
> Scary day

> Yes it is. I hope everything is ok

THE LILY NURSE

> Here's hoping. I was really looking
> forward to ball.

I know but your health comes first

> I know. I cheated death again.
> Twice

Yes you did. Scared me when you called.
I am sure you are pretty scared

> Feels like I'm dreaming
> Nope, I'm not

Lol. You still have your sense of humor
We're thinking about you

> How's practice?

It is cold but good.

Then Kim sends me a video of the boys, our baseball team. There are eight of them standing on the baseball diamond, saying in unison, with their squeaky teenage voices, "Get well, Coach Julia!"

JULIA EVANS

> From your boys. I didn't tell them anything. I just told them you weren't feeling well

> That's so sweet. Thank you.

This video brings a smile to my face, all of them sending me a genuine message of hope to get better. None of them really aware of what is truly happening, just knowing I am not there with them, but wishing I was.

I love coaching these boys. They give me such strength. They keep me on my toes, always challenging me to take on something foreign to me, a sport I really know nothing about. Striving to be the best coach and version of myself for them helps me develop them to be the best version of themselves, and I am having so much fun in the process. I encourage the team to always work together, becoming a complete unit—from our traditional push-up circle to cheering their teammates on—always bringing everyone up and never down. I provide opportunities for everyone to demonstrate their individual skills and assets, and have them bring those to the field for the team to integrate as a whole. Always building them up, never tearing them down; always building character and strength.

I love being a part of this for Titus. It's building a foundation for him. He says he loves assisting me with the drills; he helps me with researching and implementing them for his team. It builds his confidence up, and for the ones around him. Besides, it's a nice break from having to take care of me. I absolutely love seeing him as a strong little man playing baseball. This positively warms my heart! It puts things in perspective to have a time to pause from the everyday struggles and just be able to play, have fun and really enjoy life.

I replay the video several times. These boys are such free spirits. I love that they are all dancing, doing "the floss," giving me thumbs up to get better, and being silly, crazy little boys in this video. I wish I was there with them, on the field, and not in this godforsaken hospital bed.

They are such a great distraction from the shit I am being faced with right now. They help deflect the reality of what is really happening. I close my eyes and envision being there with them on the baseball field, conducting my warm up drills and laughing without a care in the world. I imagine feeling the breeze on my skin, the smell of the freshly cut grass, and the sound of the banter and laughter of everyone on the field, from all of the kids, the parents, and the other coaches. That would sure beat this stale stench of hospital I am entrapped in right now. I can't wait to get out there and run around in the open space with the team. I can't wait till I'm free to go. Back to my regular life, and away from all this strife.

My phone rings, and it's one of my best friends.

"Oh my God, Julia! Are you okay?"

"Nikki?!"

"I'm flying home!" she announces.

"Don't fly home," I reply, in a don't-be-so-stupid tone. "You need to be in Edmonton with Jordan right now!"

Nikki is a beyond-devoted and loving mother to her two children. Jordan is her daughter, the oldest, and she keeps Nikki so incredibly busy with her ridiculously amazing dance talents. They are in Edmonton for another showstopper dance competition where Jordan is dancing and up for the diamond award. Nikki wanting to drop everything and fly home with great urgency is a bit overwhelming, and a completely ridiculous notion to me. It warms my heart knowing how much she cares about me, but it does frighten me to think about how serious this whole situation might actually be.

"I'm so worried about you," she says in a concerned voice.

"I'm fine!" I reassure her. "I survived! I'm a fighter. You know that!"

"I don't believe you," she says. "You're not 'fine'. I'm going to call you back on FaceTime so I can actually see you for myself." As Nikki hangs up, I quickly reflect on our friendship. Nikki is one of those friends within your life who you never initially thought would have such an impact.

My first encounter with her was when we started working together in the hospital. At first, we were just colleagues: no in-depth conversations, no after-work meetings or gatherings. It was just a simple, plain old working relationship. Until one hilarious day when we both discovered our shared inappropriate sense of humor. It all started with one little comment about a blue Christmas ornament. It was innocently placed, but when we both saw it and acknowledged it, we laughed our asses off. It was the kind of laughter where your belly hurts and you can barely breathe; you snort, gasp, and then laugh again. This hilarious innuendo and inside joke between us started not only a deep-down-roaring laughter, but an amazing friendship too. This pure explosion of joy and laughter started a brilliant connection between us and granted us a new way to release what we dare not face, and it filled a void within our lives.

Neither one of us likes to show our true emotions or allow people into the depths we hide from. We were both in need of some sort of release and we got just that through our uncontrollable laughter. It's so refreshing to have someone to laugh with and to be on the same page as you, knowing you always have a friend through ups and downs, and the colorful areas in between.

Finding humor and joy, and a different way to cope with life.

THE LILY NURSE

As people say...
"Laughter is the best medicine."

We are most definitely the best medicine for each other, always there for each other through thick and thin. We don't have to be together for every moment of every day, but we are there when it counts. We know we can turn to one another, no questions asked, no judgment—just unconditional love and support.

I answer her FaceTime call.

"Okay, now you can see me. See, I'm fine; I'm alive! I'm alive Nikki" I mock her request and requirements to visualize my existence. I scan my room, my bed and myself with the camera on my phone so she can see and inspect everything.

"Yes, I can see you. You look like shit!" she banters back. "And put your boobs away!" She laughs.

I laugh out loud at her comment. That's the Nikki I needed! She always knows what to say to get me laughing. I love this humor and release!

As I watch her talk over the video chat, my attention is drawn to her expression. She has a panicked look upon her face. Never in my life have I seen her so worried about me. Nikki is a cardiac nurse: she is a brilliant nurse within her field. She's caring, knowledgeable, and doesn't put up with shit. My kind of girl, my kind of nurse and I trust her knowledge and experience. So, with her displaying such worry, I start to realize that this is quite serious.

"Okay, tell me everything!" She presses me for the information of what actually occurred. "Start from the beginning. I want to know all of it!"

She does this to gain control of the situation, where she cannot physically be.

As I begin telling her the story of my life changing event, the overhead announcing intercom comes on. It blares over the entire speaker system of the hospital: "Code Blue, CSU. Code Blue, CSU. Code Blue, CSU."

The very loud announcement brings attention to the medical emergency so that the right teams can be put into action and know where they are heading.

"Julia!" Nikki yells from the phone.

I had lowered the phone and went silent to listen to the code being called. It's a nurse's instinct to stop what they are doing and listen to those calls, just on the off chance they have to run and offer help.

"It's not me, Nikki!" I yell at the phone with a great emphasis, holding the camera part of the phone up to my heart monitor, so that she can see it for herself and do her own visual nursing assessment, reassuring her mind that it wasn't me coding.

"It's not me. I'm not the code," I reconfirm, before trailing off and becoming quiet.

Both of us completely frazzled by the overhead announcement of a code for the unit I'm on, we look at each other through the phone screen, not being able to hold in our emotions any longer. We both begin to cry. Not laugh, but cry!

"I should be there," she says through her tears. "I should be there with you!"

We both pause in silence, staring at each other, allowing the tears to roll down our faces and allowing the emotions to flow. This all has been so scary, and having Nikki see me like this reconfirms just how fucking serious this really is.

"It must have been so scary," she says through her tears. "I can't imagine what you're going through. I should be there with you."

"It was bad, Nikki!" My words tremble out of my mouth. I can't share any more of what I went through. I can't tell her; I'm still not wanting to face it. I can't release or let out any more, not even for Nikki. I still can't believe that this is really happening. That all of this really happened. I am going to have to face it, but I can't right now. I take a huge breath in and out, wipe away my tears, and shove all that emotion deep down.

After turning off my emotions, I calmly say to Nikki, "I'll be here when you get back from your trip. I'll keep you updated. Don't you dare fly home!"

"I should be there," she says again.

"I'm okay," I reassure her. "I'm alive, and I'm not going anywhere. As you know—I'm one hell of a fighter! I love you, and I'll see you when you get home."

"Okay. I'll phone you later to check in on you," she responds. "I should go into the theater now and watch Jordan."

"Wish her luck from me. I know she'll be amazing," I completely change the tone of our conversation, lightening up to an area that I feel more comfortable in: the area of avoidance.

Nikki can pick up on it, and once again offers to drop everything for me. "You know I'll fly back right now if you need me to!"

"I know," I respond, smiling at her. "I'll talk to you tonight. Love ya!"

"Love you too," she smiles back at me.

We hang up, and I lay my phone beside me on the side table. I'm exhausted from our conversation and I just want to close my eyes, rest and escape from all of this. I pull up my grey fuzzy blanket that lays under these scratchy old hospital blankets. Greg had graciously brought it in for me from home. Nikki bought me this blanket several years ago, after witnessing my struggles after I had been diagnosed with MS. She bought it to comfort and warm me and my heart when she couldn't be there beside me.

Even though she is miles away from me right now, it feels like she is with me. I bring the blanket up to my face, clench it tight and, closing my eyes, give it one hell of a squeeze. I envision Nikki here with me—right beside me, supporting me, comforting me, loving me, and caring for me.

I truly wish she was here with me. I can't tell her that though. I can't tell her how scared I am, and I can't take her away from her daughter. I can tell her most things, but even for me this is too big to comprehend, understand or accept. I am so scared, lost and alone. I can't make sense of my world right now. I wish this was all a scary dream, for it to be over and to be back in my own bed at home with my family. I want to reopen my eyes and be in a place I am familiar with, not to be here in this desolate hospital bed as a cardiac patient who's being closely monitored. I wish someone, anyone, was here with me. My thoughts go back to my previous questioning:

> Did this really happen?
> Is this really my world?
> Why?
> How?
> What's next?

I go back to gazing out of my window, trying to calm my mind and still it from the world around me, breaking from the sight and sounds of this hospital atmosphere. I know I need to rest and heal, but I'm struggling. My heart is weak and so am I. I close my eyes and drift off to sleep.

Chapter 9

Okay, Honey—Let's Ride!

~  ~

Greg spots me from inside our house and comes outside to check on me. "What are you doing sitting out here all by yourself?" He questions me and my motive as I sit alone in a depressive state.

It's April 26, 2016, and I'm sitting slumped over in a patio chair on our back deck. I slowly glance over to the sound of his voice, not wanting to look up at him. My back is to him, and I want to keep it that way. I am not wanting to change my position and fully face him or what I am dealing with. I hold my forehead in the palm of my right hand, tilt my head to look slightly over my shoulder and I stare at his feet. My head is tilted enough to signal I am listening, acknowledging his presence. But I don't move from my position in the patio chair, keeping my body and my mood in a slumped, closed-off, dysphoric state. I can't bear to face anything today; I can't even bring myself to say anything to my doting, loving and supportive husband.

"Sitting here pouting and feeling sorry for yourself is not going to help anything or anyone, including yourself," he informs me with a playful tone.

I stare off into the distance, not wanting to acknowledge that he is calling me out. I want the world to swallow me up. I want something, anything, to take this pain, suffering and fatigue away. I don't have the strength today. I am so tired of fighting with my mind and my body as it continuously eats away at itself. So I sit in this patio chair defeated and depressed.

"I just want to sit here in silence for a while," I plead. "I'm so tired and sore today; just leave me be."

"Well, you could sit here and feel sorry for yourself, or…" He moves his hands up and down to mime weighing out my options. "…you can get in the side-by-side and feel sorry for yourself while I drive us around and have fun."

He presents his clever idea to me so nicely—it is a valid point. He gazes at me as though I am a timid deer he has just spotted and doesn't want to spook, dangling the carrot of a new perspective in front of me in hopes that I'll bite and agree to his master plan.

"Can't I just stay here, in our backyard? I'm getting fresh air," I say.

"Nope," he says. "You're getting in the side-by-side. I'll grab you a drink and a sweater. I'll meet you in the driveway."

He doesn't wait or give me any opportunity to respond; he just heads inside to gather our things. I stare at the door as he closes it behind himself and I take an exaggerated breath. I slowly rise from my patio chair and do what he says.

I meet him in the side-by-side on the driveway. I still don't want to go on this adventure, but I play along. I'm in such a blah mood and can't see anything getting me out of it. I truly have no interest in doing anything right now and I'm surprised he has any interest in taking me as I have such a somber demeanor. I'm barely managing to play along with his plan. *He is right though—sitting and moping around is not going to help anything or anyone, including myself.*

He gets behind the wheel, hands me a sweater and a drink, and starts the engine. He gazes lovingly at me with this humongous smile pinned on his face, and says, "Okay, honey—let's ride!"

I smile while playfully rolling my eyes and shaking my head at him. I love that he is so excitable and this makes me giggle. We back out of our driveway and head to the fields behind our house. We are both so quiet, riding in silence as we joyride through the open prairie fields. The openness of these fields, the infinite blue sky, the fresh air and the rumbling engine are all so beautifully peaceful. It gives an amazing sense of freedom and calmness, something very different than sitting slumped over on a patio chair in the backyard. I can feel the wind on my face and through my hair. The rumbling engine shakes things up for me and blocks my depressive thoughts. My heart flutters with excitement as we drive through the trees and fields.

Greg frequently looks in my direction with this enormous genuine gleaming smile and loving gaze. *I love this man.* I know he loves and adores me too.

Greg loves adventure, having fun and being silly. He always says to me that he's happiest when there is a smile on my face. "Happy wife, happy life," he often says. He's very selfless. He's my strength, my rock and my light when things are dark and bleak. Greg has such a playful boyish personality and he always seems to bring a spark of excitement in everything that he does in life. It's quite intoxicating.

After several bumps, jumps and weaves, we finally stop to take a break and a breather. We exit the side-by-side and stand in the middle of an open field—just the two of us, with no one else around us for miles. Greg walks over, embraces me and kisses my forehead. I wrap my arms around his waist. I love being in his arms; it's my favorite place on earth. No matter where we are or what surrounds us, there's no better place to be than in the strong, loving arms of the man I love. The world stands still when I'm in his arms and everything seems to melt away.

We stand together looking out into the distance for quite a while. It's so breathtaking out here. The open sky and endless fields go on forever. The stillness and openness of the prairies allow us to just be. Be in the moment, breathe and let go of all the stuff that doesn't serve us.

A moment of Freedom!

Together we stand holding each other, not saying a word, but just being there and present for each other allowing the stress of our world to just melt away. This is exactly what I needed — to be in my favorite place, the place where I feel safe, protected, supported and loved. I look up at Greg, admiring him, and give him an enormous smile. He always seems know what my soul needs.

"I love you, Greg," I proclaim.

My heart flutters as I express these words to him with all my heart. As if it was the first time saying it to him, like when we were just starting our relationship and butterflies fluttered within my stomach. To this day, he gives me those same butterflies, every time he looks my way or any time I look at him. My heart exudes a love beyond no other for this man who stands here with me. He's my soulmate, my light, my love, my everything.

"I love you too, Julia," he says, leaning in and kissing me passionately on the lips. "Okay, back to the side-by-side. Let's ride!" We jump back into the side-by-side, both super excited for the next adventure.

"Which way, beautiful?" Greg queries.

"That way!" I yell with excitement, pointing enthusiastically to a new direction and destination.

We drive fast and free for quite a while, and then approach a ditch full of water. A blip to our path, a challenge on our course. Greg gives me the opportunity to choose which course to take: Go back the way we came and try to find another route, or face the challenge head on and see what happens.

"Let's do it. Drive through," I say, embracing the excitement further.

"It looks deep," he warns.

"Do it," I encourage him, disregarding his warning.

He backs up a little and puts the vehicle into drive—full speed ahead. As we go down the ditch, the water comes up quickly. There is far more depth to this water and this ditch than I had anticipated. The water is up past the tires, then up to the bottom of the seats. And we get stuck! Right in the middle of this ditch, our vehicle submerged up to its seats in water.

"Well, shit!" I blurt out. I start to laugh at this situation that we are literally stuck in. It was me that got us into this mess. I laugh even harder at that notion.

Greg turns off the engine, jumps off the back of the side-by-side and hurtles himself to the edge of the ditch. He stands on the dry land, staring at me, and he starts laughing uncontrollably at the decision I made for us. I get up, out of my seat and maneuver myself to the back of the side-by-side, to stand on the dry portion of the back seat. I am trying to stay out of the water, to stay dry, and I laugh even harder at this situation and the new obstacle I have put us in.

"Now what? You're stuck in a rut. Do you need help to get out?" He highlights what space I'm in and inquires how I want to get out. He is mirroring my mood and inquiring how I might get out of that depressive state I was stuck in. Interesting tactic—I don't believe he had this exact experience intended for me; he was, however, trying to show me a way to get out and enjoy life. Not to be stuck in a rut, no matter what obstacle we are presented with. I stand there for moment and assess this situation.

"I'm going to leap to you," I inform him. "I need your help; I can't do this on my own."

He gives me a cunning smile.

I stand on the back of the tailgate, and leap towards him. He has his arms extended, and with his help I make it to the dry edge of the ditch. Not knowing if my legs would hold out and allow me to do this. I just had to have faith and trust that Greg would pull me back, and save me. And that he did—both physically and emotionally! He really does know what I need even before I can see it or admit to it. My knight in shining armor, always there to show me the way to the light, happiness and a good life.

To Live Life to the Fullest!

As we stand on the edge of the ditch looking down at the side-by-side, we are laughing hysterically at it halfway submerged in sludgy, mucky water. What a relief to be out of that mess. I wrap my arms around Greg's neck and give him the biggest kiss. We look into each other's eyes and say in unison, "Now, how are we going to get out of this mess?"

As we are saying these words to each other, I spot a dump truck driving down the road. I flag it down and the driver helps pull us out, asking nothing in return. I give this kind stranger a hug for his generous gesture and we all carry on our day, as if nothing out of the ordinary happened. But I am aware of the significance of this little joyride. That was the point to it—riding out the joy of the experience. Greg must have had an inkling…

THE LILY NURSE

To help me
Find my joy in life again.

I'm back! I am back to being the charismatic, life-loving woman that I pride myself on being. Back to my playful, laughing self, full of life, taking on life's challenges head on, with the man I love by my side. I'm the never-give-up person I strive to be, each and every day I'm here on this earth. I just needed to be reminded of that.

"Well that was an adventure! Thank you, Greg! I needed that," I say, smiling at him.

He smiles back and replies, "I'm happy to help."

CHAPTER 10

Both Sides of the Vitals Machine

~  ~

I wake to the sound of the vitals machine turning on as my nurse enters the room. It's a subtle, familiar sound I have grown accustomed to. It's a sound that I long to be on the other side of. To be back in the role I pride myself on—the nursing role, not the patient role.

As I watch my nurse glide across the floor towards me, clipboard and pen in hand, she appears ready to chart her findings of my condition, my progress or decline. She moves towards me to complete her task at hand. Ready to chart what the machine can tell her about what is happening inside of me and what she can see from my physical appearance.

She is assessing merely my body, separating what she can't see, test or find within me—my emotions, thoughts and experience of all of this. She is unable to assess the other side of this situation, the mental and spiritual effects that are taking place alongside the physical systems: my broken heart!

My heart struggles to keep beating, and to efficiently move blood through my circulatory system to all areas of my body. It also has this enormous conflict within it, between the physical component and the magnitude of my thoughts and emotions towards what is happening around me and within me. My world has completely flipped, and I am left here in this bed to figure out all the pieces to the crazy puzzle. My reality is altered, ripped and torn apart.

My heart is not only broken anatomically and physiologically, but also on several different levels. I am not quite able to address the mental and spiritual toll bestowed upon it. I am not wanting to fully look within the depths of my heart to figure out how I am to heal from this all. I am scared to find all the broken pieces. I don't believe I am equipped to fully understand and fix all the layers of this picture; there's too many and it's oh so overwhelming.

The nurse stands there assessing my physical body, as if my body is a broken machine and requires fixing. She is unable to hear, see or understand what is truly happening within me, like what is happening through my five senses, what is playing out, and causing havoc within my mind, my reality or what is unraveling and tangling up within the corners of my mind, and my being. She is only able to assess what she is trained for: collecting data to be relayed back to the physicians. She is only to address the body's broken pieces, fix the physical problems and nothing else.

I lie here in this hospital bed, watching her quietly as she does her routine assessment of me. I stare at her, not saying a word. I'm doing my own quiet assessment and observation of my reality, and my environment, continually trying to make sense of it all. I watch as she converses with her colleagues, and I am drawn to how she would be experiencing this situation. I recall the many years of me being on the other side of the vitals machine, being the fixer, the nurse. Utilizing my broad knowledge base and years of experience to help heal, treat and fix the patient who appears before me.

I smile at her as she does my assessment; she is so kind, gentle and nurturing. She brings with her not only the vitals machine but a mothering sense about her, and she tries to tend to my other needs as well. It's in her presence; it appears to be in her nature. She seems to see more of the picture than she lets on, not only assessing my physical problems, but subtly assessing other aspects that she is aware I am struggling with. She doesn't pry for further information; she doesn't try to put her spin on the situation, to put her judgment on what I am going through, emotionally, mentally or spiritually. She does, however, bring a beautiful presence with her. It gives me the sense she would stand beside me and fully listen to whatever I really needed and required.

At this point, I don't even know what I need.
I know I'm struggling with more than what my physical state shows
But...
I am just learning what to do with this new body and state of mind.
I'm trying to wrap my head around all of this.

Nurses tend to have a more nurturing, healing approach. They seem to be more in tune with what the patient truly needs: therapeutic touch and a sense of knowing. Nurses advocate for their patients, addressing missing links to what they are physically witnessing. We are trained to look at the bigger picture, think critically about all the possibilities and create care plans and concept maps of everything the patient requires. We try to tie in all the components of the physical and mental body.

Physicians don't always listen to the bigger picture of the patients, not allowing the patient to share their voice. They tend to view only the physical attributes of the patient's condition or aliment focusing on just what they want to see and fix, and not really addressing all the other areas that they are uncomfortable looking at. Physicians tend to approach the situation with an agenda to fix what they can see, prove, scale or test. They can have an ego-driven, god-like mentality and persona, narrow-minded about the other realms around us, not able to understand the simplicity of the complexity of the body, mind and spirit...the complete package!

I believe this serves its purpose too—to have the logical, scientific mind on the horizon to do streamlined thinking, and to be able to interrupt and analyze the task at hand—for there are times we need to be fixed. It's the other components that tend to be overlooked, and in this situation, I wish I could understand how to achieve the healing of all of these components.

My mind keeps jumping back and forth to grasp and understand everything that I am going through. It's a rapid influx of information, senses and experiences. I just want to step away from it and hide in the shadows. It's easier to hide in the darkness than address the light of the situation, for in the light we are able to see what is right in front of us.

As my nurse continues to fulfill her nursing assessment of me, of my physical condition, I am now drawn to her appearance and the significance of her nursing uniform, her scrubs, and what they represent, which is being able to be easily picked out of the crowd to help, assist, and care for a patient. It holds the image of a professional who is responsible for treatment, safety, recovery and trust, attributes that coincide with all the other nursing attributes and values that I hold dear. Her uniform visually identifies her importance and role within this setting, and it brings me a sense of comfort, familiarity! Her ID badge dangles at my eye level and it makes me yearn to be back in the role where I am most comfortable, to be identified as a nurse!

Only moments before she entered this space, I felt as though I was trapped within this shell, this body, this bed. I felt alone, lost and so very scared of everything that has and is happening within my world. I was not wanting to accept this fate, this reality. I was wishing for someone, anyone, to be here and be present with me. Not someone share their views or perspectives of what has and is happening, but to be willing to listen to what all my needs are.

Even if I don't know all of what I need, I want to have someone there to listen and help me find my inner voice, my strength and my power to heal. This beautiful quiet nurse gives the opportunity to do just that, but I am not ready to face it all.

She does, however, bring me to a place I can relate to, a place of familiarity and comfort. Somewhere and someone I can latch on to and put myself in their shoes, for just a moment. A place I have grown accustomed to, the place and role on the opposite side of the vitals machine.

Oh, how I wish to be back there. I am far more comfortable being the nurse. I want to be back to the role of the incredibly caring, strong, and knowledgeable nurse, especially in this setting, the hospital where I work and where I am known for that role: Julia Evans, BScN, RN. That is all I know, or all that I believe I know, and that is all I allow people to see. This is my identity—a nurse who is strong, caring and knowledgeable, someone who always puts others' needs in front of her own to care for her patients.

I deeply care for my patients. I am strong for them, and I love utilizing my many years of education, experience and knowledge; these are some of my best attributes. It's what I know, to demonstrate kindness and compassion, and be the one who does kind things to help others in need. In essence, I help heal them by fixing what they are suffering from.

> Become the fixer, for those in need.
> It is far easier to help others;
> Fix, mend and repair
> what is broken for them,
> than it is to look upon your own broken pieces -
> Your own broken Self.

I don't know how to look at myself now, how to be the ideal

patient who accepts the need to be helped, healed or fixed. That's not my role! That is too difficult to accept. It's too difficult to look at myself here on the "wrong" side of the vitals machine. I have always been the fixer, helping with other peoples' needs. Helping them! Fixing them! Taking myself out of the equation, putting myself last, staying in the dark—not to be looked at, not at all.

It's far easier to assist others in their healing, than to look at myself and the depths that have been created over time. I deemed myself a nurse for the majority of my life—put others' needs first, helped with their pain and suffering above all else. In my mind, it's always been black and white.

This has been a core belief for me since I was three years old. After my mother's death, I started shoving down my emotions and putting everyone's needs ahead of my own. I wanted so desperately to help heal those around me. I was convinced and determined that this was my purpose and my calling: to help others with their pain and suffering and never once look at myself or my needs.

At such a young age, I witnessed the pain and suffering of those around me. The devastation of my mother's passing was so profound. She was only 25 years old. She died at home, in my father's arms. He attempted CPR, but she'd passed before he could even start. My brother and I were upstairs in our beds while our parents were going through this devastating tragedy a floor beneath us in their bed.

I remember parts of the day leading up to it: My mother complaining about a headache all day, trying to quiet my brother and I so that she could function through the pain. My father taking her several times to the hospital, wanting the expertise of the doctors. He needed them to assess what was wrong with her, to use their logical, scientific minds to fix, mend and repair what he could not see. He needed them to interrupt and analyze her pain, her suffering, her problem—her headache. We all needed their god-like persona to be just that: god-like! We instilled all our trust in them and their abilities to help her, to fix her. After numerous trips to the hospital, they still couldn't find what was wrong, so they just gave her some sedatives to numb the pain and sent her home.

She had a brain aneurysm, and it ruptured when my parents returned home. I was asleep through all of this, but my father filled me in after it happened, never sugar coating the situation.

I remember....

My memory is small but contains very significant and profound segments of the morning after my mother's death. I was unaware of what was happening within our household, my environment. My experience of this, and what happened surrounding it, was far different than what everyone else was facing. I would have just woken up to start a new day, totally oblivious to what had happened the night before. In the night, as I lay asleep in my bed, my father watched the woman he deeply loved, the mother of his two children, suffer and die right before his eyes.

He tried!
He tried to save her!

Although her time here was done—it was her time to be free and play with the angels—my dad was seeing it from the other side. He was face to face with her traumatic passing. It haunts him! He tried everything in his power to bring her back, to keep her here with her family, not wanting to let her go. He lay beside her hoping to help with her pain, but as he lay there with her in his arms, trying to protect her, she died right before him.

He initiated CPR. He attempted to get a breath of life back into her, but was unsuccessful.

His world came crashing down right in front of him.
Never to be the same again.
Feeling Broken and Lost...

THE LILY NURSE

There I was, his little girl, the offspring of their love, standing in the kitchen of our home, having my very own unique experience of this loss. I would never be able to comprehend what he had experienced, what he had gone through. I couldn't begin to imagine the extent of the emotions he was bombarded with. I had been asleep in the comfort, protection and safety of my own bed.

On the other hand, he couldn't comprehend what I was going through either.

My experience and memory of that morning is of me standing in the middle of the kitchen, my head just peeking over the kitchen counter, my eye level not quite high enough to see over it. There I was, standing in the center of the kitchen, the heart of the home. Alone, in the center of all the commotion and disharmony, completely unaware of what happened—I was just looking for my mom. Oblivious to what was happening in our house, our home, I just stood there with only one concern—locating my mother. She's my protection, my love, my safety—my mommy.

I couldn't foresee the significance of this moment, nor the heartbreak I was about to endure from the words that were about be spoken to me. This would stick to me forever.

"Where's my mommy?" I questioned anyone who would listen.

My dad, not even functional or aware of how he was supposed to address this question, harshly blurted out, "She left us. She died. She's gone."

I was so angry, hurt, scared, and lost. All I wanted was to have my mommy back, for her to be by my side in this space, to hold me, to protect me, to make me feel safe and loved. I couldn't accept this reality.

Why? Why was she gone?

As my attention switches back to the nurse who stands before me, I realize all the tables have been turned again. I have a new awareness and view of the world around me. It's giving me new perspectives. I have no idea what she has experienced, and she has no idea what I have experienced either, especially with this catastrophic series of events that I was meant to go through. No one really knows what the other is experiencing, thinking or feeling, but it is acceptable to ask to help each other heal from it all. Talk about it. Let it out. Do not be one sided and firm in your thinking, but rather put yourself on both sides of the vitals machine to understand the bigger picture.

Everyone has a unique story, with their own unique experiences.

We have to be willing to talk about it.
Share what weighs us down, what causes disharmony within us.
Talk about the experiences, perspectives and versions,
and actively listen to what is being said.

Both sides will have insight for you.
Nothing is one sided.
Be open to
the details and possibilities.

So everyone can heal.

Everyone has a story
Those stories tie us together
We heal from the storytelling
Attaching to what resonates with us, as individuals
Listening and saying what has and needs to be overcome
For a missing piece to the puzzle, may be found through the sharing
and be part of yours and/or someone else's
Healing Process.

It's all part of the journey!

There is more to healing than addressing the physical body. There are other aspects, elements, and components too—the complete package: mind, body and spirit. There is so much more to the healing process. There is so much more to everything. My eyes are starting to see that now.

Chapter 11

Debriefing

~  ~

I am awoken by a hushed chatter located in the hall, right outside of my hospital room. I hear familiar voices, whispering about me. Most of it is vague; I can't quite make out all the words that are being said, but I know it's about me. Then I hear a loud and assertive remark from my nurse.

"No, you may not enter her room," she says. "She has had quite enough for today. You may leave and I'll tell her you came by. Thank you!" I am a bit puzzled and taken back by her assertiveness, but pleased that she is advocating for me.

I am completely drained and exhausted from all the non-stop commotion that has been swirling around me the last two days. There hasn't been any pause ever since I stepped on to my unit two days ago, when my world completely changed. I haven't had time to process any of this. I have been continually bombarded by people and their extra pieces to an obscure puzzle. I am trying to put all the pieces together so that I can get a grasp of this whole picture—this crazy ordeal!

>All I want is to get home and be with my family!
>Hold them all in my arms
>and Breathe!

>I don't want to believe that any of this is real.

There are two quiet knocks upon my closed door. My nurse peeks her head in and says, "How are you doing, Julia?"

She is so genuine in her questioning and is wholeheartedly concerned about me and my well-being. This is the first time someone has actually asked me that question since all of this craziness happened. The first time I am being put into the equation, being looked at as though I may be struggling with all of this. I want to cry and release some of my pent-up emotion, but I still fight against it.

"I don't know," I truthfully respond. There is a slight quiver to my voice and tears are starting to pool in the corners of my eyes.

She enters my room and closes the door behind her. She pulls up a chair right beside me, grabs ahold of my hand and says, "You have been through quite a lot the last few days. I can't even imagine what you are going through."

My heart melts as she says these words to me.

"You need to be kind to yourself, Julia," she continues. "You are the one in this hospital bed, not them. You are the one who needs to heal. It's your turn." She squeezes my hand and quietly waits for a response. She sits there, holding space for me, giving me an opportunity to share something, anything, or nothing.

I squeeze her hand back, giving her a crooked smile while biting my lower lip. It's hard to be on the opposite side of the vitals machine, hard to let go of wanting to help everyone around me and making sure they are okay. I'm not used to addressing how I am doing; I am lost for words. I close my eyes and lay back down on my semi-upright bed and I finally permit myself to let go. I allow the tears to flow down my face, in the presence of someone else.

Finally, I am not invisible, and I have the opportunity to be heard. I'm not feeling the pressure to help everyone else process and heal from this traumatic event. I am no longer forcing myself to quietly listen and absorb what others are going through. I am finally able to have a say in how I am really doing. I am not required to listen to others right now, not required to hear their stories, their feelings, thoughts, emotions and perspectives. I take a huge breath and the first thing I need to say is, "Why did this happen?"

I take this opportunity to pose this question because I have been struggling with finding the answer. I ask this nurse, not necessarily for her to answer, but to put it out into the Universe, to ask a higher power. I needed someone else who is in my presence, someone who is right in front of me, to hear it too. I am struggling with so many layers and I don't know what I should be feeling. I can't unravel any of this in my brain; I just want to be loved and cared for, so that I can heal from this.

She can sense my yearning to be nurtured and she starts stroking my hair, like a mother does to her sad, lost, broken, alone, or afraid child. I feel protected and safe in her presence. I feel like my mother is there with me: protecting me, loving me, and making sure I'm okay.

I squeeze my eyes tight, envisioning my mother there beside me and I say, "This really happened, didn't it?!"

I open my eyes and stare at her, realizing it's not my mother, but a caring nurse beside me. I ask this question because I am looking for validation. I want to lock into my brain that this really did happen and I did actually experience this, all of this. I need someone to confirm that I am, in fact, the patient here laying on this godforsaken hospital bed.

"Yes, Julia," she says. "This happened—all of it!"

My head starts to pound from the realization of this. It's like my brain is starting to identify, communicate and process everything that has happened and is happening within my world. I start crying even harder; I'm finding it hard to breathe. I don't want to breathe in this information I am receiving. I let go of her hand and hold my hands up to the sides of my head, forcing my brain to accept this confirmation. As I have my hands on my head, I start to calm and eventually stop crying. I have locked this information into my brain and I want to start processing it, but there is a lot to process and an immense amount of healing to take place; I don't know where to start.

This beautiful, loving, nurturing nurse that sits beside me puts her hand on my thigh, and explains, "Julia, I've been monitoring your heart quite closely today. You need to rest and allow yourself to heal. Your heart spikes every time you hear someone else's version of the story. I know you don't want to admit to it, but I can see the irregularity of your heart rhythm when staff are debriefing with you. I know it hurts your heart and not just because I can see it on the monitor, but I can also see it in your eyes."

I sheepishly look down at the heart monitor that rests upon my chest. I pick it up and hold it in my left hand, cradling it as if it was my actual heart within my hand. I watch and assess my heart rate. Staring at each beat of my broken heart in the center of my hand: blip, blip, blip...

I know every beat is being monitored by my nurse and the staff on this unit. It's constantly being assessed and the staff are making sure it keeps beating at a regular rate and rhythm. It's nice to hear that she recognizes what my heart may be feeling, what it is doing; it struggles with every aspect of this whole ordeal. As she makes me aware of her findings, it reassures me that she is truly advocating and trying to protect me from further pain. She is truly allowing the first step in my healing process. She is addressing and making me aware of what often gets overlooked—the patient's mental health. My mental health.

She's right. All of this hurts my heart. It is not only trying to heal from the physical toll, but also from the emotional aspects. Even that doesn't seem to touch all the levels of pain I am coming to terms with, but it's a starting point. There has been a hefty amount of information people keep sharing with me, and she's absolutely right, every time another person shares more information and in great detail with me, it breaks my heart a little bit more. As I am allowing them to debrief with the wrong person, my heart gets heavier and weaker.

I am the patient in this picture, and no one really sees it that way. Yes, they can see that I lie here in this hospital bed, but are they really, truly aware of how this is taking its toll on me? Has anyone, other than this nurse, really taken into account all that is weighing me down from this catastrophic event? In what other scenario would staff debrief and state their experiences with the patient? That never happens! It's not right to share all your personal experiences of the event with the patient, to share all the details of the event. I understand that they watched in horror as my body was failing and being worked on right in front of them, but that was me going through it on that stretcher. I need to talk about it too!

> It was awful to be a part of,
> No one wants to see it through my eyes,
> My perspective.
>
> It's too scary to face!

I know I have permitted this debriefing to happen. It's in my nature to help other people with their struggles, pain and suffering, and exclude myself and what I need to heal from. It's far easier to help others, than fix, help or heal myself, to never look at what I truly need to face or heal from. Just keep going, pushing and moving forward.

"I'm just trying to help them through this all," I say. "It must have been awful to witness and watch me like that."

I'm flipping the conversation to avoid addressing myself, putting the focus on everyone else again. The truth is painful, and everything surrounding this incident is too emotionally draining for me to address. When I do pause and think about it, it wreaks havoc on my brain, making me so forlorn. I ask myself, *Why do I allow this to keep happening? Why can't I permit myself to take care of me?*

My nurse flips the conversation back to address my needs, not allowing me to push myself out of the picture. "One of the doctors you work with was just here, wanting to see you," she says. "I shooed him away. He wasn't even there that day and he isn't even in your circle of care. He doesn't need to bother you. I told him you need to rest; you have been through enough. I said I would relay to you that he stopped by."

I find it quite refreshing that she changes the conversation back to me. She is protecting me and is fully advocating for me and my right to heal from this. She reiterates back to me what my needs are, the ones I don't want to admit to or address. She is standing up for me, especially now that I can't bring myself to have a voice in this. She's protecting and caring for me like a mother would do. She is allowing for my need to breathe in peace, be in a quiet space to start permitting myself to see the bigger picture.

I love the fact that so many people are wanting to see me. I perceive and portray this as them loving me, respecting me. They are happy and joyful that I'm here!

It's actually the opposite; it's what I can do for them. That's why they come see me. That's why they stand at my bed side. It's for their benefit, not mine! It really isn't therapeutic for me to debrief them all, and not have the opportunity to express what I went through, what I am feeling or experiencing. Why do I have to do this? Why do I have to prove that I am still strong, for them? I am driven to helping others.

Perhaps I cannot let go of that, wanting to hold on tight to a very strong core belief—always be in Survival Mode. Show strength, not weakness. Don't let people feel sorry for you! Exist and try to live. Push through the pain, in spite of the difficult circumstances I am faced with.

> It's funny, this core belief;
> It actually makes me weaker and suffer more.
> Never allowing myself to heal from underlying issues.
> I'm good at pushing my pain down
> Not wanting or needing to find the root cause
> of my suffering and pain
> Never able to fix or heal from what really weighs me down

"I'm not permitting anyone else through your door to burden you with their pain," my nurse says. "I'm keeping your door closed, and I will stand up for you, advocate for you. Be your voice! You do not need to hear any more stories about what everyone else has experienced. I am taking a stand for you! You need to heal from this. It won't happen if you put your energy into helping them. It's your turn Julia." I find her assertive statements very therapeutic and it brings me a beautiful awareness.

"I'll be checking in on you, assessing you and making sure your heart is beating at a regular rate and rhythm. Give that part to me. Rest. Heal. I will protect you. I'll let your family in when they arrive, but no one else for today. Your heart needs this!" Her words are like an enormous breath of fresh air.

"Thank you!" I respond and I breathe that all in.

As I exhale, I am letting go and releasing the pressure I put on myself of needing to help others heal, and I breathe in the new focus and awareness of healing myself. Allowing the process to begin.

It's as though my nurse can sense exactly what I need, exactly what I wanted to say but didn't have the words to say. She is truly helping me help myself. Teaching me to find my inner voice, the one I pushed down so many years ago.

For two days I have been debriefing the hospital staff: nurses, doctors, managers, CEOs, cleaning staff, porters. I permitted it, allowed it to happen. I fell right back into my familiar and comfortable nursing role. I thought, *I may not be able to get out of this bed, but I sure as hell can sit here and help everyone else cope. I can help by listening to them and their perceptions of everything that has taken place.* It's a twisted, complex, surreal, unimaginable catastrophic series of events that happened to all of us. There is still something inside of me that is not able or willing to even start to address any of it for myself. There's still a missing piece that I am not ready or able to see, my mind just focuses on the fact that I am here, alive!

I AM ALIVE!

It's as though I have been given a second chance and I am just learning how to adapt to this new life. This new state of being. So, as I sat here before, listening to everyone else's debriefing, I was trying not to absorb everything that was being said; I was holding space for people to express their story to me. Excluding and eliminating the fact that I have a version of my own. I am trying to unscramble my brain from its thoughts so I can see the bigger picture; I just haven't allowed myself *time* to do that.

I was helping others through their pain and torment. Listening to their side of story as if I hadn't been there, as if I didn't actually experience any of this. As people kept entering my room and debriefing with me, I'd wonder, *Did everyone forget that I was the patient on that stretcher?* I may have entered the unit as a bubbly enthusiastic nurse ready to start her shift, but I left my unit rebooted and broken on a stretcher that I coded on. I have a version, a perspective and a story to share, too. I know more of the story than anyone else, for it happened to *me*!

I sat here, on my hospital bed—as a patient, not as a nurse—listening to all of them. All the staff that were there with me as I was brought back into this life. Listening to everyone who needs to debrief and hadn't gotten an outlet to do so. They all need to share and talk about what they went through, to release the heartache from what took place. But I release myself from that role. I need to be heard too. I need to heal from this and its many layers and missing pieces.

It's my turn to heal.

Debriefing is done when there is a need to discuss what has happened during a crisis or traumatic event. It's a safe place to share your feelings and let go of the craziness and hardship you were a part of. It is done so you don't carry that pain with you. So you can free yourself from the active, emotionally charged memory of it. It's so it doesn't consume you. It's a powerful tool that helps individuals and the team to reflect upon a recent experience and discuss all areas surrounding it; this also helps disassociate you from your thoughts and memories of the trauma, allowing you to disconnect from it and not ball it up inside. It's very therapeutic and healing!

I wish the staff would have had the opportunity to close the unit for more than eight minutes, allowing the debriefing of the staff to occur. Then I wouldn't have to feel the pressure from everyone debriefing with me. I wouldn't have to deal with the brunt of the pain and suffering of the staff members and everyone else that this affects—the ones who were there and the ones who weren't.

I wish I received some form of debriefing, for I feel as though I am to blame for what they all need to heal from. I hold an array of emotions in my heart and my mind. Right now, guilt is the strongest emotion; I feel I am to blame for everyone's emotional pain, because I was the one who needed saving. I was the one on the stretcher and in my time of need, I made the team go through this traumatic event with me.

I understand and can relate to the struggle and the impact this all has on them. I have seen it and I have been a part of something similar. I have my own firsthand experience of a horrific, traumatizing and haunting situation, exactly 13 years ago. I never got to talk about it or debrief and I still hold it in my body and mind. I can't let them do the same, therefore I provide a space for them to talk, but I still need someone to hear me too.

I recognize I have a lot of healing to do and a lot of things to let go of. There are just too many layers to address at one time, and I don't have the tools to find the answers to heal from this all.

> Maybe I just need to calm my mind
> So my soul can figure out what it needs to heal from.

As my nurse grants me time to be alone in my room, I am able to further reflect, and I begin to become conscious of the changes within me and my world. I start to understand the underlying occurrence that has happened and what is happening. I am now able to start addressing some major epiphanies.

> There are a lot more layers and pieces to this puzzle
> A lot more that
> I have to accept, see and say.
> Let the healing begin…
> For I am here.
> Alive!

Rebooted and Re-birthed!

Chapter 12

Lessons from My Father

Survival Mode!
Always demonstrate the illusion of strength.
Not weakness,
Never show anyone your
Hidden pain....
or gut-wrenching raw emotions.

Keep your true broken self,
Hidden...

That was a lesson my father taught me at a young age. He never actually said this directly to me, but he acted it out, and indirectly instilled his belief in me: Never show weakness, and never let anyone into your heart to see the true pain and suffering. "Don't allow anyone to feel sorry for you," was the message I received, loud and clear!

I internalized this message for my entire existence. This lesson was ingrained in me after my mother's death, when I was only three years old. I clearly remember my father portraying this message to me and my brother. I don't recall this in full detail, but I do have flashes of this very significant memory.

We were in a grocery store, and someone was expressing their sympathy towards us regarding our mother's passing and my dad's loss of his wife, leaving him alone to care for the two of us: my seven-year-old brother and three-year-old me.

"Oh, how devastating for your loss," this pretty lady said, sympathizing with us.

My dad was so broken, shattered by the loss of his wife—his love, the mother of his children—but did not want to show it. He didn't want to face that pain. He didn't know how to let anyone else into his heart and allow them to see the true suffering he was enduring within. So instead of crying or expressing what he was truly feeling, he suppressed that and turned it into anger instead. It's as though he blew a gasket; something inside of him couldn't be contained any longer. All his pent-up anguish had to be released somehow.

That's when it happened—he became so enraged at this nice, pretty lady, right in the middle of the grocery store. She was showing such kindness towards us, such compassion; well, my three-year-old self viewed it as kindness and compassion. I guess my dad thought and viewed it differently.

"We don't need anyone feeling sorry for us!" he screeched at her.

I innocently looked up at him with my young bewildered eyes. This shell of a man was so broken and hurt and was doing everything in his power not to fall apart. He was obviously holding back his tears. He was fighting against everything and anything that would break him further. Not allowing anyone to see his true emotions: his sadness, grief, pain and anguish. He kept it all in, compressed all of his internal emotions so he didn't have to face them. Perhaps he did this to protect my brother and me, or maybe to protect himself. True avoidance of what he was actually feeling and suffering from.

"Get the hell away from us!" he screamed at her.

He looked down at my brother and me, shouting at us that we had to leave. And so we just left. We fled from the store, the three of us running away, hiding from the pain and the sorrow. He made us leave everything there; we deserted it all—the lady, the situation, all our food. We left it there, right in the middle of the produce aisle. It happened so quickly.

He held my hand with a tight grip and gently pushed my brother along to leave the store. We left; we just left!

We never spoke about it. Never acknowledged that this even happened. I don't even know if my father was fully aware of his actions, or if he just blanked out for a moment, overwhelmed by his emotions, and completely switched off from his reality, to protect what little he had left inside.

I review this memory now, and I understand that his outburst was due to the pure raw emotion that he was not ready to face. Since the passing of my mother, his wife, he had completely fallen apart. Instead of dealing with any raw, painful emotion or memory, he blocked it out or tried to escape it through avoidance, overworking, and alcohol.

He became a shell of a broken man. He has never fully healed from it. He was never able to fully accept the pain and loss of his wife, and he pushed it all down to a deep dark place within himself and is unable to deal with it. He tries to escape from his reality through other sources of comfort, like numbing agents to ease the intensity of it. But in turn, he has pushed others away who have tried to show him love and compassion. He avoids people that remind him of his internal pain. Instead of feeling the sorrow, he runs away from them just like he did the nice, pretty lady at the grocery store.

In this process of numbing and altering his reality, he tries to protect what little he has left in his heart, and he continuously pushes people away so that he never has to face his raw gut-wrenching emotions, his true broken self. In his mind he's in Survival Mode, when actually it's all an illusion of strength, to hide the pain and suffering. Protecting himself, and his shattered heart.

I too do this to some extent: not allowing people full access to the vast spectrum of my raw emotions, perhaps because of this harsh realization at such a young age. I was subconsciously wired not to trust others with my underlining emotions, the emotions that most people would have a hard time dealing with, including myself. Perhaps it is not to protect them, but to protect myself.

It's so hard to face reality at times, and to deal with all the emotions and pain that make you feel broken, lost, alone and afraid. It's the fear that holds you back. The fear of how it can consume you so quickly, throwing you into a vortex of doom. It's so much easier to suppress and bury it all down. It eventually rises to the surface and you have to deal with it. For there's no point in going on; you have to break free as you can only hide from it so long. Or until there's an outburst like my father, having a misdirected explosion or until it physically and emotionally eats you alive.

Chapter 13

The Depths of My Abyss

The Depths of my abyss are deeper and greater than I could ever imagine.
I can no longer cope with this…

It is the winter season 2017/2018, and I can no longer take much more of this debilitating, devastating and unpredictable disease. We have tried many different therapies, from small things (changing my diet, doing self-care, meditating, stretching and exercising every day) to more extreme, out-of-the-box experiments that Greg and I researched. Aspirin therapy is one of the experiments; I take 1400mg per day to help with my fatigue and pain, but that only touches the surface and causes more problems, like a bleeding stomach.

I am willing to try anything to help with the symptoms from my progressing MS. My doctor is even running out of suitable options for me, and I'm losing hope to keep going another day.

THE LILY NURSE

My family is struggling with watching me suffer through this too, but they don't know a fraction of the pain I am suffering from. I am not even aware of all the pain and suffering I have pushed away, for I never wanted to deal with any of it...

Oh God... please have mercy!
I plead to you...
Please take this pain away!

I beg you...
Hear my cry!
I cannot take it for one more moment.
The pain is too deep,
It's so painful.

Don't inflict any more onto me
or upon my family
It is Destroying the ones I love.
It is Destroying me.
The FEAR of this,
Has taken me over
It has engulfed me
Brought me to the depths of the Abyss
I cannot face it.

Take it away
Take it all away!

I stand at your mercy,
For the love of God
Please...
Take it away!

I can't go on anymore!
I Surrender!

The pain! Oh fuck, the pain! It's a pain that is so unimaginable, unbelievably unbearable! It's constant, crippling, debilitating, and eats away at my inner core. All I want to do is give up. Be free of this pain and torment. Every cell within my entire being feels as though it's shaking, screaming and pleading for it to stop. *For the love of God...mercy!*

I want to scream from the top of my lungs, but instead I put on a smile, and pretend the pain is not real. I hide it from everyone, including myself. I put some lipstick on, and slap on my survivor mask. No one will even notice. It's amazing what a little makeup can hide. Wow, if they could only see the extent of it; I don't think anyone could truly comprehend all my pain and suffering hidden within. I try not to let it consume me, but there are times it does, and this time—I'm done; I cannot go on. It has literally eaten away at me.

I absorb not only the pain, but all my fear that is attached to this unpredictable disease. Denying anyone access to my internal emotions. I try to hide it from myself as well, not wanting to deal with the intensity of it. Sealing it all into a tiny little box of my mind, storing it away, never to be addressed nor faced again. The reality of this devastating disease is beyond terrifying. It's like a seed of a thought that has been planted in my brain, sprouting and rooting further fear of a terrifying and questionable future. The fear of the unknown, the impending doom and the unpredictability hold me prisoner within my thoughts.

I will not let it take me over. I will keep fighting, surviving. I do not want this disease to win. I'll keep fighting against it and pushing it all in and down to a deep dark abyss. I hold the power to keep going, but this disease has reared its ugly head again, and gives me more pain and suffering. It's as though my muscles are being ripped off my bones. And when the pain lessens, the numbness and/or fatigue surfaces, bringing yet another dimension and element to this saga.

I constantly have to deal with this pain, fear and uncertainty. I'm always having it challenging me and putting up obscure obstacles in my way. My reality spirals me out of control, spinning me into a vortex of doom. To a very dark place, a deep abyss. A place that seems endless and full of despair.

I try to claw myself out, but I am dragged back. I sink deeper and further within the abyss. Being encapsulated into darkness. Being attacked from the inside out. Having my body literally eating away at itself, and destroying me, physically, emotionally, mentally and spiritually.

Physically my body fights the inevitable destruction of my myelin sheath—the protective coating of my nerves. As it does this, the messages from my brain reach scattered, broken or frayed areas within this coating, then is forced to disperse an erratic flow of messages from my brain. Firing off nerve impulses of a different path within my nervous system, dodging current runways that have been already developed, trying to send messages but they get garbled. This then causes pain, numbness and other unpredictable challenges.

The emotional pain of all this becomes unbearable. I am struck by the raw emotions of being a burden on my family, the frustration, and the grief for my old life when I was free from this suffering. It takes a toll on me. I am terrified of having my family take care of me. Not because I am resistant to their help, but because I am saddened by the pressure they are faced with, the need to have to help me. This is my cross to bear, not theirs. This is my pain, suffering, worry, fear, anguish, and everything in between; it is something I have to deal with, not them.

There have been many times when it all has become too much for me to handle. I would find myself standing in the shower and crying, letting go and releasing the emotions I could not bear to hold on to any longer. Having the water from the shower wash it all away: my tears, my feelings, my emotions, my pain. Taking the tiny little box out of the corner of my mind. The one crammed full of everything I did not want to admit to, or deal with, or face. It would bellow out and seep through this box, one stress and emotion at a time, not wanting to be contained anymore. Bursting at the seams, until finally it would break through, and force it all out of me, making me own it. Own all of it, not letting me keep it inside any further. Like an explosion. That's when I would let out one hell of a scream, relieve myself from all the burden and all of what I had been bound to, and I would bawl. Weep like the 40-day flood, filling the floor of the shower with tears, but instead of drowning in it, washing it all away through the drain. Till the next time I would have an internal explosion.

As the tears come flooding from my eyes. I allow the shower head's forceful stream of water to saturate my face; permitting me to embrace the emotions that have been stuck within my mind for quite some time. I embrace it for just a moment. Then as the water washes away, so too do the contents of what I have boxed away. All the emotions and pain it had within it. It all washes away, for a short period of time, down the drain into the depths of a new abyss. Out of my thoughts, but never out of my mind. As this happens it would provide me with enough strength to go on for another day.

MS is an unpredictable, chronic, progressive auto-immune disease. This often-disabling disease of the central nervous system disrupts the flow of information within the brain, and between the brain and the entire body. The disease is characterized by the loss and/or damage of the myelin sheath. Antibodies attack the myelin, creating "plaques" or lesions within the brain. The damage prevents communication between the brain and spinal cord, causing numerous symptoms.

Once diagnosed, MS stays with you for life; there is no cure, and at times it feels like there is no hope. I'm losing hope! The symptoms can fluctuate greatly from day to day, minute to minute, and no two people experience it the same way. Thus, it's difficult for others to understand and believe the depth of what you are going through. It isolates you! No one truly sees what you have to deal with, or the extent of the fear and suffering you are facing. It's constantly changing, but always progressing. It's the invisible disease. It affects every part of your life, yet people are unaware because you appear to be fine. You don't "look" sick. So, you are left alone to suffer and fight what seems like a losing battle, every moment of every day. Always worrying if this is the day it takes you over. All you wish for, while in this state of being, is for it to end, vanish, and to be free of its destruction.

I don't know what changed in me! I recall many years of not knowing what was wrong with me, trying to find a diagnosis, a reason for all my aliments and symptoms. Why was I so fatigued? Why was I experiencing all sorts of pain and numbness throughout my body, slurred speech, poor vision, difficulty swallowing? And that's just a few of the symptoms I was experiencing. It was years of appointments, rushing to the emergency room, and still not knowing what was happening to me.

I flash back to the day of my diagnosis, in October 2014. Finally, I was admitted into hospital and given an MRI. That's when we all became aware of it; I had 27 lesions throughout my brain and spinal cord. It was definitive—this was my explanation for all my pain and suffering.

My MS diagnosis was a life-changing moment. Not only for me, but for my family, my friends and everyone in my life! I will never forget the moment when my neurologist walked into my room and gave me my diagnosis.

It was first thing in the morning, the crack of dawn. My new doctor, my assigned neurologist peeked through the curtain that surrounded my hospital bed. As a nurse, I knew the look on his face all too well. The look of devastation and sadness is hard to hide, because we are only human. I've had this demeanor when entering a patient's room. It hints at what is not quite being said yet, before the words clarify the truth.

I am now put in that same position of being in the presence of this doctor bearing that similar appearance. The "how do I tell the patient this devastating diagnosis" look. So, I stop him before he can say anything; relieving him of the strife associated with those words, that label.

I humorously blurt out, "Before you give me this diagnosis, let me put on a bra, because I want my girls up before you say what you have to say!"

We both laugh at my ridiculous request. I manage to get my bra on but require assistance from a very nice nurse. I blame it on the excessive amount of IV tubing that was attached to me, but what I really need is another person beside me as I started to wrap my head around this and a moment to process as I become untangled from the IV tubing and my thoughts. Once my bra is on, and my gown tied up, I signal the doctor in to enter my space. He sits on the edge of my bed beside me, sheepishly lowers his head, and very quietly confirms my diagnosis.

"Okay. So, what's the next step?" I calmly question.

He smiles the biggest reassuring smile and says, "With your personality and positive attitude, you've got this!"

I know I do, I think to myself. I know the exact place to put this fear…into my dark abyss. It's an infinite dark place I can hide from, sealing away the things I don't want to address. It allows me to keep on going; this is not going to stop me. I'm going to keep fighting!

So, I take a deep breath of my new life. I then ask the nurse for an eye patch—which I slap over my left eye and adorn with a green eyeball and eyebrow sticker—grab a coffee and start sharing my news with the world. I figure the eye patch would help with my already altered vision—my optic neuritis—and prevent me from getting too dizzy and nauseated. Now I can block the messages of my damaged optic nerve; block my mind from my obscured vision. The stickers are placed to put an element of humor to this devastating reality. Besides, people are going to stare at me anyway, so I might as well give them something to laugh at.

Using humor to blind myself and others from facing the real truth. Inhibiting them and myself from having to deal with what I had just been faced with. Absorbing it all in and trying to find the positive outcome within this. Great coping strategy, I have always led myself to believe.

That diagnosis changed me.
It changed my whole outlook on life.

I struggle on a daily basis, and I'm faced with many challenges, but with the love of my immediate family, I remain positive and strong, even when I can't bear the pain. There are many days the pain exceeds any of my worst nightmares. My legs give out, and there are times they feel as though they are 1,000 pounds of lead and cannot move. My husband then comes to rescue me; he picks me up in his arms and carries me up the stairs. Holding me tightly within his arms, he goes up the 16 steps and down the hallway to our bedroom. He helps me dress and will sit with me until I drift off to sleep. He is forever by my side and always in my corner, helping me fight each and every day. Always living moment to moment and trying not to fear the future. Both of us feeling helpless, but him never giving up on me!

Greg is my saving grace. He lifts me up, not only physically, but emotionally, mentally and spiritually. The days that I am beyond broken, he reminds me of the greatness we have within our family unit. Of how important life really is. That MS is not a death sentence or a reason to give up, merely a series of obstacles that require alternate forms of thinking and problem solving. Always adjusting and adapting to what life has to throw at us. It's not to be seen as a challenge but as a blessing! This way of thinking grants me the opportunity to review and evaluate what is really important in life. It reminds me that every moment counts; good or bad, it all has a meaning and a reason to be there in our lives.

"It could be worse!" Greg reminds me quite often.

This is his plea to me—not to give up. He cannot bear to see me suffering and in pain. He does everything and anything to bring me happiness and joy. He sacrifices himself to be there for me, to help us live life to its absolute fullest! Grabbing hold of every opportunity, big or small, which provides any form of happiness and joy! Trying to let go of anything that does not serve us, trying to eliminate the negativity, the layers of pain and suffering. Full speed ahead; don't look back—no regrets! You never know what tomorrow will bring. Try to find happiness and joy when and where you can. It's only a matter of time when we don't have enough breath in our lungs to breathe it all in; breathe in that life, and release and let go of what doesn't serve you. Surround yourself with love and support!

Greg is my biggest support. He is the love of my life. My everything! He's always in my corner, cheering me on, picking me up and never letting me go. Never letting me fall. When I am weak, he gives me strength, keeping me positive and strong. He helps me push through, never letting me feel sorry for myself. He helps me create the most amazing memories and such a blessed life, to truly cherish everything!

With all that said…

Now I find myself in a world I cannot bear anymore. It's too much for me to handle. I'm done fighting! I haven't a clue why, after all these years of pushing, fighting and not giving up, I am now ready to throw in the towel and surrender. Why now? Why I am feeling this way? I feel like I am spiraling to a dark place that I was dreading to fall into. It is the inevitable place that I was always meant to see—to find what is in the dark!

People say I'm the strongest person they know. Why? Why do I always have to be so strong? Why can't I stop, let my guard down and see what I need to face? Stop the fight, just once. One time, so I can heal!

I'm brilliant at hiding—from the world and myself—my true feelings and emotions, the suffering and the pain. I just keep going, shoving everything inside and down to a place where I believe I can hide it, and to hopefully forget it all. I pray to never have to really deal with any of the horrific intensity that has been compiling over the years, all the unresolved despair and the emotions that link to that feeling.

I can only communicate and see within myself a mere fraction of this, just touching the surface of what I am truly feeling. I never go too in-depth on the emotional, mental or spiritual aspect of it. That's a whole other piece to my story, a missing link that I don't want to face. I guess it's because of Survival Mode: Always demonstrate strength, not weakness, and never admit to my true hidden scarred emotions. Push them down, far down, and hide them into the depths of my abyss. Access denied to the suppressed, unaddressed and unidentified inner turmoil within.

Now this compilation of physical, emotional, and mental pain that I have compressed into my dark abyss has finally overcome me. It has engulfed and entrapped me in a place that I feared, a place that I have always tried to avoid. I want to be free of this place and heal from this pain and suffering. I want to be me, the person I was always meant to be. I'm done being controlled by this suffering. It has embedded its gnarled claws into me, dragging me down and this time I cannot find the strength to come back up from the depths of this abyss—I must face it.

I have no more fight.
I surrender!
I can't live one more day like this

RELEASE ME!

CHAPTER 14

DNR (DO NOT RESUSCITATE)
~  ~

It's April 16, 2018—the new moon—Greg and I are laying on the couch, nuzzled together. It's a beautiful, new and refreshing day; the kids are busy playing, and Greg and I are able to have a moment to ourselves. I love this quiet and alone time with him; this keeps us so connected and in tune with each other. This is my favorite place on earth: right up against his chest (his heart), within his loving embrace. I love the feeling of his strong arms wrapped around me; it is so comforting, loving, and safe. It's moments like this that we can just be.

> Be in the moment.

This precious time of togetherness allows us to breathe, realign, regroup, and truly be present for one another. As we lay here conversing about our day, it allows me to pause from our everyday chaos, challenges and struggles. I am able to fully breathe, and I allow the power of the new moon and Greg's loving embrace to reset an old way of thinking so I can set out new intentions for a new beginning. This space and time help to silence my mind and makes me more aware of what I was blocking out and closing my mind to. It's bringing forth a new light that shines upon us.

As Greg and I are lying on the couch nuzzled together, we talk about our day. It's nothing of great significance, just reflecting and informing each other of the happenings throughout our normal mundane day. We talk about the kids, school, work, basically whatever comes to mind, and what we believe is relevant to share, but we're truly listening to each other and holding space as we physically hold one another, taking turns talking, sharing and communicating.

We value this time of connectedness and communication within our relationship. Always trying to provide a safe and comfortable space to converse and be ourselves. Always being open and honest, and trying not to keep the other in the dark. Truly being present for each other, which instills open lines of communication. Always trusting, loving, respecting and supporting each other. We value this safe, loving and comfortable space we provide to be ourselves. It's pure bliss....

As we connect and hold space for each other, I am able to pause and free myself from the craziness of our hectic lives. I finally feel free to relax, and I am able to breathe. It's as though his embrace supports my soul, mind and body, permitting me to be still and calm. Nothing makes me feel more content, happy, safe, and truly at ease than laying within my husband's arms, nuzzled up against his chest. It helps me to be grounded and centered, and gifts me with the purest sense of protection and love. It's my safe place!

"I am so blessed, Greg. I have you. Our kids. Our life! I love you so much!" I proclaim to him, tightening my embrace and giving him a little squeeze.

He chuckles and says, "I love you so much, Julia. You are my everything!"

He kisses the center of my forehead and grips me tight. That's when it happens, out of the blue, out of nowhere. As we lay together on the couch, there's a beautiful pause within our conversation. A stillness in the air apparates. Time stops momentarily. It's a peaceful and profound pause occurring within our world.

Then I am suddenly hit with this surge of energy, emotion and thought, and it ripples throughout my entire body. This feeling rushes over me as I lay here with my head pressed up against Greg's chest. I am drawn to the sound of his loving and strong heartbeat. It's as though it is speaking to me. As I listen more intently, I have this overwhelming need to blurt out this spontaneous thought that is cascading throughout my being, to announce a revelation that surges throughout my mind. It's almost like a jolt of a new realization. It's as though something came over me. Something, or someone was speaking to me, changing my perception, altering my perspectives.

Awakening me....

After all these years of thinking one way and being fixated on one set plan, I am now presented with a new belief and a new insight. What I believed in my mind for so many years is now all unraveled and changed in a split second. A momentary pause and change to everything I was currently dealing with. I don't know what comes over me. All I know is this intense feeling, this huge shift inside of me, has occurred. A revelation! A realization! An awakening!

I quickly sit straight up on the couch, scan the room, and look down at Greg. I frantically blurt out at him, "Greg, I want to reverse my DNR status."

He looks at me with wide eyes, as if what I am requesting or saying didn't quite register, and he responds, "What did you say?"

"I. Don't. Want. To be a DNR anymore!" I methodically explain.

It's as though a reality bubble popped right in front of me, and it woke me up.

"I don't want to give up! I'm not going to let this disease take me over! Greg!" I continue relaying this new information with a hurried enthusiastic flair. "I have so much to live for! If they need to do CPR, I want them to do it. I want them to fight for me. I want to be saved!"

***

It's shortly after my second attempt at pulse therapy and my MS is progressing. I have more lesions throughout my brain and down my spinal cord, my symptoms are worsening, and I am scared beyond belief. I am unsure of what the future will hold for me and the fear of the inevitable has set in. This disease is too unpredictable, and my symptoms are getting progressively worse within a short period of time. The number of lesions is dramatically increasing and I want to save my family from the future burden and pain that my disease may bring to them.

This has been one of the hardest decisions I ever had to make! This was decided when FEAR started to rear its ugly head and really began to take over my world.

"Titus. Jayda. Come in here. Family Meeting!" I yell out to our kids to join Greg and me in the living room.

"Coming!" they both yell back from different areas of the house.

Greg asks me again, "Are you sure about this? If this is what you really want, we'll support you!" He squeezes my hand with both of his. Then he kisses me on the forehead.

"Yes, Greg," I say. "This is what I want. The pain and symptoms are getting too bad, and too scary for me. My MS is slowly taking me over."

He quietly nods in agreement. I know in my heart that this is beyond difficult and scary for him to agree with. However, he is the only one who knows the extent and the severity of this debilitating and devastating disease and what it is doing to me, to us. He's the one who sees me fall apart, physically, mentally and emotionally. He is the one who carries me through it all, not only emotionally, but he physically carries me in his arms, and when I am screaming in pain, he's the one there holding me tight, feeling helpless as he watches and supports me through it all. He does everything in his power to help me. He tries to take it all away, tries to ease my pain and suffering, and attempts to create happiness for me, for us, no matter what. I know this breaks his heart, but he completely understands why I want this.

"I don't want to end up in a place where you all have to take care of me. I don't want to be a burden to this family. I'm not giving up! I want to live a full life! But, if my heart gives out, I want everyone to step back and let me be. I don't think my body could handle the shock of it. It would exacerbate my MS too much, causing my body to completely give out. I don't want that! I don't someone to fight a losing battle!" I cry as I am trying to state and reconfirm my reasons.

He looks at me intently, with helpless, loving eyes. He would do anything to take my pain and suffering away and to make me whole and happy. It is one of the many amazing attributes he possesses. Pure unconditional love!

"I don't want to be stuck in a bed having no quality of life. I want to continue living life to the fullest, but if and when my heart does give out, it's time to let go. Let me be free! That will be the time to let me ascend to my next phase of life, the one where I'm pain free, away from all the suffering. A restart, a reboot. Away from what I cannot control; away from all of my torture!" I lay things out for him, expressing my truest worry, fear and wishes.

"Please, Greg," I plead, desperately wanting him to agree with me. "This is what I want."

"Okay," he whispers, exhaling loudly, closing his eyes and nodding his head.

The kids enter the living room, and jump up onto the love seat beside the couch that Greg and I are on. Greg and I quickly wipe away our tears. The children stop their rough housing as they see the expressions on our faces. They sit there quietly staring at us intently, anticipating what we are about to tell them, what this family meeting is all about.

"Are you okay, Mom?" Jayda hesitantly questions me. Both children have concerned looks upon their faces.

I don't know how to truthfully answer the question, so I begin the family meeting to deflect it.

"Daddy and I want to have a discussion with you both," I begin. "You both understand and know that my MS has been getting really bad? Right?"

They both nod in unison.

"You know that someday Mommy might not be able to walk, and that this disease is going to get worse," I say, highlighting the harsh truth for them. My voice cracks as I try to continue.

Titus and Jayda stare at us even more intently, hanging on my every word. Greg and I have involved them both in every decision regarding my MS—never keeping them in the dark, always being open and honest with them. They are always a part of the decisions and discussions, for it affects us all. Greg and I have always had open communication with our children, providing a safe space for them to share their thoughts, feelings, and emotions. Never shutting them out. Never having them fear that they can't be heard. We want them to know that they are not alone; they are a part of this all, and we will get through it, together. Greg and I encourage and empower them through these lines of communication, and we are continuously providing them with love, support and respect. We are all going through this. Each and every one of us, together; therefore, their opinions matter too. This is what life has thrown at us, so we might as well band together to gain strength and support from one another. We are, after all, the Evans'ssss! (That's what we call our little nuclear family unit.)

"I don't ever want to be a burden on you, or to this family in the future. So, I have discussed it with your dad, and made the discussion that I want to be a DNR." I say, verbally laying it all out on the table. Stating my living will, my wishes.

"What's that, Mom?" Jayda inquires.

"Well, a DNR means Do Not Resuscitate." I inform her in a matter-of-fact nursing voice. I break the definition down further for her, for them, so they can understand what I am trying to say. "So, that means if I were ever to collapse, I don't want someone to work on me."

"That's what you tried to do for your mom, in Mexico? Right?" Jayda questions. She is trying to form her own understanding of what I'm trying to discuss with them both.

"Yes. I performed CPR on Connie—my stepmom—in Mexico. There were other people there too; other nurses that came to help us as well. We all worked on her. We all tried to bring her back, tried to keep her here." I say.

"She died though." Titus reminds us, with a stern look on his face and harshness to his voice.

"Yes, she did," I confirm. "She died in my arms, on the beach.

She died as I was going to perform CPR on her. "I started CPR on her, in hopes to bring her back. I really tried! I cracked her ribs as I initiated CPR, and I tried everything I could to bring her back to us! I tried, I tried so hard to bring her back, back to our family. All of us who were performing CPR on her tried everything we could to bring her back. We didn't give up. We continued giving compressions, over and over again. Trying to get at least one breath in," I tell them as I am holding back my tears.

"It was a very hard thing to do, a hard thing to be a part of, working on my mother, my stepmom, when I knew she had already left us, already passed. I knew she had left us, even before I started CPR," I admit. I gaze off to the distance with a blank stare upon my face, then lower my head.

I am transported back to that time in my life. As I begin to touch on the subtle details of it for my children, it is replaying over and over within my thoughts, like a broken record. This vivid memory is ingrained within my mind, and I am able to recall what I experienced in full detail. I am brought right back to the memory of her coding, reliving it all over again.

After pulling my mother out of the ocean and assisting her to a catamaran boat parked on the beach, I encouraged her to cough up and vomit out more of the saltwater from her system. She was struggling, but remained with me, talking and moving slowly on her own. She leaned on the side of the catamaran, looking so scared. There wasn't a lot I could do at this point. So, I held her in my arms, helping her feel safe and loved.

We changed roles in that moment; I became the mother figure, taking charge of the situation and taking care of her, and she became like a timid young child, trying to fight for her life.

It became second nature to me, holding her in my arms, continually calming, cradling and comforting her. I helped her lean to the side to vomit out the saltwater, holding her so she wouldn't fall. I thought that she just needed to get it all out of her body and she'd be okay. She was going to live through this.

I remained calm as I continued visually assessing her.

Then her whole persona rapidly changed, as did her colour. It changed to the colour of death: grey. I screamed to the people around me for help. My family who were in the water with us had already fled to gather help from others. One by one they left in different directions to do what they thought necessary, running away from this inconceivable situation. Leaving me alone on the beach with her, surrounded by hundreds of people, none of them really acknowledging what was happening right in front of them.

She began to weaken at the knees, so I helped her to a beach chair to sit. "Mom, I've got you! I'm here!" I reassured her though my tears.

"Julia, I'm scared!" she said, looking at me with piercing panicked eyes. As she sat on the chair, I tried to bring my leg around to sit behind her. I was holding her, trying to help her through this.

I looked down at her, she looked up at me and our eyes locked; everything changed. I could feel her let go. Her body went limp, her eyes empty, her last breath taken. She was gone.

Then everything stopped, transformed. Nothing was as it seemed. It was as though we were taken to another dimension of the same space, like a hidden world within the same space and time of the world we knew and were in. Like we were behind the scenes away from all the chaos, people, mayhem. There's a light that illuminates around us, separating us from that other world we were in. This light is so radiant, and it shines upon us.

I remember. I saw it! I saw the light! The light! I walked side by side with Connie. We walked along the beach towards this light; towards something that was beyond anything I had ever experienced or could have ever imagined. It was so beautiful, so still and peaceful. It was as though we were the only two on the beach! It was this beautiful, blissful and serene moment. Time stood still. Nothing else seemed to matter. Everything was so calm and tranquil—the ocean, the untouched sand, the sky, and the two of us, quietly walking side by side within this place of bliss. We exchanged no words, no looks. We casually glided together, alongside the water's edge, on the beach, just the two of us, towards this magnificent light. It was so angelic!

Then I recall switching from that place and coming back into this dimension, this chaotic world. I was smack dab in the middle of a horrific scene. It was crammed with an unimaginable bone-chilling commotion. I looked down, and there lies my dead mother. The shell of her lifeless body is draped over my arms, her eyes wide open, with no life or soul left within them. I went into auto-nurse mode and attempted to do what I was trained for: CPR! I tried to bring her back. I tried to fight for her. I was trying to save her, trying to bring her back to this world, back to us! Trying desperately to get at least one breath of life into her.

I initiated CPR even though I could see within her eyes that there was no life left in them. Her soul had departed from her body. Her body remained here with us as a shell, an empty vessel, lifeless and limp now laying upon the sand. I couldn't stop what I had started. I kept fighting. I didn't want to let her go. I didn't want to give up or give her up. Every compression drove her deeper in to the sand, expelling water out of her mouth, like a pump removing the salt water from the depths of her abdomen. Her eyes remained open the entire time, filling with sand as they blankly stared off into the distance. Empty and gone.

At that point, I was strictly in nurse mode and it didn't even dawn on me what I had just experienced with the light. That I had witnessed her transitioning to a place of bliss, and now I remain here in this realm, performing CPR. In that moment, I could only see what was right in front of me: my lifeless mother on this earth.

I knew she had been recently suffering in this world. She felt lost and didn't know what her purpose was anymore. I knew she was a lost soul; she told me right before all of this happened. Her mission here was fulfilled on this earth. She didn't know what she wanted to do when she got home from our vacation. She did know that she wanted to spend more time in Mexico, her paradise.

It was as though she had prepared for this transition and was ready to move on. Her mission here was complete; her purpose was fulfilled. She was ready to play with the angels and ascend to a place where her soul would find a new path.

But nursing wasn't training me to think like that. It trained me to fix the body, help, fight, and do what I have to do to keep a person here. To survive! My knowledge base at that point was to start the heart and keep the blood flowing to the brain and rest of the body. Save her! Bring her back! Don't let her die! I was taught not to give up! I was educated to keep going, keep trying until I was told to stop. The physical body had to be saved and the other components were not always addressed; it was always a second thought—or no thought at all.

I had her upon the sand, for that was the closest and hardest surface I had to perform CPR on. I did the first compression and cracked her ribs. I looked down at her as I felt the cracking, and it finally registered in my brain that I was working on my mother, not a patient. I couldn't do any more, so I grabbed a spectator and laid their hands on her chest, with mine over theirs to assess and know the depth and the speed of each compression. As we worked I tried to get just one breath of air into her lungs, one breath of life into her.

I was yelling out the compressions in Spanish, "Uno! Dos! Tres! Cuatro! Cinco! Seis!"

No breath…no pulse. Again…again… Not allowing myself to give up on her, doing full sets of compressions over a stranger's hands, trying to feel for a pulse, trying to grab an opportunity

THE LILY NURSE

to get one breath of life to her. Over and over, compression after compression, with no breath, no sign of life. Don't stop! Keep going! Don't give up!

Bring her back! Don't leave me! My heart screamed.

A spectator, another nurse from the crowd of people, jumped in and relieved me. His partner, also a nurse, pulled me away and questioned me about my mother to get an accurate medical history.

"Let us take it from here; we're both Canadian ICU nurses. Let us take over and help your mother," she said, emphasizing my need to let go of the control of the situation, to see it from another point of view. I graciously accepted their help, and once she had my approval, she quickly went into action, maneuvering beside my mom's body, taking charge of this situation, and taking over the compressions.

As I stood over them, watching them work on my mother, that's when I saw it! That's when I realized the horrific situation we were in. There were so many people hovering around us, behind this taped-off area. They were all staring down at this scene, gawking at my dead mother being worked on in the sand, her lifeless body flopping with every compression, nearly being submerged into the depths of the sand. Her eyes remained open but empty, encrusted with tiny gains of sand, staring blankly at nothing. I looked over to the crowd and saw my father watching, helpless, broken, and full of despair.

My world completely turned upside-down,
and I can't do anything about it.
She was gone,
and we are all left behind with the last memory of her like this.

This horrific, traumatic and haunting image of her is embedded in our brains.
And I don't ever want this to be the last image of me

JULIA EVANS

> Especially when the inevitable
> turns out to be a burden
> to my family.

"It was a horrific thing to see, and to be a part of. I do not want either of you—or anyone else, for that matter—to go through what we went through," I say to my children as I come back from my moment of reflection.

I'm now back to the reality of discussing my DNR wishes with them. The image of my mother's traumatic passing weighs heavy on my heart and mind, and I try to get that point across without going into full detail of the experience of it with them. It would be too much to put that image into their developing young minds; it wouldn't be fair to them to instill that unnecessary pain and imagery. I am trying to shield them from that image of me in the future. I am asking my family to let me go when I am ready to be free from this earth, to not have someone try to save me. I don't want someone working on me over and over again, with only the end result of further pain and suffering for me and those around me.

I don't want anyone put into the position where they can't let me go. Where the inevitable outcome is me passing to a place I may not want to come back from, leaving them all here to deal with the nightmare of it.

I also fear not having any sort of quality life here on this earth, having a life that's been stripped away only to not physically lose me. I don't want to lose myself for someone's gain; I want to live! I want to be me, the fun, loving, nurturing mother and wife my family needs and deserves.

"I am asking you both, to be strong enough to let me go," I explain. "To let me go before it gets to that point where I am not me. Where it gets to a point where you have nightmares of me, and you can't remember me as the fun, loving Mommy that I am. I am asking you both to understand why I want to be a DNR. I am protecting you from further pain and suffering. I am protecting myself from a world that I fear. A world where I cannot be the person that I am."

I have outlined my fear and worry for them now. I have prepared them to be strong and insightful to what may be in the future for our family. I want them to know that quality of life matters. We talk a lot with our children: the good, the bad, the ugly and, most importantly, the truth. Greg and I have learned how to talk to them at their level of understanding, but never do we keep them in the dark. We are always open and honest with them; that will never change. I feel confident that they both have a clear understanding to why I have come to this decision, why I want to be a DNR.

"Are you both okay with everything we talked about today? About me being a DNR?" I question them to make sure it wasn't too much for them.

"Yeah. We get it," they both say in unison.

I can see that neither one is bothered by this conversation.

"I'd like to do a scenario with you both," I propose. I want to have them fully prepared for the future. If this *does* actually happen, I want them to feel confident and sure that they can handle this. We tend to do these a lot to solidify, and lock into their brains, the steps to follow in the time in which it needs to be executed. So they know what to do in the situation, and how to stay calm, and confident with what's happening.

They both nod in agreement, so I begin.

"If Dad is at work and Mommy collapses on the floor, what do you do?" I provide the first phase of what could potentially be extremely scary for them.

They both yell out excitedly, "We call 911!"

"Yes, and what do you say to them?" I continue.

Together, Titus and Jayda work out what they would say if this was really happening. "We'd say...my mom has collapsed and she is a DNR."

I question them, "Do you know what that means?"

"That you don't want to be saved. You don't want to be worked on!" They both say to me, as they are now fully understanding what this really means.

"Yes. So, what's going to happen after that?"

They both look at me puzzled. I explain to them that they are going to be safe and protected, and what it will probably look like.

"There's going to be a lot of commotion, a lot of chaos, a lot of emotions," I explain. "There are going to be a lot of friends and family around to help take care of you. It doesn't mean that you guys are going to be alone. There are going to be a lot of people coming to the house to help out. But then you are going to have to say goodbye.

"You'll have to say goodbye to me." I say, "Do you both understand that? Do you understand what this means? With us making this decision, you both know what this means, right?!" I really emphasize this to absolutely make sure that they are on board with this.

"Yes, Mom," they say, looking down at the floor.

"Are you both okay with this decision? This is a really big decision, I've thought a lot about it, and I believe this is the best for me, for us. I don't want to live a life where people have to take care of me full time because I am unable to take care of myself. It's a ginormous decision, and I want you both comfortable with it."

"Yes, Mom. We understand." They both look up at me, nod and smile with approval.

Greg puts his arm around me, and says to the kids, "This was a really hard thing for your mom and I to talk about, and for us to make this decision. We have talked about this in great detail. This was not a spur of the moment decision; I want you both to be aware of that. Your mom has a lot of life left in her. Please understand that she is not giving up! We wanted to prepare you both for what her wishes are. We wanted to prepare you before things get any worse."

I look up at Greg lovingly as if to say thank you through my eyes. He smiles back at me. We signal the children to sit with us. Both jump at the opportunity to be closer to us. Jayda plops onto my lap, wrapping her little arms around my neck and Greg's. Titus sits right beside me, nearly on my other thigh, wrapping his arms tightly around my waist and resting his head upon my shoulder. Jayda twirls her finger around a strand of my hair. Greg and I wrap our arms around this whole family unit like a protective shield. All of us together in a little cluster ball of love. Hugging, embracing and holding on to one another. None of us wanting to let go.

"I love you all so much!" I say, wholeheartedly reconfirming my love for them as we continue to grip onto each other.

Every cell in my body aches and cries over what I am asking them all to do for me, what I am asking them to let go of in the off chance that it is required. I fully believe in my heart that this is the best for me, the best for the whole family. I glance over at Greg and then back to the children.

"I'm not planning on going anywhere," I reassure them. "I'm just preparing us for the future; I needed to know in my heart that we are all on the same page. Now you all know what my wishes are.

Thank you for understanding and I hope and pray that this will never happen to us, but now we'll be ready if life tries to throw us a crazy curve ball."

"Okay, now let's go outside and play. We've spent enough time on this topic. Let's go have fun and make some happy memories," I say to lighten the atmosphere and to bring back what is truly important to all of us, to live life to the fullest and to laugh and embrace the joy of life, with the ones you love!

***

So, after all these years of having this belief etched into the back of my mind and the minds of my family, I am completely reversing my way of thinking.

This spontaneous and overwhelming notion to change my code status is as if something else was guiding me, protecting me, a tiny voice telling me what I needed to hear. *I can heal from this and come out better.*

I think to myself, *There's still so much I have to live for. So much more I have to do with my life. If I code, I want to be worked on! I want compressions to be performed on me. I want to be saved! There is a purpose for my existence!*

So once again, Greg and I gather the children together to discuss this new plan, this new decision that will be easier to come to terms with. We immediately sit the children down as I come to terms with this incredible new revelation, realization, and awakening!

I very excitedly say to them, "Mommy wants to talk to you both about my DNR status. I have decided to reverse it! I want CPR done on me. If ever I were to collapse and Daddy isn't home, you call 911 and they will do the rest. They will talk you though it."

They both seem a bit puzzled by my new decision, but also

pleased.

"Mommy has too much to give to this world and so much to live for," I add. "I don't want to give up! I am not going to let this silly disease take me down! I have too much fight left in me! And so much to fight for."

They both smile ear to ear.

"So, now if I do collapse or if anything were to happen to me, you call 911. What do you say?"

"My mom has collapsed," they say together, reassuring me that they are actively listening to the new plan. My new wishes!

"And to do CPR!" I add.

"And to do CPR!" They simultaneously and very excitedly repeat what I just said, jumping up and down with joy, with the idea that they won't have to let go of their mother too soon. She can be saved.

Greg, Titus and Jayda all smile enthusiastically. All of them are thrilled by my new plan, my new wishes. As if they all were patiently waiting for me to see it.

**I believe in my heart
I will survive
I will be saved,
and I will live a better life because of it!**

CHAPTER 15

BATHROOM PRIVILEGES

I've been in this hospital bed for two days, trapped in this room like a caged animal. People have been constantly entering and exiting my space, wanting to gawk at me—the nurse who survived a crazy event on her own home unit. All of these people, oh so many of them, keep stopping by and expressing how they feel, what they experienced through this whole ordeal. They are presenting me with their own twists and turns as they too are trying to figure out why and how this all took place. I have been laying here listening, as they all debrief with me, telling me their stories and their findings. I've been trying not to react to everything they are all sharing with me. I have my own reality to process and live with.

> I'm just happy to be here.
> Alive!
> Stunned and bewildered…
> But Alive!

THE LILY NURSE

There has been far too much information been shared with me—talk about system overload. I am the patient within this situation, not the nurse. It's not my job or duty to debrief and help everyone else cope with this. I am the one laying on this hospital bed, broken and trying to figure out how to function within my new world. I am trying to unscramble my brain, trying to put my own puzzle pieces together, trying to paint a clearer picture of the events by trying to connect all of the dots. It's a lot to process.

I need more time to process all of this; too much has happened in such a short period of time and I can't make sense of any of it. I haven't allowed myself to express my need to be heard, and I have not given anyone the opportunity to truly listen to me. There are so many more pieces to this puzzle, but at this point I don't wish to share them with anyone. I can't even begin to fathom all that I went through to be in this state; it's too much for my brain to process.

I believe in my heart that everyone who stands before me at my bedside is all trying to show their love and support the best way they know how. Perhaps I'm blocking their love and support because I am not ready to face it, avoiding everything and pushing away what I actually need to face.

I have permitted all these people to share what they experienced through all of this. I'm trying to help them cope and I'm not addressing what I want or need. I am the one who has been pushing my feelings, thoughts and experience of this whole thing down to a place where I don't want to see it, not wanting to truly address any of this. I listen to others and I use my humor any chance I can to help me cope, but what I need is to face this, understand there is more to this than I am actually acknowledging.

I don't want to be here in this hospital bed listening to everyone; I want to be back home where I feel safe. My family needs me, and I need them. I want to be back home with them, nuzzled together in the comfort of our home—safe, protected and loved in each other's arms. Maybe then I can start to accept and process all of this. I need quiet time away from here to untangle my brain from everything. I want to get back to what normal life I have and not be here as a patient.

This is just a blip,
a small challenge that I have to adjust to,
Or is it?

These people, who have been hovering over my hospital bed, don't have an inkling of what I have gone through. The focus has been on all of them and what they are going through. No one really asks me. It's quite a rarity to be in the presence of someone who came back, someone who may know what's on the other side. How do you ask? What do you say?

Our left sided, logical, linear, medical brains can't even begin to process this; it's not how we were trained to think. So, we think critically and analyze the facts, what we can see and prove, what's medically happened to my physical body. That in itself is extremely hard to wrap our brains around. Everything happened so fast and no one saw it coming! We were all placed in a crazy situation and now I am the one transmogrifying and I can't understand how or why.

I am getting asked the occasional generic question people are programmed to ask when they see someone in a hospital bed. As they stand over my frail body which we all are hoping is mending, they look at this person before them, not really sure of what to say.

"You okay?" Some ask, without really acknowledging or listening for the response.

"I can't believe this happened" and "They treating you right here?" are two other popular choices.

Then there are the few who jokingly inquire, but so desperately want to know, "Was there a light?" or "Do you remember anything?"

"Yes. I remember all of it, every little detail," I abruptly respond to them. There aren't any further remarks or questions following my response. What do you say after that? One of us quickly changes the subject, neither ready to hear the answer to the underlying question.

Truthfully, my conscious mind is not ready to comprehend what I truly experienced. It can't, especially at this point, as I lay on this hospital bed listening to the variety of people who add even more layers to this situation. My mind can't label or latch on to anything I experienced through this whole ordeal. It is beyond anything I can put words to and I just can't make sense of it. I get gentle signs, but still cannot see what's right in front of me. I require my mind to identify the missing links before really seeing the clear picture.

I have to live and experience this new world around me before I can truly accept any of this. I have to get out of this hospital and experience this new me, for being here is all too much to handle.

This is a new reality, a new life, and I possess a new knowledge and understanding. But I need to be at home, alone, in a quiet place to sit and reflect. I need to be able to breathe. Breathe it all in, before awakening to the understanding of what I had really gone through, what I needed to start healing from.

So as I am bound to my bed, my room, my hospital, I can't really fully come to terms with any of this. I need to be alone with my thoughts, to think, pause and breathe!

I have a hard time conveying this to myself. I have gone through all of this. I have been through a traumatic event and have lived through to see another day. I have been given a second chance at life. But what does that mean? What do I do with all of this? Where do I go from here? What's my next step? What's my next path? Where is this journey leading me now?

There is just too much swirling around in my head and I feel like I could explode, but I hold it all in. Hoping to have someone in my room beside me, distracting me from my thoughts, feelings and raw emotions. I don't know if I'm ready to face any of this.

Maybe my nurse will change her mind and let someone through the threshold of my doorway. I know I need to process this and heal, but I'm not ready to face it. I like having my peers in here with me. I love trying to find the humor and lightness of this situation. I do like hearing all their tales, their versions of the story, even though it is so heartbreaking to hear. I feel like I'm helping them and I don't have to share what I am feeling with this whole disastrous life-changing circumstance. I don't have to believe it is all happening to me. It's similar to discussing or debriefing a case that we have all experienced, but I put myself out of the picture. Out of sight, out of mind. Deflection at its finest!

"Julia, I have someone here to see you. She says she's like family," my nurse says cautiously, not wanting to let this person enter my space that she has been guarding and protecting all day.

I can see the woman she is inquiring about standing patiently behind my nurse, my guardian, my protector. She stands there, waiting patiently for my approval or a reaction, respecting my wishes either way.

"Barb!" I squeal. "Yes, she's like family. Let her in," I say to my nurse, giving her a reassuring smile and easing her mind that Barb is truly here for me, not just for herself.

My nurse gives her access to enter my space, and as Barb walks towards my bed, the nurse closes the door behind her, leaving us to talk in peace and quiet.

"Julia," Barb says to me. It's as if she needs to hear herself say my name to make sure I am, in fact, sitting before her—alive!

"Barb," I respond, giving her one hell of a smile. "Look, I'm here!"

"Can I get you anything? What do you need? Really anything, I'm here for you." She's rapidly shooting off questions, not really giving me an opportunity to respond to any one of them. "Are you comfortable? Do you need water, food? Are you feeling okay? Are you okay I'm here? Are you warm enough? How's your heart? Does it hurt? How do you feel? What can I do?" She rambles away, trying to hold in her tears. Trying desperately, with everything in her power and being to help and be here for me. She would be willing to give me her heart if it would help me.

"Barb," I try to stop her rapid firing questions. I know all she wants to do is fix this and help in any which way she can. "I'm here!" is all I can say, looking directly in her eyes. I do this so both of us can come to the realization that I am here, and alive.

She stays with me for a very long time, tucking my sheets, getting me water, coffee, lotion and lip balm for my excessively dry skin. Making sure I am comfortable, and not in any physical pain or distress. Addressing if I needed emotional comfort too, providing several opportunities for me to share, but not being pushy. Listening intently to anything I want to talk about, never once trying to tell me her side of the story.

She allows me to process what others were saying to me. I tell her how everyone was coming to visit and debriefing with me; telling me their side of the story. Describing to me in great detail of what they saw as the event unfolded and took place right before their own eyes. It must have been horrific for them." Barb, do people not realize this actually happened to me?" I ask.

"None of us can believe this happened to you," she replies. "Do you even believe it?"

"No, I don't," I reply. "I can't get my head around any of it."

"Barb. I keep listening to them tell their versions and it's so very frightening, but I don't know how not to listen. I want to know it all. I want to be able to understand everything and I want to help them all through this, but it's all too traumatizing to face."

I am so thankful for having my nurse outside my room right now, having her guarding and protecting me, denying access to anyone else entering my room. This visit with Barb is very therapeutic and I'm pleased we're not being disturbed. Barb is truly listening and being there for me. Up to this point, the odd person has subtly inquired, but never genuinely asked me about how I was doing. Other than my nurse earlier, no one has really asked what I experienced or how I am actually feeling with all of this. No one, including myself, really wants to accept that this all happened to one of their own, one of their colleagues, one of their work family members.

I realize I opened the gateway for everyone to feel like they can share with me; this has always been my nature and it's a hard habit to break. Especially in circumstances like this, where everyone needs to heal from a piece of this puzzle. Honestly, the sheer magnitude of this whole event is beyond overwhelming and extremely hard to take in and perceive; the layers just keep piling up and it's hard to focus on just one piece of this.

We hear a knock on my door. My nurse excitedly enters the room and announces, "I have good news from your cardiologist: You have bathroom privileges!"

"Yes!" I blurt out; doing a double-handed fist pump. "That's fantastic news!"

Finally, I have enough strength to receive the privilege to emerge from my bed of solitude and walk to the bathroom without assistance. Without a nurse—or two—standing beside me. I am free to pee without someone watching over me.

THE LILY NURSE

"I'll watch her," Barb says to my nurse. They are both a little resistant and reserved about letting me walk to the bathroom by myself, not knowing if I have enough strength to complete this venture and not collapse as I'm doing it. Also, we all are a bit leery about how I am going to react to what they can see and I cannot. Opening that bathroom door, by myself, may be like opening Pandora's box. Once I'm in there and see what others can see, it may just finally hit me.

Barb stands up beside my bed, avoiding her need to assist me. Oh, how I've been longing for this moment—to pee freely, without assistance! I'm feeling more independent and stronger. *Yes! I get to spread my wings a little.*

Barb lowers my side rails and I slowly get out of this godforsaken bed. I stand on my own two feet to gauge my balance, allowing all my blood in my body to adjust to this new position, making sure my blood pressure won't bottom out and send me to the floor. I am assessing if my heart and body can withstand this triumphant moment. I stand marching on the spot for a brief second. Yup, I can still feel my feet—this is just fascinating and exciting to me. I can feel my feet on the ground. No pins and needles, no pain, it's just the sensation of the socks on my feet and the miraculous feeling of having the ground beneath my very own two feet.

Barb is watching my every single move but restrains herself from assisting me. I would have never even considered that this would be such a memorable moment in my life: Standing up from my hospital bed without assistance to walk towards the bathroom on my own, and being able to feel every single step that I am independently walking to my area of triumph. I can pee in peace, with the door closed, no one hovering over me.

"I'll be right outside of the bathroom, listening if you require help," Barb says, trying not to put her fear on to my little victory.

Even when nurses are not at work, we never veer too far away from our nursing role, especially if it's someone we care about. I can sense Barb is worried about leaving me unassisted in the bathroom but doesn't stop me from this amazing privilege.

I reach the bathroom, close the door behind me, and finally breathe. I sit upon the throne and have a little tinkle. Wow, it's nice to do without needing assistance; it's very liberating. I make my way to the sink of this bathroom and finally look up at myself in the mirror. This is the first time I've really been able to gaze at myself since everything flipped upside down. I don't fully recognize this person staring back at me, this reflection in the mirror. I know it's me, but everything appears to be so different.

Barb calls from the other side of the door, "Are you okay in there?"

"Yes," I reply. "Can you get me a facecloth and soap? I'd like to wash myself."

"Of course," she replies. I can faintly hear her through the bathroom door, passing on my wishes to a fellow nurse.

I giggle to myself. She is not willing to leave her post; we are all still a bit leery of this new adventure or privilege that I am granted. She stays close by, just in case.

I look down at my oversized gown; I'm swimming in it. I take my heart monitor out of the strategically sewn pocket on the front of my gown, and place it meticulously on the flat surface beside the sink. I then slowly undo the strings at the back of my neck, holding this tent on me. I open the very top of the gown and I allow it to caress the back of my shoulders as I take it off. Feeling the fabric slide down my shoulders, I extend both my arms and let it fall off, dropping it to the ground, stripping it away from me, so I can see what's underneath. I look into the mirror again, this time startled by what I see, the wires and leads that reside on my naked chest.

I lean in closer to my reflection and notice the areas where the defibrillator pads were located. I hold my hands over both spots. My right hand rests on my right upper chest—above my breast, below my collarbone—my left hand under my left breast. I stare at the reflection as I hold these two spots, hiding from my eyes what's underneath.

There's a knock on the door and Barb asks, "Can I come in?"

I quietly respond, "Yes…"

She opens the door, soap and towels in hand. "Are you okay?" she questions, staring at how I'm holding my body.

I lower my hands from where they are resting, and meekly say, "I'm burned, Barb." I start to cry. "This really happened! This really happened to me!"

She drops what is in her hand and holds on to me tight.

"I died!" I cry out in horror. "Barb, I died!"

"Yes, you did," she validates. "But you came back!" she emphasizes, clinging onto me tightly. She is squeezing and holding me within her arms as both of us soak in this realization together. "I'm sorry I left you! They pulled me away. I'm sorry." She bawls uncontrollably.

It's this gut-wrenching emotion that you feel within your core— that center spot underneath your heart and lungs, right in the middle of your diaphragm. It burns at this spot and cascades an influx of emotion which travels up to the back of your throat, preventing you from speaking. This then forces your eyes to close shut! Your body tries to resist this intensity of emotion. Not wanting to deal with it. Not wanting to internalize it. Not wanting the pain it holds in its possession. You try to resist it all by not allowing yourself to let go. But this intense internal emotion is just looking for a way to escape, pressing until finally your body is unable to hold it in any longer.

Your body finally submits to this process by releasing the deepest exhale, allowing the body to fully let go. You actually feel the pain, the hurt, the true raw emotion. As you exhale, your body releases tears that pour out of your eyes, down your face to the floor. Allowing you to fully submerge yourself into the intensity of the emotion.

That's how my body forces me to live through this. To deal with all that I need to feel. It's beyond difficult to be forced to feel the pain and the hurt, to be fully immersed into this type of emotion. Releasing and letting go! All of this is necessary to feel in that one moment of time. But it brings up so much pain with it as I release my tears. My body shakes with the sobs, as if every cell in my body is experiencing and dealing with every intense emotion that was hidden within. All the feelings and emotions that are attached to this memory expel from the depths of my being, totally releasing at a level I didn't want to acknowledge.

"I died!" I declare out loud. As I come to that realization, I start coming to terms with the other aspect I hadn't wanted to face yet. Through all of the commotion, trauma, chaos, and the series of unfathomable, surreal events, it hits me.

"Oh my God, Barb! I came back!"

We stand there sobbing uncontrollably in each other's arms, tears flooding from our eyes, saturating our faces. I'm finally allowing myself to address and accept that this is all factual and not a fabrication within my mind. This actually happened! I weep and breathe in all of this information. We stand in this tiny hospital bathroom for several minutes, until there are no more tears to be shed.

I squeeze her hard, not wanting to let go of her, and she squeezes me back. We embrace each other quietly, and I start to get the giggles. I whisper in her ear, "You do realize that you're holding me, and I'm naked?"

We both snort out gut-roaring laughter. She leans back, smiles, and then goes into auto-nurse mode. "Now let's assess those burns." she says assertively, but lovingly.

She helps me wash and applies burn cream to my wounds. Then she walks me back to my bed and sits with me until I close my eyes. A sense of calm trickles through my body as I drift off to sleep. It's a whole new world, and I'm ready to face it.

***

It took me nearly a whole calendar year to really comprehend all the events that transpired that day, back on my home unit of the hospital as I was about to start my shift and have my world change forever…the day when everything in my world flipped, never to be the same again. It took a year for me to really open my eyes to it all.

On the anniversary date of my reboot, my re-birthday, all I need is a quiet space to breathe and start saying the words out loud. I turn on my iPad and start recording. It is a rainy day, and I sit in my favorite chair in my living room, in front of my bay window. Extensions out, no makeup, no bra, just sitting there comfortably in my pajamas; ready to say what I needed to say.

Chapter 16

Something Bigger Than Us Is Always Listening

~  ~

An aha revelation has come over me,
An epiphany...
All of this happened for a reason!

Remember the Universe—something bigger than us is always listening.

It is us who turns a blind eye to its
Messages.
These messages can be through song lyrics, feathers, dimes, déja vus or catastrophic events,
It can slap you right in the face, or right where it hurts.
Giving you a wake-up call.

There are always messages from something bigger than us to help guide us

THE LILY NURSE

to the path we are always meant to be on.
To help us face and heal from what has always been right in front of us.

My prayers have been answered.
My plea has been heard.
It may not have been the way I had anticipated
It had to happen the way it happened...
So I can see it, face it and heal.

There is more to this realm,
This world.
And so much more to this story.

As I view this in a different light,
A different point of view...
I can see it.
I can see what has always been right in front of me.
I wasn't quite ready to focus,
Wasn't ready to deal or heal.
But it's time...

I remind myself of something a friend said to me,
Something that really resonated...

**"When you are aware of it
It's probably time!"**

I am becoming aware.
The time is now.
No more hiding, or closing my eyes to it.

I am Awakening

This happened!
And it all happened for a reason.

I am starting to see that now.

Chapter 17

Here Is My Story

As the clock strikes nine I am brought right back to where I was a year ago.

It was a year ago, to the day, to the minute; I was ready to start a regular shift. Moments before entering my unit, I was walking up the stairs from the locker room, messaging a very dear friend of mine to wish her a happy birthday. Then my attention, thoughts, and focus were drawn back to my baseball team. The thought of their disappointment weighed heavy on my mind as I recalled how utterly disappointed they all felt about their first game being cancelled. I've orchestrated a fun practice for tonight to replace that disappointed feeling of the team and instill some fun and excitement in our lives.

As I was approaching my unit, all I could think about was sugar—of all things, sugar! I was concentrating on the sugar I needed to purchase after work, before practice. I was planning on surprising the boys with an array of fun drills, and a sweet treat from their coach: homemade cotton candy. I thought this would cheer them up, preserve the cohesion of the team, brighten their spirits and keep their excitement alive. This was my last normal thought as I opened the doors to my unit. The last normal thought from my former life.

Sugar!

Reflecting on this, I realize I have been begging and pleading with the Universe to change my world, to take my pain away. My entire being wanted to heal from everything that I had suppressed inside for far too long—all of my emotions, the grief, anger, joy, trauma, pain and suffering. Never permitting myself to heal.

I wanted to preserve the sweetness in Life.
To be, who I was meant to be,
Bring back my Light!
Let my soul shine
Find my Joy!
Be Alive,
Live!

Live, like I was always intended to live. I have forgotten how to communicate that within myself, with my body, mind and spirit. My soul thirsts for my inner child to heal. Bring me back to where it all began, at that ripe old age of three, when my mother left me—when she died! It left me lost, alone and afraid, without knowing what path to follow. I was stuck in a place I was unsure of, a place that I needed to heal from.

May 10, 2018: the day the Universe decided to give me my biggest wake up call.

I open to the door to my unit
Opening the door to my new beginning.

"Good morning!"

I begin to greet my colleagues. It's my morning routine. I always do this when I'm about to start my shift, acknowledge everyone as we start a new day together. They are my team, my work family, and I trust them with my life. I greet them to show my love, respect and admiration for them all. We're all in this together to help heal and be a part of people's lives, providing our expertise and knowledge to help them through whatever they are facing here on this unit. Saying good morning establishes good rapport. A good rapport with your colleagues provides a great work environment and it puts everyone on the same page—working for the greater good for us and our patients, cohesion at its finest to provide the best care we know how to give.

I look to my left, turning my attention to the recovery staff. "Good morning," I cheerfully greet everyone.

"Good morning," they all reply.

As I am walking by, greeting my colleagues, I say to one of my work friends, "Oh, I forgot to grab those jeans that you nee…d…ed…."

And as I'm trying to get the words out, my throat begins to feel really scratchy. Like I've swallowed sandpaper and I can't get out what I was trying to say to her.

I cough a few times, trying to clear my throat.

I continue walking towards the nursing station, the heart of our unit. I'm heading there to put my purse away before I go to the lunch room where we put our lunch bags.

My throat is getting tighter and tighter. I'm discombobulated by what is happening. I'm not sick; I have not come into contact with anything. I'm doing a rapid assessment of myself. Then I look forward and spot this beautiful bouquet of Stargazer lilies. The stunning huge bouquet sits right on the desk of the nursing station. They're merely a few meters away from me, but I'd know that scent anywhere!

What the fuck are lilies doing on my unit?

My lily allergy was identified 18 years ago, and I try to avoid them at all costs! Hence why I work in a scent-free environment and not a fucking greenhouse.

These beautiful Stargazer lilies seem as though they are staring at me and I'm staring right back at them, like a deer in headlights. I frantically yell with what breath I have, to anyone who can hear me, "You guys have to get these out of here! I'm allergic to lilies!"

Everyone gives me a funny look, as though they are all thinking, "Who the hell is allergic to lilies?"

My throat is closing up. This is happening, very quickly. In the past, I've always been able to get out of the vicinity of the lilies—ASAP—and it hasn't caused too much of a reaction. I'd have a slight coughing spell, followed by very slight tightness of my throat and lungs, but I had always been able to cough it out, get some fresh air, and carry on.

This is new! This is scary!
This is happening too fast!

Someone picks up the lilies to remove them, but it is already too late. The smell of these spectacular flowers has already infected the area with its powerful aroma. It has permeated throughout the entire unit; it is out of my control to escape its deadly fragrance.

It is taking me down!

I attempt to escape by entering our conference area, our lunchroom. I'm coughing, wheezing, and my throat is just getting tighter and tighter. It's getting harder to breathe. I'm trying to catch my breath. The harder I try, the more my throat closes.

JULIA EVANS

I enter this new area and scan the room, looking at the late-shift staff, my colleagues, for help. I'm desperate! I sit on one of the chairs, trying to cough it all out of my lungs. The sound of this horrendous wheezing radiates through this room, down the halls and to most of the unit.

One yells, "I have to call your husband." She frantically runs out of the room.

"I have to get you Benadryl!" another blurts out to me. "I don't know if you can even swallow the antihistamine!" She seems puzzled by what she has to do, and rushes out of the room to find some medication for me.

I hold my hands up to my neck to give the universal sign of choking. It feels as though I am drowning in air!

Another nurse jumps up from her seat. "I have to get you a wheelchair; you have to go. We need to get you to emergency!" she yells while running off to fetch a wheelchair.

This leaves me and another co-worker alone in the room. Just the two of us staring at each other. She can't take her eyes off me; both of us are paralyzed in fear.

There are now two nurses in the doorway with a wheelchair; I try to get up and move to it. I don't even have enough oxygen or strength to get out of this room. I'm fading fast. Getting weaker by the second. It's extremely difficult to breathe.

I'm terrified!

I manage to get into the wheelchair, for I know what's happening; I'm hypoxic at this point. My closing airway is not allowing adequate oxygen to enter my body and I am turning blue: cyanotic! Not enough oxygen in my blood steam. I need more oxygen—I'm drowning in air!

I CAN'T BREATHE!

I'm in the hallway of the procedure rooms. I am starving for air, struggling for life in this wheelchair, and my colleagues are arguing and yelling at each other about what they should do.

"We've got to call a code," someone yells. "There's not enough time to run to emerg!"

As they are trying to figure it out, the overhead speaker blares, "Code Blue......"

Someone has already pushed the code button. Someone has foreseen the crisis that is unfolding before us and has made the executive decision to initiate the code protocol—this is a medical emergency! We need more hands on deck; we need the code team here and fast!

Fuck! That's for me! I'm the Code Blue!

This is when my world completely flips upside-down and my life as I know it changes and never will be the same again.

Code Blue is an overhead call that signals staff of a medical emergency. It is activated when there is an impending medical threat to a person's life; the patient is in immediate danger and every moment counts. The code team rushes to the location of the patient and responds within minutes. The witness or first responder initiates necessary action prior to the code team's arrival, doing whatever they can to keep the person alive, trying to prevent death or further trauma.

Shit just got real and fear has set in for everyone.

The procedure room doors open up. I'm in front of procedure room two and a very good friend of mine, Barb, pops out and yells, "Oh fuck! It's Julia Evans!"

As a health care professional and provider, that's one of your biggest fears: one of your own is in trouble. That emotion sinks in, locking that image into your brain and piercing their look of terror into your heart like a jagged dagger, cutting you open deep to get every little bit of love out of you for them in their time of need. You try to push the fear and panic to the side, but it latches onto you with such a great force. You do what you can to save them, but you are scared beyond belief.

I look down at procedure room one and see another colleague emerging from that room. He gives me a horrified look, and then grabs whatever medication he can from his cart. Barb takes charge, spins me and the wheelchair around and runs as fast as she can down the hallway.

"Open a bed!" she screams down the hall.

Spot seven is right in the middle of our unit, in front of the nursing station. I have barely any breath left in me, but I find enough strength and fight to get up onto that stretcher. Barb has barely stopped the wheelchair when I am jumping out and up onto the stretcher.

This is my only chance!

I expose my arms, fall back, and point my body up to towards the ceiling, up towards the heavens, surrendering to whatever comes next. Yoga teachers call this position Savasana, or corpse pose. That's how I feel.

Nearly dead and done!

Someone save me!
My thoughts are focused....

Fight, Julia! Survive!

I have no breath left.

THE LILY NURSE

I watch as the intravenous and medication is put into a vein in my left arm, my antecubital vein, and I can feel another intravenous being poked into my right side as well. I see the looks on everyone's faces. I can hear everything they are saying. But I cannot do or say anything. So, I lay helpless on the stretcher, having to instill all of my trust in them and their abilities to save me from all of this.

The code team from ICU arrives. I look up to them, seeing so many familiar faces surrounding my bed—all of them trying to save me. Fighting for me to stay here with them and not drift off to another place. I open my mouth, thinking someone should put an endotracheal tube down my throat to intubate me—to open my airway so I can breathe. Get oxygen to my lungs. I'm fading fast and I don't have any other way to breathe, other than the use of artificial ventilation. I can see a mask being placed over my face, but don't feel the tube; I don't even know if it is in or required. I know they are bagging me, manually forcing breath to my lungs. I can feel the oxygen from the oxygen bag entering my body. Whoever is on the other side of that bag is attempting to squeeze breath back into my lungs. I feel my lungs rising and falling.

Barb is there squeezing my hand. She is on the right of me, not leaving my side, not leaving me. I can't speak, nor move. All I can do is trust. Trust them to save me. Trust that they will fight for me.

Save my life!

I start breathing on my own. It's the greatest relief to be able to inhale and exhale, and to do it all on my own. I'm not suffocating in my body, not drowning in air.

I cheated death!

The commotion around me is out of this world. My colleagues, my work family, the people I have been working with for years, surround me with panic in their eyes. There is so much crying, commotion and yelling. They are still working on me, making sure I am here to stay.

> To run and be a part of your own code as a nurse is awful!
> I am breathing, but barely.
> My Everything is exhausted!

One of our doctors pleads with me, "Julia, just breathe. Breathe. Just take some breaths! Breathe!"

I finally take a full breath! I'm now breathing a bit better, but my throat and lungs hurt so bad. I throw my safety glasses off my head. The glasses I was wearing as I started my shift. I was meant to be working in the procedure room, being a nurse to others, not fighting for my life—not being a part of my own fucking code! I pull my lanyard from my neck and throw that off too.

"Well, this is a shitty way to start your shift!" I joke, with a touch of anger and relief for those around me to hear.

> My heart starts fluttering.

I frantically start taking off my warm-up jacket. Shit's about to become real again! My world and my reality take another turn.

I grab my chest and start screaming and crying, "My heart, my heart! You guys have to get leads on me. This is bad!" I grip my chest tighter.

One of the nurses beside my bed, whom I have never encountered before, tries to explain and reassure me, "Oh no, It's the epi. It's okay. It's the epi," she continues babbling, "I had epi in my finger; makes your heart race, and it's the worst feeling."

"Fuck off," is what I want to say, but I restrain myself. *You have no idea what I'm going thorough right now! This is not some epi prick on the finger!*

THE LILY NURSE

I try to reinforce what I mean by saying, "No, this is different! This is bad; this is bad!" I clench my chest, my heart, again. It feels like my heart is coming though my chest, popping through my rib cage. I quickly glance at the vitals machine. I am trying to visually assess and confirm what I am experiencing. My eyes widen at the sight of my blood pressure and my pulse.

It's high!
Dreadfully and Drastically High

One of the nurses sees what I am witnessing, which validates what I may be experiencing within the core of my body. She panics and says, "Holy fuck!" then turns the machine around so I can no longer see the numbers.

Let me see it!
Don't hide this from me
I'm the one living it!
I need to know,
I need to see this with my own eyes,
Solidify proof that this is happening.

My heart rate is well over 200 beats per minute. My resting heart rate normally sits at 52 beats per minute. My blood pressure is skyrocketing too! But I can't further assess what's happening visually, because someone turned the fucking machine around and away from my sight. I'm losing control of what is happening to me. All of my nursing skills can't help me now. I have to trust in my team!

I can feel what my heart is doing. It feels like it's exploding within my cavity wall. It's going to burst! My heart is breaking! There's nothing I can do to stop this!

I feel like I'm losing control of this situation again, and things are about to turn really bad, really fast! I yell at the team, "Someone get that patient out of spot 12! They don't need to watch this!" I point to the patient across from me, trying to gain some control over what is happening.

I continue trying to get my scrub top off, trying to rip it off my body to expose my chest so they can see this happening, so they can assess my heart.

> Put the fucking leads on!
> My heart is exploding!

"Here, Julia, open your mouth," someone from the code team says. I'm given a few sprays of nitroglycerin under my tongue in hopes that this will alleviate my chest pain.

I'm sensing further panic in the air, and it's not just mine.

My heart is pounding profusely. An ICU nurse and I are now both attempting to take my top off. She finally senses the urgency, and tries to help me.

"You have to get leads on me! I'm going down!"

My heart is now at its maximum capacity, and cannot endure any more pressure, so it pushes the pain to my head. The back of my skull is where I feel the most pain and pressure. This pain is the most pain I have ever felt in my entire life. It feels like I blew the back of my head off with a shot gun.

"It's like 20 out of 10 pain!" I scream.

Barb is still holding onto my hand, and I grip it so tight, crying to her, "Barb, it hurts so bad." I am holding onto the back of my head with my other hand.

"I know it hurts," she says to me through her tears.

"Make it stop!' I beg. Then I pull her closer to me, and whisper, "Barb, don't leave me." I am absolutely petrified of the state I am in. We both are. We both can see where this is going. We both can foresee what's going to happen next.

She stutters as she promises to stay with me. "I wo..won't, I wo... won't leave you. I won't leave you." She tries to get the words out as we hold each other and bawl uncontrollably. The words don't want to come out of her mouth. They don't want to be spoken, for when they are spoken, we are admitting what's happening next. It is the inevitable ending to this equation; the process of life.

I unconsciously start preparing her for the inevitable.

"Barb! You know what to do. Make sure Greg is okay and that my kids are cared for. Call Marie." Marie is a mutual friend of ours; I had previously discussed with her what my wishes are, what my living will is. She needs to be notified, and she needs to be there for our dear friend Barb, the strongest person I know. I need others to help her, to help my family and my friends cope with what is about to happen.

As I say this to Barb, I look deep within her eyes to confirm she is there with me till the end and that I know she can handle this. I squeeze her hand with all of my might, and then I look to the left of me. Away from her, so she can't see my eyes fade away.

I am not alone, and I am not scared.
I am ready to let go.
Release me.

And that's when everything stopped.
It all Faded away,
It all went silent
& Dark...

Chapter 18

What Is Happening to My Body?

"Everyone! Quiet!" a nurse yells out to the crowd surrounding my silent, limp, grey, flaccid body. "She's unconscious! Someone check her!"

Unresponsive
Start compressions

My body lays upon the stretcher,
Lifeless...
Grey – The colour of death.
One second talking,
The next gone into something we all dread and fear.
Silence...

Barb is pulled away by someone feeling the need to separate her from my limp body as it lies before everyone here on this unit. Ripping her away from the promise she agreed upon, deteriorating her relationship with me. Stripping away and adding this to her last memory of us.

"Don't leave me!" My words echo in her thoughts.

What is happening to my body?

What happens to a body when it goes unresponsive? What does that mean? When a person is reported to be unresponsive, they are considered unconscious—possibly dead or dying.

Why start compressions? If the unresponsive person is not breathing and has no pulse, no blood is pumping through their body. Manual assistance is required to pump or push oxygenated blood from the heart to the brain. Lack of oxygenated blood can cause brain damage within minutes. Compressions are initiated to preserve the brain, in hopes of preventing permanent brain damage.

That's what is happening with my body, but what about the other components?

Chapter 19

Where There Is Darkness, There Is Light

Everything is so calm, dark, and still; I'm floating in a void of nothingness. I try to adjust my eyes to see in this vast darkness, but that is all there is, and all that I see—darkness. There are no walls, nothing surrounding me but a state of being. Here I am, alone in complete darkness. I have never knowingly experienced a place like this before. It's darker than anything I could have ever, possibly, imagined. It's as though I am blinded by what is right in front of my eyes. It frightens me.

There is a stillness to this place, like a subtle pause from everything and anything from the world I know. That world I know is gone—vanished! How did I get here? What is this? There is nothing here, nothing surrounding me but complete and utter darkness. It's just me, here, alone, in all of this blackness, and yet it's not even black. There's no label to put to this place, this state, this dark nothing.

THE LILY NURSE

Are my eyes even open?
Or are they completely closed shut?

Nothing is familiar! I am somewhere else, somewhere beyond anything I can put words to. It's so dark! My senses are unusable, dysfunctional. Nothing is computing in my brain from any one of my senses, other than this sixth sense that I'm in a different realm, or pause from the world I know—it's blank consciousness. This vast never-ending darkness that I am engulfed in, separates and strips me away from everything and anything I ever knew. Only my thoughts are with me, scrambled, and oh so scared at this point. I feel lost, alone, and afraid. So very afraid!

There is no sense of time. It stands still; it doesn't seem to exist. Nothing seems to exist, not even me, and this leaves me feeling even more empty, alone and afraid. I am terrified! I cannot see, hear, smell, taste, or touch anything. My mind is racing and trying to grab hold of something familiar, trying to process what is happening, which terrifies me more. I cannot latch, label or grab onto anything. It's so dark, and I'm in a sea of nothingness, a waiting area or a drastic pause from the world or realm I am familiar with. I am surrounded by silence, and complete darkness. Everything is so still. I feel like I've been put somewhere to be lost and forgotten.

There's no one here, no one with me. I'm alone. Have I been brought or taken to some place, to be lost and forgotten? Am I in purgatory? Perhaps a waiting room of some kind. *It is not my time.* I released myself. I surrendered. I asked for this. I want to go back. I am not ready. I can fix this. I can heal.

Open your eyes, Julia!
See what's right in front of you!

I try to scream, "I'm here! Someone, anyone come save me from this darkness. I am so scared!" I can't speak; nothing is coming out, not a sound. I cry, but the tears don't flow from my eyes; it's my heart that weeps. My attention is drawn to my heart—my desolate broken heart. It's not my mind or my thoughts; it's my heart that needs to heal.

I envision that I am shrieking within this state of being at the top of my lungs, trying to emphasize my terror and fear of this place. I am within the core of my soul, the sacred depths of my heart. It's scarred, shattered, and damaged from the great abyss of darkness that I had created within it. I want to be healed from this destruction. I assure myself that someone will hear me now; I cry out, with all of my heart,

> I want to be Saved!

Out of this darkness, my sense of hearing is ignited by a familiar voice. My birth mother's voice apparates from out of this darkness, and she announces in the most loving, nurturing soft whisper, "Julia, don't cry Honey. Mommy's here."

Then I hear this eerie, bone-chilling, shrill of commotion around me. "Julia! Come back to us! Breathe!" There are so many people yelling though the darkness. I can hear it all now.

I feel this sudden jolt! I find myself back in the world and chaos I thought I had left behind. I am on the stretcher where I had left myself—my shell, my body—only moments before. I open my eyes, wide. I can see clearly now this horrific scene and situation that I am encapsulated in. Back to the world I was ready to let go of, and now I find myself smack dab in the middle of this unimaginable dreadful commotion.

"She's back!" someone yells.

I scan my environment, wide eyed and full of fear, relief and confusion.

As my eyes begin to focus on this overstimulating environment, I can see myself on the stretcher. I am looking down at myself, as if I'm hovering over my body and watching this horrific scene unfolding before me. I feel as though I am not fully part of my physical body. I look up, away from myself, towards the people surrounding my bed. Still sensing that I am not fully there, not fully back to this world with them. I am paralyzed with fear, and completely disillusioned with what is currently happening to me in this dimension. My thoughts are scattered and my being is disassociated from everything that is happening.

I can see all these people around me, my colleagues, my friends all surrounding my stretcher. Crying, yelling and working on me—frantically working on me. I hear so many people through this commotion, desperately yelling at me from all sides of the stretcher. One person to the right of me, a familiar voice, encourages me to show any sort of movement: "Julia, squeeze my hand!'"

Nothing—no movement! I can't physically move anything! I have no messages to relay from my brain to the rest of my body to get it moving.

"Move your feet," a doctor yells from the end of my stretcher.

I maneuver my gaze towards the end of the bed, towards my feet. I can see my feet, but I can't get them to move. They cannot compute any information from my brain to initiate movement. I perceive that I can only move my eyes, and nothing else.

I feel panic setting in. My world is swirling out of control. There is so much yelling and commotion surrounding me. I can hear them, but I cannot feel them, any of them. I can see and hear that they are trying to provoke me to move, to demonstrate signs of life, no signs of deficit.

They are poking me, touching me, yelling, crying, all trying to get me to move from their tactile and auditory stimuli. But alas, all I can do is look at them. Look at all of them with a stunned, bewildered, and frightened gaze.

I can't even feel my eyes move, but I know I am looking around. Perhaps I'm still not fully back into my body. I can see all of them are attempting to save me within this chaotic situation. I can also hear everything—every last little sound and frequency—but my body refuses to move. Not even one minuscule muscle or cell within this body of mine, will show that I am there with them all—maybe not fully, but I'm here!

I'm here!
I can see you all!
I can hear you all!

SAVE ME!

I look to the left of me and I see an old colleague of mine, scared beyond belief. I can see right into his eyes, his thoughts, and soul; I can see his fear and worry.

"Julia," he cries. "Please…please…squeeze my hand. Come back to us."

I can't! I scream in my thoughts, for no voice can evacuate out of my mouth.

I have no say in what is happening to me right now!

I look up towards the ceiling. Blocking out the sounds of the yelling, crying and chaos around me. *Oh fuck!* I cry out to myself. *This is why I wanted to be a DNR! This was what I was afraid of… FUCK! I didn't want to come back to this, my MS. I knew this was going to happen! This fucking disease took over my entire body. I cannot move! How can I live like this? I am completely useless!*

Send me back!

I didn't want to come back to this! I didn't want to come back to be a burden on my family. I'm stuck in this shell, this hell! This is my worst nightmare.

THE LILY NURSE

I want to go back!
Please take me away from all of this!
Take me back!

PLEASE....
WITH EVERYTHING IN MY BEING....
I beg to go back!
TAKE ME BACK!

I am at your mercy!

I want to see my mommy!

Everything fades away again...

I faintly hear in the background as I drift away, "We lost her again!"

But then all that fear, and the pain, and all of the emotions and everything that I have ever experienced just went away. Gone. It all just disappeared!

I am brought to a place of love, pure, healing love. Infinite happiness, trust, and being. There is no suffering here. No pain, absolutely no pain, truly no suffering. Everything is still. And calm. And oh, so beautiful. Absolutely beautiful. Tranquil. I'm in a place where I can breathe. It's what I asked for.

A place to heal. It's everything and yet nothing. It's so freeing!

I am brought to this angelic place. All of the love you can possibly experience is all wrapped in one little package within me. It's so blissful! It's so beautiful! Time stands still. It stops. Here I am... Being! Breathing! Believing!

I can sense this incredible infinite love
Beaming through me,
Around me,

JULIA EVANS

Within me....

A Love so powerful it radiates Light!

My Mom, and those who have died before me
Are here.
All of them
Standing alongside me.
All of us within this Light!
So Pure
So Majestic

There's so much Love
Surrounding me and radiating within me.

This is a place of pure Bliss!

I can Breathe!
I can Heal!
I am finally Free....
Free of Pain!
Free of Hurt!
Free of the suffering from my past!

I can finally just BE ME!

There are not enough words in our realm or this lifetime to articulate this state, this dimension, this light. So pure, bright, and loving—you want to just give yourself to it....

It is Absolute Bliss!

**There is a divine creation and it is of pure love!
It breathes Life into you!**

Chapter 20

Rebooted and Re-birthed

~  ~

"Clear!" an authoritative voice calls out, and 150 Joules of electricity surge through a defibrillator into my body.

I'm being ripped, pulled, pushed, and forced away from my current place and state of being. Away from my place of bliss. I am slammed, thrown, ejected (rejected from remaining in a place I was not meant to stay in) back into my former body.

> I was pushed back.
> Pulled back,
> Shocked back
> HARD!
> With this intense mighty force.
> Zapped right back into the former body and life I knew.

I feel this hard jolt of electricity and energy surge through my entire body, propelling me to a fully seated upright position. Theewhack! Back to this reality, this body, this world.

JULIA EVANS

I am Physically Alive!
Here;
I am Back!

I am sitting straight up on this stretcher, stunned and dumbfounded. Trying to switch back to this familiar and yet new reality I have been forced back into. Unable to fathom the intensity, and the magnitude of all the components and levels I'm experiencing all at once. I am trying to process everything I am experiencing, and I question….

Am I Alive?

I am momentarily unsure of my surroundings. Where am I now? Am I really back into my previous world that I knew—I know? I am waiting for my conscious mind to realize that I am, in fact, alive—in this realm, in this world that I tried to leave behind. I realize now I am in a different space, realm or dimension, not in my infinite place of absolute bliss. But I am still enveloped within this healing, loving light; it's blinding, and I cannot see beyond its radiating beam.

I feel like I am being recreated from this radiant and angelic light, as if I am being reborn like a phoenix rising from its ashes. Transforming from death and a former life of despair and destruction. Re-birthing into a new beginning, a new purpose, a renewed, rebooted, restored life. Resurrecting from death and a previous life of pain and suffering. Emerging into a new world of healing potential and strength. Not just to survive, but thrive and truly heal from my past. Moving towards a better future and life that I was always meant to be in. I am a survivor and I have the strength, the need and the desire to be here!

I deserve to be here!
Strong and in tune.
I am worthy!

I can sense that I am here on the stretcher. Every cell within my entire body is awakening to this new state of being. Although I'm back to my former shell, or body, everything seems new and heightened. It is as though I am experiencing everything for the first time within this new life. I am being birthed again into this new world through an infinite loving light. My attention is drawn to and fixated on this light that surrounds me. It is within me, embracing me in this immaculate intensity of healing love that exudes a light like no other, shining on and illuminating the areas that need to be repaired and healed.

This love encompasses me, projecting to and from my heart while mending the broken pieces of the erratic transmissions of my body. My previously misconducted communication of my nervous system is now being completely rebooted, like a computer's operating system starting up again. This reboot fires up the communication to initiate more of the healing process throughout my entire being. This place and state of unconditional love illuminates my being to radiate from this infinite love, rather than a place of hurt and pain. All of my systems are rebooting so I can truly start my healing process, igniting my awareness to the things that are essential to heal from. It's a wake-up call and I'm finally able to see what I need to face, heal and learn from. I have been given another chance to live and to be me — be the person I was always meant to be.

I am Here! I am Back!
I am stronger than ever.
I am Alive!

I begin to spontaneously open and close my hands, while raising and dancing my feet upon this stretcher — proving to myself and my surroundings that I can, in fact, move.

I'm moving!

I am utilizing and initiating my sense of touch, for this is the task I couldn't perform prior to entering a different realm or dimension. I am grabbing hold of whatever — or whomever — I can, unable to see anything or anyone. I purposely exaggerate my movements to lock into my brain that I am here, back and alive, in this place. I am trying to latch onto my new world by grasping onto anything that activates my physical sensation of touch, completing my transition from a place I was not meant to stay in. I'm metamorphosing from the confinement of my broken self to something pure and beautiful. Out of the dark, deep abyss I had bound myself to for far too long, and now I transmogrify to a spiritual state of being able to spread my wings like that of a butterfly or an angel, encompassing and radiating love and light.

This activation of my sense of touch allows my mind to process my body mechanics and activates new neurotransmitters and renewed pathways of communication within my mind, body, and spirit. It initiates the wholeness that I was lacking within my former life. Squeezing hands and fingers, and moving my feet allows my conscious mind to fully grasp that I am...here! On this earth, in this realm, in this dimension to heal.

I am beginning to feel, but I cannot decipher much at this point. My mind is torn by the influx of my senses and the remaining stillness from this radiant light.

This loving light still encapsulating me, I can see this vivid, even-more-brilliant light projecting from me, my soul and my being: my true form. It shines a spotlight to where I am needed and meant to be. It places me back. As if it's a vortex, a tunnel (both light and dark) pulling and pushing me, like a mother pushing her baby out of her womb. I am exiting the comfort, safety and protection of the realm or space I feel most comfortable in. I can feel the love of my mother and her internal strength, love and protection, hugging me, and preserving me to live—now pressuring me to live. Outside of this physical attachment, to face the world for myself, learning and experiencing my world in a different light. I am becoming me, birthing me into a world I am meant to be in. A world I am meant to exist in. Be free to be me!

This time, I am being re-birthed into this world head on. Not frank breach—or ass-backwards like the first time I was birthed from my mother's womb—I am facing this world and my new life head on, with my eyes wide open, illuminated with a new sense of awareness, insight, knowledge and enlightenment. I am blessed to be given a second chance, to be re-birthed from this pure loving light, facing my new world head on—with eyes wide open, ready for the world I was always meant to be in. I'm ready and willing to face my former self of destruction, pain and suffering, and look at my world —in a different light, from a different perspective, from a place of love within.

> I have been Consecrated, Blessed and Transformed
> From the loving light of the divine
> It's a Love that is so pure, unconditional and healing
> I hold it in my heart
> And it wraps around my entire being.

This is all I see at first: this infinite radiating angelic loving light that I am being birthed from…being re-birthed into this world from a place of healing love…from something greater than us.

I can feel my body! Every last little cell and particle of my being, I can sense it all! I can feel it all—every little thing within me and surrounding me, every last little particle of my being and beyond this universe. Everything seems so clear, heightened. I am aware! I am awakening! I can finally sense it all, and my conscious mind has decided that I am here. I am back.

> I am Awake
> I am Alive

I am frantically moving my limbs, grabbing hold of anything that I can sense. Triggering my memory to remember a life that I know. Allowing myself to complete my re-entry into this new life, by fully pulling myself back here of my own volition. As much as I want to stay in this place of bliss and let go of all that pain and suffering that remains here in this realm, I want to be here! I want to be with my family! I want to be back for not only myself, but for Greg, Titus, and Jayda. They need me and I need them.

> I need to be here for them!
> I'm Here!
> Awake, and Alive!

> I am not ready to fully let go of the beauty, and potential that our world offers.
> I have so much **Love** to give.

I can move! I can actually move! I sense others' hands beside me, so I squeeze them. I dance my feet to prove that I can. I move to prove that I am here, back in this body. I am really here, not hovering or looking down on this. I am here: body, mind and spirit. I'm back completely with everyone in this area, this space, this world.

> Alive!
> Back to this world, to stay.

As I look around I cannot see anything or anyone from my previous life. All I can visualize is this brilliant, beautiful, angelic light surrounding me. My mom and all the others deceased before me are here beside me, giving me more love, light, and protection. All these people I needed in my life are now with me, supporting me and loving me, pushing me back to a new life, birthing me into this new world through this infinite light & love.

> I am worthy of this love
> It encompasses me!

My sense of taste is activated. I am able to sense the savory sweetness of life that has been divulged to me, nourishing my soul, self worth and self love. To love, be loved, self love, I finally have it all.

My sense of smell is slowly getting ignited as well. I smell a scent of flowery smoke, parallel with the robust aroma of alcohol swabs, which cohabitate in my nostrils. The smells trigger different areas of my brain, activating both an alarm that questions my sense of safety, and also soothes me with the familiar known attachments and labels to a sense of safety; I am in a place I know and am familiar with. Our sense of smell either draws us to or away from people and situations that are good or bad for us. It is the most useful sense for survival.

As these smells become stronger, so is my sense of hearing. My hearing is being heightened by my sense of smell.

I can now hear the commotion of my colleagues. This frequency of white noise is faint at first, but it is getting louder. The frantic chatter rings through my ears and I cannot quite make sense of the words. It's just sound to me, a lot of white noise.

As their voices get louder, I can see an image standing before me at the end of my bed. I can't decipher anything else. The image before me is radiating its own light. It's like there's another light at the end of this tunnel that I am being pushed, pulled and forced through. This so-called tunnel and its light are blocking any other visual imagery.

This person that stands before me is the male charge nurse from the emergency department. His image and appearance are quite striking and profound for me. I see his strong, kind stature, with long lush hair wrapped up in a man-bun on top of his head. This imagery stays with me, representing both sides of what I believe.

I don't realize the significance at first, but as I process this over time, I am brought to an awareness, an awakening: Just as I am becoming aware of my surroundings and self, I am awaking my new state of being, my new life. Both worlds are combining together in more ways than one!

This being standing before me is simultaneously a silhouette of Jesus and representation of Buddha. Both are intertwined in one single being, standing here before me. Comforting and highlighting both sides of my beliefs and views.

My Christian, left, logical, western brain, latches onto a figure that represents the fixer, the savior—Jesus, the one who shows us the way, saving us from our sins, our punishments, our broken life. He heals us by fixing what we can and cannot see is the problem. We can willingly instill all of our trust and faith onto him and His power, releasing our inner demons and sinful ways repent from what doesn't serve us. We can choose to follow His way to a better life, follow His path to become healed, saved and be in the power of the almighty. Following His words and His steps, His knowledge and wisdom, believe it is the only and right way to salvation—saving one from death and separation from God. Have Him lead the way with His god-like persona, for he is the Son of God; the all knowing.

Buddha represents a more abstract, less rigid way of thinking: to think for one's self, listening to one's inner self, inner voice, innate wisdom. This stems from self love, inner peace, meditation, and the mentality that nirvana can be achieved if we live in the present. We have the knowledge and power within each and every one of us. Buddhism incorporates universal consciousness and connections, energies and the knowledge that everything is connected within this universe. It brings in the other, often overlooked, components: the power to heal within, connecting to the power of self. It represents the right side of the brain, the intuitive, imaginative, holistic or holism mindset.

Both of these hold a form of truth. They should not be separate from one another, instead they should be brought together like yin and yang, integrating both sides to make us whole and addressing who we truly are. For at the end of our given path we are all just being—with no labels, no wrongs/rights.

Just being!

As he stands before me, he seems to be opening his heart to me. He is standing before me with open arms, waiting for me to choose what I truly want from this. In life our paths are already chosen for us and we create the illusion that we get to choose what our purpose is. When our shell, body, castle, temple — whatever you wish to call it — is damaged or broken beyond belief, our soul cries out to heal and go home to a place of love. When our soul cries out, it's not our soul that needs to heal, but that which protects us. That is when we are brought to a place to gain back the knowledge of love that has always been inside of us, providing and permitting the healing to occur. It is so our outer being can better protect our soul, allowing us to follow the path we were always meant to be on. We are sent back when our purpose is not fully completed and we are led to believe that we are the ones to choose to live, but in fact it is a higher being, something greater than us, that continues to send messages and guidance to pursue the already chosen path.

We think we choose when to give up and when to keep going. And as this image stands before me, it is as though he is giving me a choice to either take his hand and be guided into his light, or to look down to my new body. The choice has already been made; my time here in this realm is not over and I have a purpose to fulfill. My attention is instinctively drawn down to the appearance of my physical body. My body now becomes completely visible to me. As I look down, I see that I am naked! Physically naked from the waist up. Everything is stripped away, leaving me completely exposed, just like an actual baby being born.

Everything has been stripped away — physically, emotionally and spiritually. I am fresh, brand new, and at peace. All of the things that do not serve me anymore are stripped away. The unwanted beliefs and thoughts that caused me pain, distress and suffering from my previous life are now peeled and stripped away. This is so I can become anew.

I am getting a restart to life, a reboot, a re-birth, a re-do!

Finally being able to be Me

JULIA EVANS

> Free as I was always meant to be.
> I am whole, healed
> Ready to start my new life.

The first thing I blurt out is, "Who cut my bra? That's my favorite blue bra."

A silence falls over the commotion and the man bun nurse calls out laughing, "Inappropriate behavior! She's back!"

I am completely stupefied by his comment and outburst. I respond, "Back from what?"

I feel the nurse to the right of me place her hand upon my shoulder. She calmly and assertively states, "I brought you back."

"Back from what?" I question her, totally baffled about what she and the man bun nurse are referring to. I glare at her with an utterly confused expression upon my face.

"I did compressions on you and we shocked you twice. I brought you back!" She is adamant as she says these words to me, while gently giving my shoulder a little squeeze, like she's pinching me a little so I can realize this is real and I am not dreaming. This triggers my conscious mind to see what all is in front of me.

As these words register within my brain, I look to her in horror. I've been on the opposite side of this situation before. I know and completely understand what she is confirming for me.

> I was the code blue!
> This happened.
> This actually happened to me!

This is when it all comes together, the details of this traumatic, and horrific situation I fell into. Everything quickly plays out in my mind. My previous life rapidly flashes before my eyes. I move my glance from her piercing eyes to her hand that rests on my

THE LILY NURSE

shoulder, then down to my chest. My exposed chest. I can now see the defibrillator pads: one on the upper right of my chest, and another under my left breast, which carries my glance to the cords that attach to the crash cart. I look to my chest again and see leads scattered all over it. The stickers, the metal clips, the wires protruding out of them, are all attached to another machine—a heart monitor. I haven't seen any of this until now. Up to this point all I could see was my bare naked chest.

My gaze continues assessing and processing down the rest of my body, which resides upon this hospital stretcher. My scrub pants are still on, intact and covering the bottom half of my body. There is garbage resting on me and on my bed, highlighting the quick-thinking chaos that took place and materialized into a horrific and chaotic situation for everyone on this unit. There are packages from the medications, intravenous, oxygen tubing, tourniquets, alcohol swabs and an unsettling energy lingering over all of us.

Then my blinders come off; I am aware and now can finally see the people, the hysterics, and the crying.

As my mind accepts this new awareness and environment, it's as though single spotlights are illuminating specific areas of this situation. It's like the light in a gymnasium or hockey rink—the huge ones that take time to actually activate, but when they do, they shine a lot of light on the surrounding area and really illuminate the environment. When the spotlight shines on one layer of this, it is locked into my mind and then another is illuminated. It's as though my mind is a blown circuit-breaker switching back on, permitting me to visually accept this into my conscious mind.

My mind can't withstand any more. This is so much to take in at one time. My mind panics with the influx of information. It quickly diverts my attention back to the ICU nurse who stands beside me with her hand upon my shoulder. I only want my eyes to lock on her.

I whisper to her, "Good thing I lifted my DNR status." I had to tell her. It's like she already knew, as if she had already spoken to me two weeks ago, changing my mind to revert to a full code status.

She takes a step back and shrieks at me, "What? You're a DNR? Are you kidding me?"

"I was! I just reversed it two weeks ago!" I reassure her. I can't look away from her, can't take my eyes off her. There's something about her; I just can't distinguish it among my current thoughts. I'm too bombarded with everything that is happening in such a short period of time.

She slaps my shoulder, starts crying and says, "I would have jumped on you regardless!" She then takes a further step back to take a breath from what I had just presented her with.

"You were a DNR?" someone in the background questions.

"Not anymore! I guess I knew I had to come back. I reversed it two weeks ago." I emphasized the significance of this new code status.

I did know...
I had a feeling,
Someone or something was guiding me.

My body, mind and spirit had to reset;
I had to experience this
All of this...
To become anew.
To initiate my healing right from my core.
I had to be rebooted, and re-birthed!

My plea and my prayers had been answered
I remain with the illusion that
I was given a choice

THE LILY NURSE

To leave this place or stay.
Despite what other hardship I may have to heal from.

I feel as though I got to choose
I realize that my time and my purpose is not done.
And the "choice" was already decided for me,
But...
I believe I chose to come back
Of my own free will

I choose this Life
Rather…
I choose to LIVE!

I had to go through
The code and all of its elements.
To become me again.
Reborn into something I was always meant to be
Whole
Healed
Not broken

To be the ME
I was meant to be, ME!

I have the love of the Divine residing in my heart
I am worthy
To have and feel that Love
I believe in a higher power
And all of its glory.

I choose to be here
To see and share
Love and Light
of this plane, dimension and realm!

Allow the freedom and knowledge gained from this to be who
I am meant to be, ME!

JULIA EVANS

There is still more hardship and healing to endure
before coming to terms with this fully.
The story doesn't end here...

Chapter 21

Through My Family's Eyes

My immediate family did not have time to process this surreal life changing experience that we were forced into, nor were they really able to understand it all. They weren't given the time nor the opportunity to understand and comprehend what was happening. I went to work—like a normal, typical, regular day—with the intention of returning after my workday, to meet them all at our house, our home. We were supposed to reconvene from our day, eat supper, carry on with our evening and go on our merry way to our next scheduled endeavour. The day and evening were all planned out before I left the house that morning. And it all changed.

> No one could have anticipated this.
> No one could have foreseen this happening.
> No one could have prepared for this.

Through all of this chaos I was experiencing, everything I was submerged in, my family had no idea—no way of knowing, no inkling of what was happening.

Me, in the staff lunchroom at work…drowning in air! Everyone around me scatters to a task to help me in this situation.

- One to get some medication

- One to get a wheelchair

- One to call my husband, unaware of the extent and the seriousness of this situation

- One sitting there paralyzed in fear, shock and disbelief, not taking her eyes off me

And others frantically trying to assess the situation, the seriousness of it all.

While every ounce of my body is fighting, trying to hang on, trying to survive, my husband is at home, enjoying his quiet morning routine, just about to pour himself a coffee. Then one of my work friends calls and says, "Greg, Julia is having an allergic reaction!"

He responds calmly, "Oh, to lilies?"

"Yes! How did you know?" she inquires.

"Well, she's allergic to lilies!" he shoots back to her, as if this was an obvious, known fact about me.

His perception was nowhere near what was actually happening for me at that very moment. He had no way of knowing. He could only understand it through his past experiences and current knowledge. He had experienced this before with me, watching me have a reaction to lilies. I would get short of breath, cough, wheeze, and in all of those incidents, I turned out fine.

It had never been a crazy ordeal, just a minor hiccup to our day. I would struggle for a very short period time. But in all of those instances, I would very quickly remove myself from the environment that contained the lilies, cough it out and carry on with my day. It would make me quite tired, and left with a sore, raw airway, alongside with a weak and timid voice for a portion of my day. But in the end, it always turned out fine!

His mind then concluded from these referenced lived experiences, that the worst-case scenario would be: I'd require an antihistamine, Prednisone (a steroid), and perhaps a nebulizer to decrease the severity of the reaction and improve my airway.

No need to panic.

So, Greg finishes his morning coffee, goes to the washroom and moseys down to the hospital. And then he waited to see me, totally unaware of what was actually occurring. In his mind, I was probably just getting a few medications, thinking to himself, "She'll be fine and she will probably even go back to work," but he still loved me enough to be by my side, showing his support.

So, after everything that had happened to me during the code blue, I am brought to the emergency department. I am still laying on the stretcher I coded on, still attached to the defibrillator and the crash cart, all the other pads, stickers and leads upon my chest. I'm continuously monitored and continually checked on. My vital signs are displayed for others to see and assess: my heart rate, blood pressure, respirations and overall status.

The constant beeping of monitors and chatter around me echoes in my ears. Staff come in and out of my room, like there's a revolving door, keeping a close eye on me. A co-worker still stands beside me, never leaving my side, trying to calm the situation, perhaps trying to calm herself by mothering me, trying to soothe the pain of the experience. She softly caresses my forehead like she does to her children when they are scared, tired, and need to rest. She leans over and whispers to me, "I'm not leaving you. I'm staying until your husband arrives." Her voice cracks as she continues to reassure me. "You are not alone!"

I silently lie in my bed, my stretcher, stunned. Scared! I don't want to believe or understand this whole situation. Tears roll down the sides of my face as I stare at the ceiling above me. And we wait. We wait for him to arrive.

"Close your eyes. Rest. Get some sleep. I will stay beside you!" she tries to convince and reassure me.

"I'm too scared to close my eyes. I'm scared I won't wake up," I admit to her. "Do you know where my husband is? Is he is coming?"

"I know someone called him," she informs me. "I'm sure he'll be here soon."

"Can you call him again? He should be here by now!" I desperately need him by my side. Nothing feels real to me at this point; nothing feels normal.

She collects my phone from my belongings, from the items that were stripped and cut off of me and shoved into a bag. She dials the number on my cell phone and holds it up to my ear. The phone rings and Greg answers.

"Hi, beautiful," he says lovingly.

"Hi Greg," I cautiously start our conversation, forcing back the tears and fear in my voice. "Where are you?"

"I'm in the emergency department, stuck at triage," he says. "Julia, there was a bad code. They still haven't called it off yet." His voice has changed to a factual and concerned tone.

He was here this whole time. He was on the other side of the wall at the triage desk. Over an hour had passed since he got the call.

THE LILY NURSE

He was oblivious to it all. He was probably even sitting there before I was stable enough to be transferred to emergency. He was probably even here as the code team was frantically working on me, doing everything in their power to bring me back, keep me alive.

My heart sinks…

He has no idea!

"You better get in here," I say. "Someone will bring you to me."

We hang up and I look up at my co-worker in horror. "He has no idea! You're going to have to tell him." I close my eyes for a moment to escape from what is about to unfold for him—for us! I gather my thoughts before he enters my room and is exposed to this new world, before he is aware of our new reality.

Time drags as I wait for Greg, the love and light of my life, to be by my side. I've been yearning for him to be near me, to hold me, to be there beside me in the same room, to help me feel safe and loved. To help me decipher something real. I want him and his love; that is real, that I can get my head around and focus on.

It's a very short distance for someone to guide him to me from the waiting area. Although it felt like an eternity, it was only just a few minutes for him to be brought to my bedside. I lay there frozen in my bed in anticipation after talking to him on the phone, dreading what he is about to face. I am trying to get my wits about me, trying not to completely fall apart as he walks through the doorway. In my mind, I am trying to figure out a way to lighten the blow of what he is about to walk in on, the hell he is about to see!

He thought this was something minor…

He was in NO rush.

JULIA EVANS

He finished his coffee.
He perceived that...
There was NO need to panic!

He came to the hospital
To be by my side,
Support me,
Love me.

Allowing for the proper procedures to take place
Trusting the process,
Believing that everything will be,
Fine
Golden
And we would be able to continue on our day,
Like it's a tiny little blip.
No need to think otherwise!

And there he sits
At triage.
Oblivious to this all.
But still,
He was here
This whole time...
Waiting!

As I lay in this room within the emergency department, I am unable to sit up, roll over, or hide. My thoughts are racing through my head—what my husband is going to think and feel, what hell he is about to experience as he sees his wife lying before him on the same stretcher she coded on. The one I died and came back on. He will see me still attached to the cash cart they used to shock me back, the one that sent a surge of electricity to my heart in a desperate attempt to keep me alive, to not lose me again; it stays attached to me in the off chance someone may have to shock me again. The wires, the IVs, the tubing, the sheer chaos of this.

I hear him approaching...
Then he turns and enters the room.

THE LILY NURSE

The way my stretcher is positioned I cannot see him as he enters. It's pointing to the opposite door in the room—the one that faces the core of the department—so the nurses and doctors can glance over and do a quick visual assessment of me.

His idle conversation stops as he enters the room.

"Julia?" he says loudly in disbelief, as if his brain is questioning and rationalizing what his eyes are seeing—his wife, the love of his life, his everything—lying on a stretcher before him, almost lifeless.

This was beyond what he had imagined to be the worst-case scenario. This was a thousand times worse.

I still cannot see his face, his reaction. All I can hear is my co-worker timidly telling him a brief summary. He doesn't say a word. I don't even know if at that point he could speak, hear her or understand what the hell was happening or what had happened!

He then takes a step towards me. I muscle up enough strength to tilt my head in his direction. That's when I saw his heart break. His world came crumbling down like the Berlin Wall. Shattered and helpless!

He couldn't, he just couldn't…
He just stood there
in disbelief,
Shock!

There was NO time to process this for him.
NO time to really understand or grasp the magnitude of this.
All he saw was what was presented there before him.
His frail wife…

He stands there, frozen. Staring down at me. Listening to my colleague explain what happened. I don't think one word really sunk in for Greg. He just keeps staring at me with this blank look upon his face.

When she finishes telling Greg, she leaves us alone in this emergency room. He pulls up a chair and sits beside me. It is as though our world has stopped, completely and utterly stopped. There is hustle and bustle around us, lots of things happening, but he just sits there beside me, quietly. We both sit quietly, trying to absorb it all. Not saying a word. Staring off in the distance.

What the fuck happened?

CHAPTER 22

TOO MUCH EPI

Greg has been sitting beside me for several hours in a chair he pulled up to the side of my stretcher from the corner of this room. He sits there not saying a word, not touching me nor the stretcher that I lie upon. Both of us are silent in each other's presence, observing the chaotic world around us.

He is listening and observing, but not comprehending what is truly happening. Everyone has been in and out of here giving their own point of view, perceptions, hypotheses of everything that has occurred. They debrief with us—the two who just want to sit in silence, think things over and breathe. This whole time he has not been able to pause and look at me or this situation. He hasn't been granted any time to adjust to any of this. He's not able to look at me directly or at the situation we are both forced to face. He and I are not willing to submit to the occurrence of this traumatic event. This was supposed to be a typical day in our world and reality.

He sits there quietly in his chair, watching the array of people entering and exiting this room; he seems to gaze off into the distance, at the floor or his hands. His hands are continually moving, constantly squeezing and ringing out the fear, worry and emotions from the center of his palms. He doesn't know what to do or what to say; he's helpless! So am I!

For the brief moments when all these people aren't in my room, we remain silent, still, an eerie feeling over us. Neither of us want to accept this reality.

I stare at Greg longingly, but he can't bear to look at me. He hangs his head, not saying anything, not a word. Oh, how I wish he could see me, look at me and see what is happening right in front of his face. It feels as though if he looks at me, truly sees me here upon this stretcher, we have to accept, acknowledge and submit to this fate.

This has to be the worst of it. I died and came back! I am weak, frail and adjusting to staying here in this realm, this world, this life. I am still fighting with my spirit and mind to stay here and not fade away. This has to be all of the puzzle pieces I have to deal with, to face and to heal from.

Greg sits here so quietly, watching and observing the constant stream of people entering and exiting this room. I watch him intently, waiting for some sort of reaction, emotion, anything. I wait for him to realize the severity of this, for him to want to hold me, to embrace me tight in his arms, and protect me from all of this.

I feel so lost, alone, and unsure of everything. I am yearning for that connection, to be reunited with him again. I need our souls to realign. I need to escape from this reality.

I want him to take me in his arms and protect me from all of this turmoil. I need to be nuzzled up against his chest—his heart. I need to feel and hear his heart beat, and for him to hear and feel mine. I need him to touch me, to know that I am here! I so badly want to be in my safe place right now—my favorite place on earth, in his strong, loving, protective arms. I want to be safe within his embrace, to pause for just a moment, to be present, to breathe. I desperately need to feel safe at this point, to be comforted, loved, and protected, to be shielded from all of this unfathomable reality and strife that swirls around me, and resides within me.

I can't take it anymore, not for one more second alone in this room without his strong arms around me. I'm back! I'm alive! I'm here! Acknowledge my existence! I telepathically yell at Greg. Alas, he cannot hear my thoughts.

I finally verbalize to him, "Greg! I need you to hug me! I need you to wrap your arms around me. I died today," I cry to him. "I'm back, but I died."

He finally looks at me, both of us realizing this harsh and yet blissful notion. I came back! I am left with pretty shitty conditions right now, but I am back—back to him, back to our family, back to this world, back to this life.

It is as if he needs permission to embrace me, permission to acknowledge this catastrophe. He quickly stands from the place he had resided for more than four hours, and finally leans down to give me a hug. He very carefully and very gently embraces me, the whole time trying not to interfere with all of the tubing, wires and medical equipment that are a necessary part of my continued survival.

Once he has me in his grasp, we are both able to breathe. We exhale and fully evoke the emotions and tears that we were with holding from each other, finally acknowledging this fucked-up situation.

"Greg, I died," I cry to him

"I know," he whispers, squeezing me harder, not caring about the external things attached to me. He conceals his head within the nape of my neck, tears now rapidly flowing from the both of us, flooding the room with emotion.

"You're back. I didn't even know you left me!" He sobs heavily, with his shoulders quivering from the outrageous influx of emotions. He can't hold them in any longer.

"Am I really here?" I inquire. I'm still absolutely dumbfounded.

"Yes, you are! You're here with me. I love you so much, Julia," he heavily sobs.

"I love you too," I respond. "I can't believe this is happening. I just went to work, Greg. Why did this happen? I just went to work!" I howl and bawl intensely.

We squeeze each other with all our might, not wanting to let go of each other ever again. Wanting to be entwined and in tune with one another. Not wanting to separate from this safe and loving embrace, but to stay connected and protected from this hectic chaos we are enduring. Time stops for a moment as we reconnect, having our hearts feel and hear the other's heartbeat. We take a moment for ourselves to grab hold of what is truly important to us: our life, our love. We are now able to be still, calm, and breathe—a little slower and a little deeper. *Ah, my safe place!*

As we are in this embrace, a new doctor enters the room. He sheepishly perches himself at the end of my stretcher. Greg and I regrettably separate. Greg sits back on his chair, positioning himself to face the doctor, but not letting go of my hand. He gives it a little squeeze, reassuring me that he is still here with me, being present both physically and emotionally, by my side, in my corner, taking on this new obstacle together. I feel that I am not alone, having him here with me, holding me, and acknowledging me and this situation. We are able to take anything else that is to come our way now. We are together, connected and strong.

I am alive and that's all that matters right now. He looks at me, gives my hand another squeeze, and presents me with a loving, nurturing smile.

"It has been quite a shocking day," the doctor informs us, as if we didn't know.

"Literally, twice!" I factually and inappropriately blurt out, holding two fingers up to really get my point across.

Greg and I laugh out loud at my quick response. This is a fantastic coping mechanism: inappropriate humor. A little humor goes a long way, and right now it's an amazing distraction from my true emotions. It helps me ease the intensity of this situation. It also helps those around me, or so I believe. I think it really helps others get through the uncomfortable situation of not knowing what to say to me. It clears the path to see the silver lining within the shittiest of situations. Besides, life is too short to always be so serious. It's best to laugh when you can.

The doctor is stunned by my remark and graces us with a small smirk. Then his persona gets very serious again. My weak heart sinks....

"I don't know how to tell you this," he begins, before taking a long dramatic pause as he looks down at the paper in his hands.

Greg and I fearfully glance at each other.

"I have never been put into a situation like this," he continues. "I just want to start by saying I am so sorry you had to go through this Julia. What I need to share with you is quite serious."

I squeeze Greg's hand, and think to myself, *Fuck, now what?*

"I am led to believe," he pauses, "you were given the wrong dose of epinephrine. I can't be sure at this point, but it appears that you were given 10 times the amount of epinephrine—that the intramuscular amount was given to you intravenously." He states what others have been hinting at. Numerous people have asked me if I remember anything.

I remember all of it!
Every last little detail!

"I got your results back, and you have global damage to your heart," he says. "Your ejection fraction is at 35 per cent and we are unable to determine if the outcome will be permanent damage. The heart damage would reflect the excessive amount of epinephrine you endured." He pauses, as if he is lost for words.

Greg speaks up, rapidly firing questions to the physician. "So, what does this mean? What is the extent of this damage to her heart? What does 35 per cent ejection fraction mean? What is global damage?"

I lie there silently. Here I am lying on the stretcher that I died on and then came back to this life, twice. I am stunned and shocked, but how else do you explain what happened as I felt my heart pounding through my chest, and the pressure in my head caused by my excessively high blood pressure. Clinically, I know what all of this means.

But Greg doesn't.

"That means you both have to consider what to do next," the doctor explains. "Seek advice. An investigation has been initiated. I can't imagine what you are thinking. The damage is affecting both sides of the heart—both left and right systolic dysfunction—meaning the whole heart is damaged. Julia, your heart is only able to pump blood to the rest of your body at 35 per cent of its normal force. The amount of blood being pumped out of your heart is less than what your body requires and needs."

Fuck. Heart Failure!

I can't believe there are even more pieces to this horrific story. Not only did I go through this unimaginable experience, but now I have to deal with this too. I become completely numb and switched off from the world with this new information. Words rings in my ears: "global damage" and "it may be permanent."

"You are going to be admitted to the Cardiac Surveillance Unit, to be closely monitored," he continues. "I pray this damage is not permanent, and the doctor who administered it has been swirling around this unit wanting to talk with you. I am so sorry you are faced with all of this. I wish the best outcome for you, Julia. We're all so happy you're back!"

"So, I can coach my baseball team tonight?" I question the physician, as if I didn't hear one word of what he said to me.

"No Julia, you are not coaching tonight. You're going to be monitored in the hospital for a while." He gets up from the end of my bed to vacate my room. He faces me one more time and says, "I wish you all the best with this. Take care of yourself." Then he exits my room.

Greg and I don't even speak about what we have just heard. He leans over and embraces me again in his arms, both of us desperately needing each other right now. Our world has flipped once again. All that is familiar to us at this point, the one thing that hasn't changed in our world, is the love we share for each other. So, we grab hold of that notion and don't let go, for we are in this together. I came back for a reason and a damaged heart is not going to stop me.

> It's going to be one hell of a journey.
> Now all I have to do is survive the night.

I abruptly release from Greg's embrace. "Oh my God, Greg! The kids! We have to tell the kids," I blurt out, frantic and anxious at the thought of them having to hear what happened today.

We locate a cell phone and call our neighbor—one of my dearest friends and the one my kids trust most. We have been neighbors and friends for a short time, but she has always been there for me and our children. I trust her and need her more than ever to assist in this unfathomable situation. I need her there for our children. I need her to protect them, comfort them and bring them to me.

"Hello," she answers casually.

"Kristina, I need your help," I say, trying to hold back my tears. "I need you to go to my house, make a snack for my kids and bring them to me. Greg and I are in the hospital."

"Of course! What happened? Are you guys okay?" she asks with fear, worry and concern in her voice.

"No," I respond. "Well, yes and no." I give her the Cole's notes version of the events that took place and led us here.

"What do you want me to say to them?" she questions, not hesitating for a moment to step up and be the short lived pseudo-parent to our children, wanting to do whatever she can to help in this situation.

"Act natural," I say frankly. "Tell them you are bringing them to us. We will tell them everything when you bring them here."

I don't even know what I am going to say to our children, or how. This moment is going to stay with them for the rest of their lives; how do I not scar them more?

"Are you okay?" she asks, nearly crying. I can hear her holding back the emotions.

"I don't know. I just need my children beside me. I need to hold them," I say and then end the conversation.

Chapter 23

Is It True?

Greg and I sit in this emergency room, in the middle of this horrific situation we have been placed in. There is no time to process any of this. No one seems willing to talk with us about how we are actually doing with this whole situation—not just the physical broken pieces to this puzzle, but the draining emotional and mental aspects too. Not one person is showing true compassion towards us, everyone seems to be too busy scrambling and worrying about how this affects them—how *my* horrifically traumatic event makes *them* feel. We have to come to terms with this all by ourselves, with no help from anyone else. We are just supposed to accept all of this, and not have it affect us in any way.

I can't even begin to untangle this web we are in; I am not in any fit state to even try. All I am trying to do right here, right now, is to survive this day. I have to make it through until tomorrow, for tomorrow is another day. I want to put this day behind me, forget that it even happened. But the fact is, it did happen, and

I am the one who gets to live through it all, live through all the repercussions of this. I am the one who will have to heal from all the layers of this whole unsettling situation.

I wish I could get out of this bed and run away from this place, never to look back, but I can't. I can't even lift my head off this pillow or move off this stretcher I died in. I'm still connected to the crash cart, intravenous, oxygen and monitors, and I am too weak to do anything about it. I have to instill my trust in everyone here and pray that they have my best interests in mind, to supply me with the proper care I deserve.

> How can you heal from something that is such a major external factor in your demise?

I don't know how I'm going to live through this. I'm here and alive; I'm thankful for that. I am going to have to keep reminding myself of that. I'm alive. Thankful I'm here. I'm alive.

I look over at Greg; he looks so devastated, broken, lost, helpless. I wish I could get out of this bed, jump in the side-by-side with him and forget all of our troubles. No amount of laughter or jokes can lift any of this pain away.

I'm so torn—happy I'm back, alive, but distressed. Can all of this possibly be? I was just going onto my unit to start a regular shift to help people in need. I shouldn't be the one here on this stretcher, being forced into this situation, because of things that shouldn't have even happened.

"Greg, what are we going to do?" I ask.

"I don't know, Julia." he says. "I can't even think straight. We should concentrate on the fact that you are back, here, alive." He is desperately trying to stay positive and strong for the both of us. He places my hand in his hands, holding his hands in a prayer-like position, lowers his head and says, "I can't lose you. Thank God you're back."

I start crying at the thought that I almost didn't come back. He could have lost me. We close our eyes for a moment, trying to block out what's happening, only to spontaneously open them back up because this presence standing at my bedside. It's the doctor who gave me the epinephrine. He's just hovering over me, staring down at me like he's seen a ghost.

I have to ask him. I have to know, for my own peace of mind—not to blame or point fingers, but to know what actually went into my body. What was forced into my body without me knowing.

"Did you give me the intramuscular epi through the IV?" I ask.

"I did what I had to do," he responds quickly, as if this statement had been rehearsed. "You're here, aren't you?"

He walks away.

Greg and I stare at each other, unimpressed with his response. We're stunned. But at this point, this is the least of our worries. This isn't even an area we want to give our energy to. We are just concerned with the aftermath and how it affects me and our family unit. How can we find peace and a blessing from this?

Chapter 24

Good Night and I Love You

It is late in the evening, and it's time to say good night and goodbye to my family. They have been here all afternoon and evening. It has been one hell of a day. I am petering out from the excitement of the day's events and I can see my family needs rest too. They need time away from this environment to process and calm their minds from everything that has happened. They need to step away from this turmoil and chaos. They need time to be able to feel what they need to feel and process what they have experienced today.

It's time to part paths.

This time it's so much harder to say "Good night, I love you and see you tomorrow." It is the hardest and most emotional set of loving good night wishes I have ever given to them. My family has seen me in a hospital bed before; they have seen me in pretty rough shape thanks to the harshness MS forces us all to accept. Our children have had to experience leaving me alone in a hospital bed. They have had to say their good nights, goodbyes, and I love yous, needing to walk away to be in the comfort of our home, leaving me behind. They have had to experience this unpleasant reality before, but not like this. This time it is so much harder, different and difficult.

This time, none of us want to bid farewell to each other; after we said our last I love yous this morning, our world completely changed. Unaware of the happenings I was experiencing, they all were experiencing their day in a pretty normal, mundane way. Greg at home, with his quiet morning coffee, and the kids in the comfortable and safe environment of their school. They were all living a normal day. They were experiencing their own world without even a thought of what they were going to be facing later that afternoon. These events inevitably would change our family dynamics and how we see the world.

Our children are now forced to deal with this and make sense of the happenings that occurred earlier that day. Their mother left them behind and also came back. I experienced some horrific and remarkable things. They cannot begin to fathom what I have gone through; they can only see the result. They have to process all of this. I can't even process it and I was there.

The walls of my world came crashing down within moments of smelling the pungent aroma of a Stargazer lily. My life flashed before my eyes. Then everything faded away as I entered a dimension or realm like no other. I was brought back to a world I am not sure if I am worthy to be in. I surrendered, begging to escape this world; I pleaded with the Universe, the divine, something greater than me, to release me from the pain I was enduring. I hold guilt in my heart because I gave up. I permitted myself to let go, leaving everything and everyone behind. I am not sure if I even want to be back here, in this realm. I don't feel worthy to have survived. I wanted to stay there, in absolute bliss.

I experienced both sides of the spectrum: Death and Life! Broken and healed, and then broken again, this time at a totally new level. I haven't experienced heartbreak like this any other time before. My heart is completely broken physically and emotionally, ten times the amount and even more. I am never to be the same again, now feeling broken, lost and unsure if I can make it through the night. I am scared to even close my eyes, for fear that I may not return to this life.

I look at my family and my heart aches at the thought that I was ready to leave them. I wanted to stay in the light, with my mom. I am angry at her for leaving me and angry at myself for almost doing the same thing to my children. She pushed me back to show me the way to another light, a light that has always been there, right in front of me: the love of my family, for "the love of a family is life's greatest blessing." The light comes from my children and my soulmate, Greg. This love is exponential, unconditional, never ending, infinite! Our love radiates light!

As our children said their goodbyes and I love yous to me this morning, they didn't know that would be the last time they would say it to the person I let go of, the person I left behind. None of us had a crystal ball to inform us that I would die and come back—back into my former body, but completely and utterly changed. No one could have foreseen that.

***

Before Titus and Jayda became aware of what was happening in the hospital, my place of work, where I go to most days of the week to earn a living, to help financially support our loving family, before they learn of what had transpired after they said their goodbyes and I love yous, earlier this morning, they would enter our house after school, just like any other day. They would be totally oblivious of the drastic change that had occurred; they would be entering the house with the excitement to get everything ready for a fun and exhilarating evening at the ball diamond. That's when their world started to flip, and life as they knew IT would be forever changed.

They enter the house and are greeted at the door by one of my best friends, the one I called and gave instructions to help our family out at this difficult time in our lives. She is trying to keep her emotions in check, following my instructions to feed Titus and Jayda and then bring them to me, to the hospital to learn of the new reality we all have to face.

"What are you doing here?" the kids question her nonchalantly.

"I am here to take you to the hospital. Your mom and dad are there," she matter-of-factually responds. She does the best she can to comfort them, mothering them by feeding them and not making a big deal out of the situation, hiding from them what has actually happened. Waiting for Greg and me to inform them, telling them of our own accord and through our own choice of words. All of us trying our hardest not to emotionally scar them, trying to protect them from the harshness of what they are about to learn.

Our children's world starts to crumble. They are thinking the worst. Their first thought is their parents have been in a car accident and are in critical care. Little do they know or are they able to comprehend the severity of this situation they are about to endure. They create their own worse case scenario within their minds to prepare them for what they are about to face. Their little minds can't even begin to imagine the actual reality as a possible outcome of today's events.

As they are brought to the hospital, to be with us and learn of what actually happened, they are completely blindsided by the reality that their mother, the one who lays before them, died and came back. They can only comprehend what they can see in front of them: a frail, broken women, their mother, laying on a stretcher with wires attached to her and a red crash cart, IVs, and a monitor to display vital signs that they can't make sense of.

How can the person that lays before them be the same person, same mother to whom they said, "Goodbye and I love you" to earlier this morning? How can this all of be real?

***

So after spending the afternoon and evening with my family in the emergency room, I am finally settled in a new bed on the Cardiac Surveillance Unit. I am on the CSU to be closely monitored and now the time is upon us to say our good night, goodbye and I love yous. Jayda does not want to leave my side, and Titus is trying to keep it together—trying to be strong for all of us, not surrendering to his overwhelming perceptions and emotions. He's being like a soldier: staying strong and brave for his family, watching with cautious observant eyes, taking on all the facts and none of the emotion. Later on, in his own time, he'll feel this. I know him; he'll fall apart when it's just us, when he's alone in the safety and protection of his mother's arms.

"Mom, I don't want to leave you," Jayda cries into my shoulder.

"I know you don't," I whisper to her. I am so weak at this point that I can barely hold her in my arms.

"I don't want to leave either," Titus speaks up from the end of my bed. He has been standing there this whole time, watching and observing, not saying a word, just like his father did all day.

"We can stay a little longer," Greg announces. "Not too long though. Your mother needs to rest. Her heart is very weak, and she has been through a lot today."

He puts his hand upon my shoulder and catches a glimpse of the heart monitor that lays upon my chest. It had slipped out of the strategically sewn pocket of my gown. He leans in and has a long stare at it. I look at the monitor too—my heart rate is 27 beats per minute. We lock eyes as this number registers in both our minds. That is an extremely low heart rate; you don't have to be in the medical profession to know that.

"Julia," he whispers to me, squeezing my shoulder.

"I know," I whisper back, shutting down any further conversation regarding this.

My heart is so weak and it can't supply enough blood for what my body requires. It feels like it's shutting down. I feel like I'm shutting down, too frail to fight. I can't even wrap my arms around Jayda. A single tear rolls down my cheek; I can't even wipe it away either. My breathing is becoming more laboured, so Greg puts the oxygen tubing back into my nose. I give him a "thank you for everything" smile.

That's when it hits him; that's the moment when I could start seeing his world come crashing down. He's finally seeing me. His emotions overcome him. It is like I was looking at my father 35 years prior to this moment. During the outburst in the grocery store, I remember looking up at my father and seeing a helpless shell of a man, broken and doing everything in his power not to fall apart, just trying to care for two children, a boy and a girl, four years apart.

The difference here is that Greg lost me—without even knowing or seeing, having no time to grieve that part. Then he got me back. Completely broken, but he got me back, all in the same breath that he found out he lost me. Greg, similar to my father that day in the grocery story: he doesn't know how to express his locked-down emotions from today's events, and bursts out to the children. "You both do realize what happened today?"

Greg says this not to hurt the children, but to question his and their knowledge of the events that took place. Then he finally says the words.

"Your mother died today! She came back, but she died!"

My heart sinks as I hear these words and the tone in his voice. Greg is stating the facts to our children, not sugar coating or helping them cope or adjust to it. It's like déja vu of when my father was speaking these words to me, in the centre of our kitchen, about my mother. I quickly react to these words, trying to unravel their little brains to the notion of me dying. I don't want them to latch on to that. I don't want them to think their mother is gone, even though they can see me. I want to try to erase those words, prevent them from sticking to their minds, like it did for me. I had a lifetime of pain and suffering because of similar words spoken to me, and I am not about to repeat history.

I find whatever strength I have left in my body and interject, "The angels didn't want me to stay. They just wanted to play with me for a little while. I'm here! Alive! The angels didn't want to play with me long, so they sent me back to be with you. I know my heart is broken right now, but I have so much love within it and so much love surrounding me. I will heal from this. I have so much love in my heart to share and so much love around me to help heal my heart."

Jayda still looks fearful and panicked, grabbing and squeezing my side tighter, perhaps to fully feel me, to really lock into her little brain that I am here with them. I am back! I'm not dead; I'm here! Alive with them!

"Jayda," I whisper. My breath is weak from the limited amount of blood flow in my body and lungs.

She looks up at me, inquisitive of what more I am going to say.

"I need you to do something for me," I begin.

"Yes, Mom?" she replies.

"Can you go into that bag that says 'patient belongings' and get my necklace out of it?" I start telling her what to do—step by step, but unaware of where this bag is.

Greg hands Jayda the white bag, and has her place it onto the bed to find my necklace inside. This holds all the clothes the code team cut off of me as they initiated their protocol to save my life. They needed to cut it all off, to expose my chest and attach the leads and resuscitate me—not just my clothes, but my necklace too. It's the one I wear each and every day. My necklace is a moonstone wrapped in wire, hanging from a simple black cord. Jayda knows the significance of this necklace; she knows what it represents. It has a beautiful meaning and purpose to it: to bring out my joy and take away negative emotions and thoughts, such as overpowering fear and worry. It helps to protect my feminine energy that knows how to heal and bring me back to *wholeness*.

She finds it for me, puzzled what to do with it.

"I need you to hang onto this for me," I say. "I need you to protect it until I get home. That way you'll have a part of me with you. Hold it close to your heart and my heart will start healing. I may be here in this hospital bed for now, but I am always with you. Mommy will be okay. The angels are protecting me."

She holds it tight in the centre of her palm and then presses it up to her chest, close to her heart. She bows down to my abdomen, for she can't lay against my chest because of the monitor. She lays there and weeps. Although she weeps to mourn her former mother, she is starting to see the new life we are blessed to have. She is processing this experience in a different, more pleasant and heart-warming manner, a new light and perspective.

I look towards Titus. I lock eyes with him, looking into his soul of what he needs and requires from me, and I question, "Titus, are you okay?"

He looks deep into my eyes, seeing only his mother before him, alive. He erases this environment from his mind. He just needed to look deep into my eyes to see that I am here—not gone, but here with him.

Greg takes this cue to vacate the room and take our children home. They all have a lot to process and adjust to. Greg leans in, kisses my forehead and whispers, "Good night Beautiful. I love you."

I smile at him and say, "I love you too."

Greg picks Jayda up into his arms to carry her off and then wraps an arm around Titus. The three of them begin to walk off into the depths of the hospital—away from this room, away from this place—to be in the comfort and safety of our home, united, protected and strong. The Evans'sss band together, gaining strength and support from one another, especially in times of need.

As they exit my room, we all instinctively say, "Good night and I love you!"

I watch them step away from me, from my hospital room, to face the outside world, leaving me behind, needing me to find the strength to live through the night. My heart sinks seeing their backs trailing off, away from me. I have to find my strength within my heart to live another day, to see them: my family, the light and love of my life.

I reflect on what I said to Jayda. I am flabbergasted by the events that brought me to here. Did this all actually happen? I become more aware of the magnitude of the catastrophic situation I am in. I am realizing how weak I actually am right now. My mind starts racing and I start pondering so many questions.

What if I don't wake up, after I close my eyes?
What if I don't survive this night?
What would my family do without me?
Who's going to help them, protect them?
What if I hadn't been brought back?
What if?
What if?
What if?

THE LILY NURSE

I lay here, alone in my hospital bed reflecting on the course of the day. I stare out my window to the vast darkness of the night and try to analyze, *Am I in the dark or in the light? Where am I now?*

My door swings open and this radiant, angelic nurse stands before me, illuminated by a light—perhaps her inner light? Or from the iridescence of the hallway's fluorescent lights, or maybe from something or someone else? At this point it doesn't matter where the light is illuminating from, what I see is heartwarming and she is beaming with light. She gives me a sense of comfort and peace. She enters my room holding a Lorazepam.

CHAPTER 25

CAN THIS BE?

~  ~

It is now a day after the traumatic and catastrophic series of events I had been thrown into. I am blown away by the fact that I endured all of this in less than 24 hours. I wake, alone in this hospital bed. It is a new day in my new existence. I am opening my eyes to it after a full night of rest, for the very first time realizing this is neither a dream nor a nightmare. This is my world, my new world, and my second chance at life. This is truly a day of awakening. I awake to the dawn of a new day on the CSU. I am a 38-year-old woman in heart failure. I am forced to stop—pause— and see my world in a different light.

This morning, when I wake up, everything is different; my world seems so much brighter. It is as through I finally *woke up*—not just from my slumber, but from a state of dis-ease. Everything around me and within me is different and new. Everything seems heightened, refreshed, cleansed and recharged. While I'm not quite sure what I am actually experiencing, what I do know is everything is different. Oh, so different. It is as though I have been supercharged, granted a gift that only I can see. I am the only one aware of this precious insight, feeling, and knowledge I have been bestowed with.

I have been saved, blessed, and reincarnated back into my former body. My body that was broken, used and abused, the one I wanted to let go of. Although I feel as if I'm back in my former body, it's not really me—everything has changed. Everything is different.

My eyes are open to this new world, this new me. Everything is so surreal, quiet, and I am trying to adjust. I am weak, frail, and totally unsure of what is supposed to happen next. I am calm and at peace with my world; a stillness and pause within my entire being has arisen, allowing me to take small breaths of this new and unfathomable precious life I have been gifted. There is still more to this picture, still more to the story.

I am not able to sit up on my own, so I lie here in the stillness of the eerie, cold—yet beautiful—peacefulness of my hospital room. I am beginning to sense my new body, my new being, trying to rationalize what is happening. I am adjusting to yet another component to this new reality that I am faced with. It's a feeling I haven't had for years!

Can this be real? I question in my head, querying all explanations for what I am truly experiencing and feeling.

"Am I actually feeling this?" I bewilderingly question. This new sensation has been hidden and not communicated within my body for years. I wiggle my toes from underneath the synthetic flannel blanket. I am astonished by my new discovery.

"I can feel my feet!" I say aloud to myself within this vast open and empty space. I'm beaming, exhilarated, and smiling with a bit of disbelief. I am grinning from ear to ear. I can't believe this! I can feel my feet, both of them! There's no MS pain anywhere in my body! No tingling of any kind, no pins and needles that signal the misconducted communication from my brain to my body! I can feel the blanket caressing both of my feet. My mind explodes with excitement.

For years, every morning when I woke up, I would have this ritual upon getting out of bed: I would slowly awaken my body to the daily fight of the uncertainty and unpredictable world of MS. Most mornings I would struggle with pain, numbness and/or tingling. I would have to psych myself up to sit at the edge of the bed and take that day's first few steps, leery and full of fear. Thinking *this is the day I won't be able to walk*, adapting to the early morning challenges I was made to face each and every day.

I was always trying to put positive spins on what I was faced with. What daily challenge was in store for me? I always had to bear the fear from this unpredictable and debilitating disease. Although it was constantly changing, fluctuating in the degrees of pain, it was always there, always creating new challenges for me. I was led to believe that I was stuck with this unpredictable, devastating disease for life, not knowing what each day would hold for me. Once diagnosed, MS stays with you for life. There is no cure. You just have to accept that fate and keeping living the best way you can, but you are constantly dreading what the future holds for you.

Every morning as I did my daily ritual of getting out of bed, it was always mind over matter! I would not allow this invisible and unpredictable disease to take me down that day! I would start this ritual with my toes, wiggling them to see the extent of my pain, numbness, tingling, pins and needles. I would then attempt to maneuver both my legs. Some days, I would have to move one and then the other. Occasionally, one worked and the other didn't. I would slowly wake my body to the new day, continually assessing the extent of the disability my body and mind had to endure that morning. As I began moving my lower body, I would also be waking up my arms, hugging my body tight to see if I could, in fact, carry on with the day. Some days I couldn't, and I had to stay in bed longer.

THE LILY NURSE

And now today…it is all different. Today, I am not faced with any challenge that MS provides, not even having the fear or worry that I contained inside for so long. I have none of the physical debilitation that MS used to challenge me with daily. Up until yesterday, I always did this morning routine and ritual, but today…today I am starting my day with a new body, new outlook, and new exciting sensations. Not only can I feel my feet, but I have no MS pain.

I glance to my left—and I can see! I have no blind spot in the corner of my left eye! For four years I have had optic neuritis—a slight deficit in my peripheral vision. I always had to adapt to this small area of blindness. But now it's gone. I can see clearly! I keep looking forward and then to the left, thinking that the spot may come back, but it doesn't. My MS is gone! Out of my mind, out of my body; it's indescribable and unfathomable. It's gone!

I have no one to share this new discovery with at this time. No one to understand or be able to fathom this breakthrough, this miracle! I just lay here alone in my hospital bed, staring at the ceiling, thanking my blessed stars!

This is a new life!
A new and renewed me!
A fresh start!
A complete systems reboot!
I have been re-birthed!

Now to wrap my head around it all. No one is going to believe me. I can't even believe this myself! There is no cure for MS! *Can this be? Are my symptoms really gone?* Maybe there is truth to going to the other side—to a place of healing. Perhaps when my soul cried out to the Universe, something greater than me was listening. Maybe I was finally willing and able listen to what my body, mind and spirit needed? Maybe there was something there that I needed to see, feel and heal from? After begging and pleading to release myself from my former life of pain, I realized I was not meant to stay in that place of bliss. I did, however, need to experience that loving light to realize what I had been suppressing for most of my life, ever since my mother's death when I was three years old.

It was not my time to stay; I know that, but what's next? *Why did this healing have to come out of something so horrific and scary?* I am so very blessed to be here, resurrected to live a new life. *But what do I have to heal from next? Why am I brought back with a broken heart? What else do I have to see?*

I came back from the other side in more ways than one and I am here to live. Other than getting home to my family, nothing else matters.

Who can I talk to about this? I don't know how or who to discuss this with. My head starts spinning, scrambling with disbelief that this has occurred. How do you talk about being in a place of absolute bliss and then coming back to having my MS symptoms to be nonexistent? Even I'm not convinced. Maybe it can all be explained medically; perhaps it was just the sheer shock to my system, new nerve impulses being generated. But I don't believe that would explain what I experienced. What did I really experience? I know I went to a place of bliss, a place where I felt love like no other, a place that radiated light from that love. But how else can I explain this? How else can a person go from such a devastating, debilitating state—full of anguish, pain and strife—to this: happy to be alive and symptom-free from a disabling disease?

> Miracles happen every day,
> I am so blessed to be part of one.

This new discovery and the thoughts around it exhaust me, so I close my eyes and drift off to a blissful sleep, shutting down my mind to this new world. I allow my mind to enter back to the world of deep sleep, allow my brain waves to rest and slow down. There is a lot to process; my neurons are rewiring, and my conscious mind is awakening to my new reality. I have to give myself time and permission to process this—every element and layer of this is a lot to comprehend and accept.

Chapter 26

Walking Around the Unit

I have been bound to my hospital bed for two days now. I've been unable to tour the unit or exit my room, fearing my heart won't be able to withstand the strain, having the nurses and doctors coddle me and worry about breaking me more. They have to be sure my heart is, in fact, strong enough to venture on the simple little tasks of any mild physical activity.

My body and mind yearn for movement, momentum, and a different space and atmosphere, somewhere other than this hospital room and bed. I just want to escape and be with my family in the comfort of my own home, away from this place, away from all this turmoil; I want to be free and breathe in the fresh air of the great outdoors.

The evening nurse enters my room. "Julia, are you ready to try walking around this unit?" she asks. "I got the doctor's permission for you to do so."

I smile the most enormous smile at her. "It's like you know exactly what I am wanting and needing," I reply. "Can you hear all my thoughts? I'm dying to go for a walk and get out of this room. Well, not literally—I've already gone down that road." I snicker and pause for dramatic effect, staring at her and awaiting her reaction.

She smiles back at me and chuckles a smidge. I believe she's getting use to my inappropriate humor and jokes. It's how I lighten up my world and my environment; it's how I cope.

"I think I know you well enough Julia," she says. "You are a fighter, and we are going to get you back home to your family as soon as we can. I can't begin to imagine how awful this all is for you. It breaks my heart knowing what you have gone through—not just with this, but with all of your challenges and struggles with MS too. You don't deserve this, none of this. I know you; you will heal from this! You're going to find enough strength to get you back to being you. The strong, never-giving-up woman you are known as."

She leans down and gives me a hug—a genuine, loving embrace. I've known this woman for years; she truly does know of my hardships. Now she is faced with being my nurse, having me in her care. I need her to help me with my healing, trying to mend my broken heart. This moment is so heartwarming to me. It's so comforting to have someone speak to me like this. My heart fills with love, blanketing me with the comforting notion that someone really does care about me. She recognizes and subtly validates what I have gone through. This supports and supplies me with more determination and drive to get better, to heal. She is encouraging me to start healing from not only my physically broken pieces, but from the shattered pieces of the tremendously overwhelming emotions that I bear inside. She is providing me with external strength to keep moving forward, to keep on my path and journey to recovery—in essence to find what it is to be me again!

JULIA EVANS

> I will get to where I need to go
> I will get home soon enough
> I will heal
> I will heal with the love that resides within my heart
> And from the love that surrounds me.
> I just have to start by taking the first step
> Baby steps to my recovery
> My journey away from self deprivation
> To my new renewed existence.

"Now let's get you out of bed and moving," she says excitedly.

I am beyond enthused about maneuvering around this unit, seeing yet another new layer to the world I am learning how to be in. She lowers the side rails of my bed and watches me sit up. I position myself to sit on the side of the bed without any assistance.

"You ready for this?" she questions me, knowing how excited I am, yet both of us being so fearful of what may happen as I venture off on my own around this unit.

"I'm going to be able to do this, right!?" I question my own ability before taking my first step.

"Yes," she encourages. "I believe you are. I will be assessing your heart on my monitor the whole time. Be free to walk the unit, but stay within the circle, so I can continue to watch your heart rate and rhythm. You can do this Julia!"

I stand beside my bed looking towards the hallway. I look beyond this room, beyond this space that I have been imprisoned in and bound to for far too long. I am eager to take on this new world, this new adventure and freedom, to test out my new sense of being and this new reality that I am forced to face.

Am I really ready for this? I question myself. Yes, I think I am! I am ready and willing to take on my new world and path, one step at a time.

THE LILY NURSE

Come on Julia, you've got this!

I spot Jayda, Titus and Greg walking towards me from down the hall. My eyes and theirs lock together. Jayda comes running down to greet me, giving me a ginormous hug, wrapping her little arms around my waist for the first time since this whole scenario happened. Titus is moments behind her, wrapping his arms around me too. Greg is beaming at me with the most beautiful smile upon his face. He leans in and kisses my forehead.

"They said you get to walk around the unit," Greg says, grinning from ear to ear. "You ready?"

I smile at him and squeeze our children in the most loving embrace, absorbing every last ounce of this monumental moment. The love of my family surrounds me as I take on my new world and my first steps to my new path of growth and recovery.

"Ready, Mama?" Jayda speaks up from where she buried her head into my side. I look down at her, both of us beaming and knowing that this is a step closer to me coming home and putting this all behind us.

"Let's do this!" I say to the three of them: my family, my everything, the ones I came back for.

My nurse steps out of the way and presents us with the next phase of our new reality. Jayda grabs hold of my hand and I take my first step away from this room. I start walking around the unit in its circular path with my family by my side, encouraging me every step of the way.

I walk past the nursing station where my heart is being observed on a monitor. The nurses all give me a smile, for they all know how empowering this walk is for me. I am figuratively walking in the right direction—away from the confinements and the boxed in area I surrendered to, the tiny space of my hospital room.

Then, I am circling back to where I had started this journey, at the threshold of my room: number 13 of the CSU (the same number as the stretcher I coded on was labeled).

According to those, including me, who believe in the spiritual meaning of this number, it is not that it is unlucky. Rather, it is a sign you should live life with love, combining the powerful attributes of strength, energy, inspiration, passion, and motivation. It signifies a sign from the angels to live a happier life, helping you find and see your inner joy. When that joy is illuminated it will burn out the pain. When this number is seen repeatedly, it is an angelic guide for your soul to align with its purpose.

This has always been one of my favorite numbers and it shows itself periodically throughout my life, reminding me once again to live my life not in fear but with love, light, and joy; to trust the process that I am being guided and reminded I am living the life of my soul's mission. Knowing this, and seeing this number representing my room, provides me with even more incentive to keep moving forward to the renewed and preserved life I am blessed to be brought back to. I am healing my broken heart with the love that has always been there, and now—after being in a place of the purest love—I am able to start freeing myself from the burden and pain of my past. I am able to begin healing from the broken pieces, looking at pieces one by one and gaining new insight, strength, and internal power.

I am not ready to go back into my room, so I begin walking another round of the circular path of the unit. Up ahead I see an elderly woman attempting the same walk. I am pushing through my exhaustion. My family is growing concerned with my labored breathing, but I just keep going, following close behind this little old lady.

I reach the halfway point of this second go around. I look towards the hallway of the hospital, beyond this unit. I am not quite ready to face the world, but I yearn to keep moving to the next destination. I want so desperately to take a breath of the outside world, away from this hospital and chaos within it, to be able to fully breathe in this new-found life! I want to keep going, like a bird ready to spread its wings and fly away. Away from the world that confines me, the one that shuts me up, and boxes me in.

"Mom," Titus yells at me with concern in his voice. "Stop! Why are you pushing yourself?"

My breath is starting to get compromised from the exertion placed on my heart. This walk around the unit is taking its toll on me. Although it's a short distance to someone whose heart is functioning properly, mine is only working at 35 per cent. My determination and stubbornness don't like to view my body in this manner; my drive to heal keeps pushing me forward. I need to continue on this path, to get moving more, further in the right direction to get home, to be with my family.

I don't want to share these thoughts with my family, but I know they are feeling the same way. They just want me to be at home with them. But I also know that they would push me to stay in this place to have the staff of the hospital there to fix, mend, and repair me. I know within my heart that I am the one who's going to heal my heart; I just don't know how I'm going to do it. At this point, I don't know how to share this knowledge and new insight with them or anyone else for that matter. So, I respond in the way that best suits me at this time—humor!

"Do you see that old lady ahead of us?" I say, stopping in my tracks to catch my breath and pointing to the woman ahead of us to give him insight about why I am pushing myself.

Titus nods, reassuring me that he is in tune with what I am about to say.

"I can't have her win the race around the unit! She's nearly 92 years old, with oxygen, a walker, and two nurses. She's cheating!"

I spurt out with laughter.

"Mom, you're so silly!" Jayda burst out with her gut-roaring laughter.

Titus smirks and shakes his head at my comment. He has had many more years of my weirdness, but he gets me, my humor, and my ability to lighten the mood, atmosphere and environment. It does provide a sense of ease and relief, even if it's not the whole truth. He accepts my silliness. It's my cross to bear, not his or anyone else's. When I am ready, I will face it.

I finally get back to my room and my bed, completely exhausted. We are all still laughing at my comment about the little old lady cheating and trying to win this race around CSU—even though she is unaware that I am racing her, and calling out her cheating tactics. It is very similar to Titus and Jayda racing me around the block on our bikes: me not knowing I was even in a race, but them just needing the motivation and triumph. That's our life, supporting each other's motivation and small little triumphs to keep moving forward and supporting each other in the process, no questions asked. That's the blessing of my family—love and support!

Titus, Jayda, and Greg tuck me in and say good night, leaving me on a good note, not sad or full of despair and fear, but rather the notion that I am getting stronger and I will be home to them soon enough. I close my eyes feeling the triumph of walking the unit two times. I am getting that much closer to facing my new world, and the path of the underlying healing the Universe is providing and presenting to me. I am not fully ready to face it yet, nor to fully let go of this place. I need the comfort and protection that this environment delivers to me. It is the only place of healing I know… or I think I know.

CHAPTER 27

BROKEN HEART

~  ~

I awake to a fluttering heart. It startles me from my peaceful sleep; I was in such a deep sleep I forgot where I was. I actually forgot all about this crazy and surreal life I am in right now. In my slumber, my brain latched onto the thought of it all being some sort dream or nightmare. I was dissociated from it for a short period of time, and now I am back to this reality.

I lay here alone, in my closed-off room, upon my hospital bed. My nurse is protecting me from everyone entering my room and debriefing with me. Permitting me to shut away the world, the unit, the hospital, and everyone who wishes to share their feelings, thoughts, and emotions with me. It's quiet in here, and so very empty. There's no one in here to distract me. No one here for me to help except myself. It's just me, here alone with my thoughts. Thanks to the protection and advocacy of my nurse, I am able to start processing some of what has occurred.

What is really happening within my world, my reality? This is the golden question I have for myself.

Can all of this really be? I ponder further.

I look towards the closed door. I feel a sense of comfort and relief knowing that I am on my own in this closed-off space, away from everyone and their chatter. I scan the room: it's so empty, cold and surreal. The bed across from me is vacant, perfectly made, and waiting for the next broken soul and heart to lay upon it.

My nurse's words echo through my ears: "You are the one who needs to heal."

Heal. How can I heal myself and my broken heart?

What does that mean? How can I fix this? How can I possibly heal from all of this? There are too many layers, too many questions, and no one to help me. How? How can I possibly start healing from this? I can't even get out of bed on my own.

Why on earth is my nurse so persistent about me processing this on my own? Why does she feel the need to protect me from further heartache? What does this nurse know that I can't see? What am I missing?

I look to the window and recall the last thoughts I was thinking as I gazed to the outside world, and I pose the question to myself for the umpteenth time, *Did this really happen?*

Further words my nurse had spoken to me earlier ring in my thoughts. "Yes, Julia. This happened! All of it!"

This is when it hits me: a sudden flash, a shift, a realization—like the buzzer of your alarm clock. WAKE UP JULIA! I'm starting to see it now. She's right, all of this *did* happen. All of it!

I was given a second chance
I was saved!

THE LILY NURSE

I was brought back.
Guided to this life!

I was actually rebooted and re-birthed.
I have a chance to heal from it all
All of it!

All of this happened!
Every little thing that I recall
It all happened!

I put my hands to my chest over my heart. I take a large inhale and yell, "Oh my God, they did CPR on me!"

This is why she was so persistent in me having my own space to process this on my own time, with my own thoughts. I had to permit myself to process it, to finally see it, be aware of it, to address what I truly need to heal from. I needed to look within myself, heal from within—listen, observe and assess what I truly need at this point. She was protecting me from the external struggles, while I start to deal with my internal broken pieces; they are all connected! I see that now.

She permitted me to look within myself to see what I really need to heal from, and by not having the distraction of everyone else's emotions, thoughts, experiences and version of the story to hinder my healing. I am free to process this on my terms. I scan the room. It's just me in here, me and my thoughts. I am a bit uncomfortable with this. I don't even know how to begin this healing process, but I know deep down in my heart, I will find the answer.

This seems like this is the first step
to mending
My broken heart.

It's getting stronger already!

JULIA EVANS

Now to get home to be with my family
Take a breath
And learn how to heal from the love that radiates and sings
within my heart.

I just have to remember to listen
to my heart strings
and not the chatter from others.

My brain is still trying to compute everything: my broken heart, my lack of MS symptoms, the reality that I'm here in the hospital, the investigation, their stories, my stories and memory flashes, and this whole entire experience. Wow, it's a lot to take in, a lot to process, a lot to cram into my brain in such a small period of time.

I will come out on the other side of this. I thank my blessed stars, moon, sun, and everything in between from light to dark; I thank the heavens and this earth, for I came back. I was in a place like no other; I have the love of the divine and it resides in my heart, my being. I just need to figure out how to utilize it. Who can I tell? Who do I trust? What would people think, if they only knew?

I close my eyes and inhale the sweet aroma of my fresh new beginnings. It would be more beneficial to take a breath away from this place; the smell here is hindering the sweet scent of my new life. I wonder if I smell? A bath would sure be nice. I would love to soak in a tub and wash everything away: my torn emotions, the memory of the code, the views from everyone that sticks to me like glue. But I don't have the doctor's order or privilege to do that yet; I'm not strong enough.

Chapter 28

My First Full Breath of My New Life

Ever since I walked around the circle of the unit with my family, I've been trying to get up and out of my bed and move around my room as much as I can. I feel as though I am getting stronger, but still I struggle to be up out of bed for any length of time. These few days as a patient feel like weeks or months. I feel like I am improving, but maybe it's a mask to keep pushing forward, for I desperately want to be at home with my family, away from this place, so I can breathe and really find my inner strength to heal.

I no longer need extra oxygen, although I do get quite short of breath and my heart is still weak. This shortness of breath is due to my heart's inability to work optimally, but that doesn't stop me. It's just something I need to adjust to. I worry about my body's ability to be more active, and I'm afraid to explore beyond the confinements of my room, but I keep that fear and worry hidden. Keep pushing through, encouraging myself to keep healing.

> Determination and Drive
> Isn't always a good thing when you are hiding
> from what is right in front of you.
>
> Running away from your problems
> and not addressing
> what you need to heal from
> can damper your spirit
> suppressing the underlining root cause of your situation and ailment.

Only a few days ago I was running on a treadmill with no chest pain or shortness of breath. I recall even before that, before my MS diagnosis, I was running on a regular basis, even doing half marathons. It gave me a sense of power, joy, and drive to be able to do anything I put my mind to.

After my MS diagnosis, the scattered communication from my brain to my body wouldn't allow me to run any real distances. I had foot drop, pain, numbness, an unsteady gait, and I looked like a Tim Burton puppet when I attempted to run. I was physically unable to use my body mechanics how they are meant to be used. For years, I stopped even attempting to run and that's when I found my passion for pole fitness/dance. It's an amazing feeling to move and flow my body around a pole, to dance freely, beautifully, confidently, not worrying when my body would fail me, for I had the physical support of the pole anchored to the floor and the ceiling. I had fluidity, grace and an empowering sense of self. It's invigorating!

My nurse pops her head into my room. She's checking in on me, for I am just standing in a daze beside my bed, staring at the ceiling lift. To her, it probably appears that I'm staring at nothing. Really all I'm doing is pondering life and not wanting to be confined in my bed any longer. Then my inside voice speaks out:

"I wonder if I could do a pull up on the ceiling lift?

"No one has ever talked about doing a pull up on the ceiling lift before," she says with a puzzled smile, "You make me laugh. You know, you are the strongest person I know, Julia. Your drive and determination is inspiring—just don't push yourself too hard and too fast! I'm going to suggest to the cardiologist to give you further privileges. I'll put a request in so you can have a bath today."

"That would be fantastic!" I shout out with enthusiasm. I wish I could jump and cheer with joy, but my heart isn't quite ready for that. "So, does that mean…I can take off my heart monitor?"

"Yes," she confirms. "But there will be a nurse with you, just on the off chance something happens."

"I'll take it!" I squeal. My heart almost skips a beat with the thought of washing my hair and body, washing off all this emotional trauma: my feelings, emotions, and the scattered and puzzling thoughts that are stuck to me. I'll have the opportunity to wash it off and then watch it all drain away—off me, down the drain, to a dark abyss. Out of my mind and away from me!

Besides, I don't think I could physically do a pull up right now. It would just defeat me, forcing me to accept that my physical strength isn't where I want it to be, even though I want to try. I am curious to see what my body and new life can do. I'll take this baby step of having a bath first and see where that takes me. I'm so excited!

She exits my room to contact the cardiologist and to get me off my heart monitor. Too excited to be contained in my room, I step out cautiously and ask my nurse, "Can I wander the unit?"

"Yes you can," she says. "Stay on the unit so we can continue monitoring you, but walk around as you see fit. Try walking to the family room; there's a television in there and some books.

Also, there is a little hall you could wander. It has a lot of windows; you could get a little sun."

I start my venture. This is the best I've felt since this whole ordeal happened three days ago. I'm excited to really start testing out this transformed body of mine. What leaps am I willing to take? What is stopping me from my true healing potential? I've had such a dramatic change and shift the last few days. *Look how far I've come, I say to myself. Perhaps I really can heal my heart.*

My next step in this recovery is to get home, be with my family and breathe in the glorious fresh air from the great outdoors.

Breathe in my new life!

My thoughts flutter. I can't wait to get out of here and see what I can do. My body, mind, and spirit are calling out for me to move, dance, run, spread my new wings and learn what this metamorphosed body can do. I'm eager to release those beautiful endorphins through physical activity.

I find a brilliantly lit hallway. The sun is shining through all the windows as I enter this space. I rest my weary body on a lonely chair in this hallway, closing my eyes and allowing my body to feel the warmth of the sun beaming down on me. My mind goes to that blissful moment standing in my driveway after racing my children around our block. I imagine standing there, in the sun, feeling like the warmth of the sun is cradling me in a giant hug, soothing me from the outside in, filling my outer and inner being with warmth, love and light. I inhale this all in; I can feel the love and the light in my heart and it is getting stronger.

"Julia," my nurse interrupts my Zen moment.

I open my eyes. "Yes?"

"You have visitors," she says. "Are you wanting to see them, or should I shoo them away?"

"I'll be right there," I say with a gracious smile. "Thank you for that." I feel as though I'm getting some of my power back, some of me back. I wander over to my room and get myself back into my bed. I had been wandering the unit for quite some time now and I am a bit tired.

I converse with the people in my room, and I am feeling really good. I share my excitement that my heart monitor may be coming off so I can have a bath today. I explain how exhilarating this is going to feel for me.

That's when my cardiologist walks in. I don't recall even seeing him up to this point.

"Julia?" he questions my name.

"Yes, good afternoon," I greet him. "Are you here to tell me I can take my monitor off and have a bath?"

He seems puzzled by my question, ignores it and starts rattling off all sorts of information that I did not want all of my visitors to know. He just starts spewing out things that I had so many questions about, but he doesn't give me any opportunity to even comprehend what he is saying to me. I feel as though I don't have a voice and he doesn't have an ear to listen to me anyway. He doesn't ask permission if he can discuss these things with people in the room. He has no idea who these people are, or if I want my medical information shared with them.

He doesn't even see me! I'm just another name, another chart for him to look at, diagnose and carry on with his day. He's not even really looking up and seeing how this is affecting me. What he is saying is ripping my heart apart and I am trying to hold it together, to not fall apart in front of my visitors.

My girlfriend Kim can sense that I can't handle all of this, that I'm on the verge of having my world come crumbling down again before me. I can't take much more of not being heard or seen!

> Someone please hear me…
> See Me!
> I have been through a traumatic experience
> I am a person!
> Not a thing to disregard.
>
> This all affects me,
> In all areas.
> Why can't anyone see that?

"So, you're good with everything I said?" the cardiologist asks, still oblivious to how this is affecting me.

I haven't even begun to understand any of this. All I got from his spiel is incomplete bits of disconnected information.

- Too much epi…yes, maybe, perhaps, looks that way…

- Something with my MS medication—a one per cent chance of I don't know what…something about heart problems?

- I'm being discharged, right now.

- I'll be on two heart medications and a diuretic. (No explanation of why, how it will affect me or if there are any limitations to anything: work, exercise… side effects?)

- **NO** salt. **NO** potassium. *What the fuck am I going to eat? I'm already on a strict MS recovery diet.*

- I'll have an appointment at the Congestive Heart Failure clinic, and should see my family physician in two to three weeks. *What the fuck? The CHF clinic?*

- Limit exercise. *What can I do? What should I avoid?*

- Go back to work on Monday—in a day and a half—no restrictions. *Really?!?*

And that's just what I managed to hear or process in my brain.

"So, I get my heart monitor off today?" I meekly ask, knowing damn well the answer is yes, but I don't even know what else to say. I am dumbfounded and crushed. I can't even comprehend that I have been through this whole crazy ordeal—at work. This all started from a Stargazer lily that should have never even been there in the first place, which then initiated this cascade of surreal and unfathomable series of events and now has landed me here, in this state. Am I good with everything he is saying to me?

Fuck no! I'm not good with any of this!

Is what I wanted to say. Instead, I just sat there—quiet, timid, and broken. I deflected his horrendous discharge and try to save face. I threw in the odd inappropriate joke to help me cope with knowing these people are listening to this all and are taking what they want from my situation and story.

Kim notices that I'm not being my assertive self within this situation. I'm not advocating for myself, and so she starts asking some of the hard questions before the cardiologist leaves the room—trying to make a few things clearer. She asked about things I liked in the past—well four or five days ago, before everything in my world changed.

"Can she drink? Can she coach? Can she have sex?" Kim inquires.

"Drinking? Shouldn't, but may have one, occasionally. Coaching? Sure, if she wants. Her ejection fraction is at 35 per cent. Sex? Sure. Be careful."

Then he walks away, leaving me to adjust to and absorb

all of this. My visitors start asking me questions that I can't answer. They share with me their views, their beliefs and their perceptions and say, "See, this isn't so bad. You're fine."

Fine? I hate that word! No one ever uses it properly. It's non-descriptive, no emotion to it, and it is often used to deflect a true emotion that someone is facing. How on earth could anyone be fine with any of this? For one moment, I just want someone to see it from my point of view. See the layers and the turmoil it has created and stirred up inside of me. I wish I had the words and a voice to be heard, have someone, anyone listen.

I just want to be heard!

My visitors leave and my nurse comes swooping in. She is just as shocked by all of this as I am. "Sweetheart, you're going home," she announces to me.

I completely break! I start crying uncontrollably. "I'm going home!" I yell through my tears.

She embraces me tight in her arms and lets me cry upon her shoulder. My mind is racing a mile a minute and I cannot stop crying. I'm excited and scared to leave this place. To leave the care of my nurses who advocate for me, protect me, comfort me and make me feel safe. Am I ready to go home? I thought I was just going to have a bath today.

The Congestive Heart Failure clinic, those drugs…oh my God, is this actually confirming my state, my new condition? Why won't anyone admit or confirm anything for me? Why am I only getting parts of the truth? Why can't anyone be transparent and honest with me? Why can't anyone see the bigger picture here? Why can't I see it or admit to it? Why? What? Where am I going?

What's next?

***

THE LILY NURSE

I'm home with my family!

It's been three days since I walked out the front door of this house, our home, to begin a normal day at work. Never would we have expected this kind of outcome. Everything in my world has completely flipped, shifted and I know this is only the beginning.

After hugging the children and entering our house, the first thing I do is walk out our backdoor to the patio. I'm standing here looking out to the openness of our backyard and I take in the biggest breath of this glorious fresh air. I walk up to the railing, so it doesn't block my view; I want to see all of the open blue prairie sky and I want to absorb this moment. I take another breath in, even bigger than the first one. I close my eyes and exhale the largest breath I have evacuated from my body. I then lean on the railing, clasp my hands together and keep breathing in the bliss of the great outdoors.

I can finally breathe!

I can feel every blade of grass. I can hear the trees singing. I can feel this majestic influx of energy all around me. I am part of it as it is part of me. I feel every bug, bloom, everything. I can hear it, see it, sense it. I have never felt anything like this before. I can feel the life in everything around me.

Greg walks over to me, wraps his arms around me, and stares off to the distance as well. He whispers in my left ear, "Are you okay?"

I tilt my head so he can see my expression and my true form, my true emotion and I say, "Yes I am. I feel amazing! I feel like I have been re-birthed into an amazing new world. I feel supercharged!"

I turn my gaze back to the openness and infinite beauty of everything surrounding me. I am in awe of the beauty and vast amount of energy I sense surrounding me. I feel like I am awakening for the first time in my life. It's absolute bliss!

I feel supercharged. I cannot articulate all of what I am experiencing and feeling in this moment. It's bliss! I'm not struggling with the pain I have been fighting with for years. I feel different. I'm me, but I'm not! I am a new and improved version of me. The me I was always meant to be.

> I'm Rebooted, Re-birthed,
> Supercharged!

I try explaining what I am feeling and experiencing. My spirit is starting to spread her wings, and I can now feel the vibrations, frequencies, and energy for every little thing and being within my environment. The best word to describe it is supercharged! I try to put further words to it but am lost for the creative description of what I am currently feeling. I try to put a label to it, to put words to something that is not fully explainable. So, the best relatable representation I can think of is a vampire movie.

Hollywood does an amazing job of capturing that significant moment when the vampire becomes awakened to the dawn of their new life. Everything is so beyond—beyond beautiful, beyond color, beyond light and dark, beyond life and death—just beyond anything you have ever allowed your mind to think or feel. Everything seems heightened and new, as if you are seeing a new world through your new eyes for the very first time, seeing beyond what everyone else sees. You feel stronger, all of your senses are heightened and you possess this new awareness and knowledge.

I needed to step away from the hospital. I needed to clear my head and sense what I really needed to feel and really needed to do. I just needed to...

Take My First Full Breath of My New Life

Chapter 29

Strength and Baseball

Sunday is my first full day home with my family since I was discharged from the hospital yesterday evening, and my baseball team is about to embark on their first game. This is the first time seeing them all since before the incident on Thursday morning, and it's also my family's first outing, together in the public eye.

We drive up to the baseball diamond and set out to face the real world. As I pull out my equipment and water bottle from the trunk of our vehicle, I can feel the kids' and the parents' eyes glued to me as I walk towards the dugout. It's as if they have all seen a ghost. There's a hush over the crowd as I walk past them to greet my team. The boys patiently wait for me to enter the crowded space of the dugout, staring intently as I quietly set down my coach's bag, none of them knowing what to say.

I close my eyes and take in a huge breath of fresh air to gather my composure, then fully exhale. The whole team watches me in anticipation of what I'm going to do next.

I'm soaking it all in, thinking of how blessed I am to be here, in the great outdoors surrounded by this great energy that the team exudes. I love how their spirit is so alive; and so am I! Ah, I am here. I am alive, outside in this glorious space, and not stuck back at the hospital in that drab secluded bed. I am away from the chatter of the hospital staff regarding my incident and back to where I love life the most: having fun and new adventures with my family.

Life moves on. It's your choice to keep moving forward with it, or to stand back and watch it all fade away. I've been given a second chance, and I'm not going to waste any second of this. I open my eyes and look at the team. I smile at them, relieving the tension of this atmosphere. You could cut it with a butter knife. I smile the biggest smile, and I blurt out, "So who's ready to play some baseball?"

The team lets out an enormous exhale in unison, as if they were all waiting for me to take the first step of the conversation. It's not that often that you come in contact with someone who's been on the other side.

"Welcome back, Coach!" they all say together, with enthusiasm, beaming with smiles.

"It's great to be back!" I smile back at them.

One of the boys sitting sheepishly on the bench, pipes up. "Is it true? Did they shock you back?"

The boys all look at him in disbelief that he asked such a question, and they hold their breath awaiting my answer. They all seem quite curious and intrigued about what I am about to say. That's the beauty of children. They don't fear asking the hard questions.

I raise my eyebrows. I'm impressed he has the balls to ask what everyone wants to know the answer to but is too afraid to ask. I nod to him and say, "Yes it's true."

The boys exhale and seem relieved that the elephant in the room is finally addressed. Now the questions start coming all at once. I smile at their inquisitive minds. I love that I am finally being asked so many questions. They all want to ask so many questions and at the same time. They start yelling out in enthusiasm.

"Coach, coach—what's it like?" one asks.

"Yeah, was it like the movies?" another asks, holding his hands out in front mimicking a reenactment of shocking someone—just like in the movies. "Clear!" He plays out the role for everyone to witness, rubbing his fists together, and pretending to shock an invisible person in front of him. All the boys laugh at the dramatization.

I giggle watching his very elaborate display of how it would have looked as I was being shocked back to life.

"Yes, just like the movies," I conclude for them all and snicker at how they are all processing this information. I then gesture to all of the boys to come in, close to me, signaling with my hands to draw them into a whisper's distance. They all lean in intently—wide eyed, anticipating what else I'm about to say. Like I have information from the other side for them all to hear.

As I have all of their undivided attention I look around at all of them to make sure that they are all actively listening to my every single word, and I quietly say to them, "I see dead people."

All of them pause, paralyzed by my response, wider eyes and mouths open. Wrapping their little heads around what I have just said to them.

"Really?" they all slowly say, looking at me like I am a mystical ghost or creature from beyond the grave.

"No!" I burst out laughing. "Now get out there and run." I deflect my inability to discuss it any further and to get their heads back into the task at hand. Play baseball! I love utilizing humor, especially in situations I don't know how else to deal with. I also love the imagination of children; it's fun to toy with it. Besides, I could tell by the expressions on their faces that they were all thinking about it. It's the questions that people think, but don't have the courage to ask. I applaud their fearless questions.

The other coaches and manager laugh hysterically at my response. Kim, our team manager, already knowing what kind of fun I like having, gives me the biggest loving smile, puts her hand on my back and energetically hugs my soul. She was in the hospital visiting me as I was released into this new life that I now have to face. She was there as another set of ears and as the voice that I wasn't ready to use yet. She helped by asking the doctor the hard questions for me, by being by my side then and being here for me now.

I know in my heart that I am surrounded by the right people and the right kind of love—genuine, pure and a two-way stream! Love that heals the soul, helping me find my inner joy and happiness in life's simple pleasures, and having the knowledge that someone is there beside me, helping along the way.

"Are you sure you can do this today, Julia?'" one of the other coaches asks, giving me the opportunity to back away from this, if needed.

"I've got this," I assertively whisper, patting his back to reassure him I will be able to do this. I walk away from the dugout leaving them there. They watch me walk out to the field, to do what I do best: warm up the team, condition them and pump up everyone's spirits, including my own.

I love being part of this team, part of this journey. As I coach these boys, I'm teaching baseball and valuable life lessons: Never give up on yourself. Love life! Keep going. Live for the moment. Laugh whenever you get a chance. Love what you do. Find what makes you happy, because life can change in a second and you don't want to miss the opportunities that make you feel alive. And in turn, they provide me with the utmost strength, lifting me up and teaching me a thing or two as well, how to be a kid at heart and several lessons on baseball—it's now one of my favorite games to be a part of.

When I finally reach the team out on the grass in left field, I find myself short of breath. My heart is still only pumping at a fraction of its ability, but it feels so good to be out in the open air, under the hot sun's rays and away from my drab hospital bed. I'm not giving up on this life and my ability to heal; my heart function is just an another obstacle that I have to adapt to. At that point I was bound and determined to surround myself with everything and everyone I loved. I was brought back for a reason and I will heal from this! I will gain so much strength from this, for this is a new body-mind, a new beginning, a new me and I'm going to thrive.

I signal to the boys to "bring it in," to surround me in a huddle to hear what the next drill is. I can only use hand signals at this point, for my breath is labored. The boys come running towards me, and Titus is instantly aware of my struggle. He looks at me with a worried expression, doubting my physical ability to actually do this. I place my arm around his back and shoulders, bring him close to me, and give him a reassuring little squeeze. I smile at him so he knows I'll be okay; I just had to catch my breath.

"Okay, boys, you all know that I just got out of the hospital," I say, pausing frequently to catch my breath.

They all nod in unison.

"I need you all to be really good listeners," I explain. "I don't have enough breath to talk over you. My heart may be weak right now, but every day I am getting stronger. As I get stronger, I'm going to help make you all stronger. I'll be cheering you on and encouraging you all to be the best you can possibly be, and you can help and encourage me to do the same. We're going to work together, as a team, and become the best team around. We are going to work with our own personal strengths and encourage each other to have fun, and play hard. We're in this together. Now let's go play some ball!"

Even though my physical strength is not where I'd like it to be, I am showing the boys how important life is. Be outside, breathe in the fresh air, see what the world has to offer. Take care of yourself, exercise, and build each other up. Be encouraging and positive. Everyone here has a purpose: We are all here for a reason, to help one another. I try to ingrain this into their minds. They have the power of greatness—each and every one of them.

I do this so the kids can be kids.
To have fun and enjoy life.

Their energy is invigorating and infectious
And that energy is just what I need to get stronger.

Coaching them gives me such a drive to do good,
to be the best I can be,
and it makes me feel like a kid too.
It encourages me to be outside,
soak up the sun,
and breathe it all in.

There's nothing like the great outdoors!

CHAPTER 30

THE GREAT OUTDOORS

It's time I start adjusting to my new, but former, life. I've been up since the crack of dawn, ready to start my Monday. I've been back home for two days since my discharge from CSU, and just like any other day at home before my three-day stint in the hospital, I awake in our bed, but Greg has already left for work. I adjust my eyes and body to this new day and my new world. I focus on the view of our backyard and what's beyond that, out our bedroom window which faces the rising sun. I look towards this endless prairie sky; it is a beautiful sight like no other. The majestic and radiant colors of the sunrise give me a sense of warmth and peace. I'm back to where I need to be; I'm home! Back with my family and it feels so good to be here, alive. Oh, thank god, I am alive!

I may be waking up on the same side of my bed at home, but this morning there are several differences to my regular routine. I don't need to do my old routine of slowly waking up my body and assessing my physical disabilities of the day, the ones that my dreaded MS normally presented to me. This morning, I don't even give it a second thought. I have none of the MS symptoms or deficits I did prior to me coding, none whatsoever! No numbness, no pain, and I can even see clearer out of my left eye; the blind spot is nonexistent. It's a whole new world!

But this incredible miracle I have been given doesn't really dawn on me, for my new aliment—my broken heart—takes over my thoughts. It struggles to keep pumping, and to keep me here. It physically challenges me and constantly makes me choose where I want to exert my energy. It makes me analyze what is most important in my life. I have limited energy and strength; it should not be wasted on the things that do not serve me or give me purpose.

It's almost like my heart is testing me, to see if I really do want to be here, alive on this plane. It gives me time to pause and learn how to live, to understand and acknowledge my true potential. Can I find my internal strength and power to heal from the broken pieces of my heart and my past, to become whole again on a whole new level? Do I choose to listen to what I truly need to heal from? Am I willing to do so or am I going to fall back into a world of pain and suffering? Am I ready to hear the internal dialogue of my innate wisdom that has been lost but is now ready and willing to be heard? Perhaps. I believe I am starting to awaken to it, but I'm not quite able to face all of it. Not yet.

I am eager to get back to my former normal life, for that is the life I am most comfortable in. It's familiar and I don't really know anything different. I'm trying to latch onto something familiar, for the world I was brought back to is mind boggling and surreal. All I realize at this point is that I'm back home, alive, and with my family. I know I'll find my way to heal. I am a fighter, but I'm just not quite ready to fight through all the pieces to this mind-altering situation. I am not ready to see what's right in front of me. I could close my eyes to this and stay in bed all day—closing off and shutting down, never to face anything within my world—but that is not me and I have two children depending on me to show them what it is to live. Even if you are faced with both internal and external factors that seem clustered and chaotic within all the areas of your thoughts, you keep moving forward, grabbing hold of whatever it is that keeps you going. Life is precious and should not be taken for granted. I know all too well how quickly life can be changed or gone. So, I get out of bed to face my day, to face all the bliss that has been granted—and the ugly truths.

It's as though 7,000 puzzle pieces have fallen before me. But it's really only a 1,000-piece puzzle; the other 6,000 are other people's thoughts, beliefs and perceptions. I have to look at every piece and see where it all fits, discarding the pieces that don't serve me or have a purpose in creating the full image. It creates mayhem within my thoughts, so I push it away for now. At this point, it's easier to grab hold of what's most important right here, right now: my children. The two of them and the fact that I was brought back to be with them is the only thing I want to concentrate on. The rest will come with time.

This morning I am not allowing myself to feel the hardship and further heartbreak by analyzing everything that happened to me within the last few days. I don't want to start facing it all. So, I turn off the part of me that feels the immense, invasive emotions. I decide to shove those pieces back into a box, but instead of completely storing it all away, I allow it to linger in some of my thoughts. I am able to start addressing and viewing it as I see fit, slowly processing it. I do, however, push the incident of my code to the back of my mind, and I try to adjust to my new reality of my physically broken heart. I'm just so happy to be alive and home with my family; nothing else seems to matter, so I hold on to that.

I don't know if I'm ready or willing to face anything right now. There's a lot there to view and process. I don't want my energy to be depleted by concentrating on all this garbled pandemonium that swirls within my thoughts. I'm holding on to what little energy I can, only giving up enough energy to go downstairs to be with my children and start their day as normally as I can. I want to start their day on a good note, with hope, love and a little shine, to have them see me in their presence, alive and at home.

So instead of addressing all of what I am feeling, I lock that away and look at this whole ordeal in a different light; it's a blessing, a second chance at life. I am full of a powerful force that radiates light from love. I believe in my heart that I will heal; I was brought back, MS free, and now I am ready and willing to live an even fuller version of my life. If I can conquer MS, I can heal my broken heart. I possess the power and love within.

I am completely aware that my heart is weak and so am I; it's only been four days. Though I am getting stronger each and every day, I have a long way to go. I'm taking the rest of this week off of work to start adjusting to my new reality; that's all I have been allotted. My nurse in CSU had to beg the cardiologist to give me time off of work to heal. He initially wanted me to be back to work today. My nurse convinced him to give me more time, explaining that I had been the nurse who coded on her own unit. He then prescribed me one week off work. He figures I can jump right back into work, no questions asked after dying and coming back right in the centre of my unit. I guess he, like many others, figures I would have no emotional trauma or pain from the horrific incident. He's the doctor; he should know what I need.

I have to get my head wrapped around everything that happened to me and I have to do it within one week. I have to limit where I put my thoughts and energy. A week is not enough time to adjust and heal from all of this. Hence why I have to adjust my energy to my physical distress first and foremost; I have to start conditioning my heart within a week to be able to complete a full shift in the hospital. I am being forced back into my former life and I only have seven days to figure everything out, but today is not that day.

Today is the day for me to breathe it all in. It's too much to deal with, from my physically broken heart to the emotionally broken status I am immersed in. Something has to give and be put away, so I choose my emotions. I turn the switch off to the areas that shine a light on my emotions and feelings. It's my physically broken heart that would be the one to kill me, not my emotions, right?!

> I switch all of my emotional energy to that of
> Peace, Love and Blessed to be Alive.
> Only permitting myself to feel grateful for the life I have.
> I do this so I can concentrate on
> My inadequate heart function.
> That's my weakest area
> It requires more of my energy.
> For without a beating heart and blood flowing in my body
> I won't sustain this precious life I was brought back to.

Now to get the kids off to school. Breakfast is eaten, lunches are made and it's time for them to catch their bus. Greg has already left for work and this leaves me alone with Titus and Jayda for the first time since this whole ordeal happened. We've spent the morning getting ready for the day, all of us involved in our regular school day morning routine. We are all trying to get back to our normal lives the best way we know how, trying not to acknowledge everything I went through.

Yet we are all well aware of my heart failure. Everyone watches over me, making sure I take my heart medications (a beta blocker, an ACE inhibitor, and a diuretic). Three pills to treat high blood pressure and heart failure—which was never an issue for me before—that prevent heart attacks and keep excess fluid off from causing swelling and breathing difficulties. Heart failure causes fluid to accumulate in areas that cause more problems, so to further protect me from more dis-ease I take these medications. All of us are cautious about the food I ingest. My new cardiac diet has very minimal salt and minimal potassium, since I'm on a potassium-sparing diuretic.

My family is babying me. It gives them a sense of control and power within this whole situation. Cooking, lining up my cardiac medications, and reminding me to take them are easy to do. They grab hold of that small portion of control with full strength. They lost me once and they are not willing to lose me again. They are also very wary of the amount of exertion my body is permitted to endure. Our children are very observant and come to my aid when they see me petering, fading, short of breath, or physically struggling with the reality of my heart failure. They just want their mommy to be okay and will do anything in their power to help in any way. It's my job to help them with their struggles and it hurts to know they are so scared and broken from this all. My heart is so weak I can't take that burden away for them. I can't absorb that pain for them; all I can do is help them cope by showing them love and my ability to keep going.

"Okay, kids, the bus is almost here," I try to hurry them up a bit so they don't miss their ride. Jayda runs over and gives me a hug.

"Love you, Mom," she quickly says.

"I love you too," I say, hugging her back and kissing the top of her head. "Have an awesome day at school."

Titus saunters over to me and gives me the biggest hug. He buries his head into the crook of my neck and pauses, not wanting to let go. I wrap my arms around him, placing my left hand on his mid back (close to his heart) and my right hand upon the back of his head. Holding and cradling him in my embrace, absorbing this beautiful moment between a mother and her child. He squeezes me tight and his strong soldier-like body collapses to a mere frightened little boy. My baby—my first born—is glued to me, not wanting to let go.

Our arms are wrapped around each other, embracing one another and time stops. Life as we know it stands still, and my boy, my strong little man, completely breaks! He begins to cry, weep and sob this uncontrollable release of emotion. He squeezes me harder, burying his head deeper into my shoulder. I tighten my embrace too and hold him in my arms as I did when he was a tiny little baby crying for his mommy to protect him and make him feel safe.

My eyes well up with tears and my heart sinks at the thought of what he is going through, the pain and strife he is feeling. His world is now crashing down before him. The fear and knowledge of losing his mother is too hard to keep in. I know that pain all too well; I lost both of my mothers. I know the anguish that encapsulates him. Titus has more emotion to deal with for he was presented with both sides of the spectrum of emotions with this situation. He lost and gained his mother back all in one breath, not having the opportunity to be able to cope with either one of the outcomes. This is his breaking point; we are alone and he's in the comfort and safety of his mother's arms. This allows for the overwhelming emotions to spew out at his realization of the magnitude of this whole messed up situation we are all faced with. He is paralyzed in fear of losing me again.

"I could have lost you for good," he whimpers.

I am crying so hard I can't even respond. I glance over to Jayda and realize she has been watching us this whole time. Watching her older stronger brother's heart breaking and completely falling apart, right before her eyes. She starts bawling too and rushes over to join in our embrace. Both of my children needing the unconditional love of their mother to feel a sense of safety, comfort, and protection from the harshness of this real world.

As a mother this is one of the hardest realities to face, having your children experience such raw emotion and not being able to shield them from this pain they are experiencing. There was no preparing for this, no protection from this harsh reality. The raw gut-wrenching emotion they are both faced with at this moment is so hard to witness, but I hold them tight and let them immerse themselves in their emotion, helping them let go of it. I don't want them to have to push and lock it down to a dark abyss, to be addressed later in life as a complicated mess of pain and suffering.

The three of us are latched and intertwined together, crying, taking this opportunity to let out some of our pent-up emotion through our tears. I am finally able to speak, and I make a suggestion. "Would you both like to stay home with me today? Let's turn off from the world and just be together. We'll go to the lake and walk around, play, laugh, and just have fun in the great outdoors!"

They both look up at me smiling and nodding. I kiss them both on the forehead and squeeze them tight together. "I have to call the school and take some of these calls I have been trying to avoid. I'll be quick. I'll turn off my cell phone when I'm done and we'll have a day of fun together. I want you both to see how very much alive I am and you need not worry. I love you both very much!" I give them one more squeeze before releasing my grip.

Knowing they are both satisfied with the plan, I walk them over to the couch so they can continue to comfort one another. They still hold on to each other, waiting for my return.

I go upstairs, leaving my children sobbing on the couch, to deal with all the phone calls. All I want to do is be with my children, but my phone won't stop ringing, forcing me to step away from them. I don't want them to know this side of my code: the investigation, the confidentiality breach, or any of the other issues I am forced to face. I am not being given any time to actually adjust or process any of this, and no one seems willing to help me. No one wants to hear me or my side of the incident, the event, the horrific reality of my world. Everyone is describing it through their eyes and experience, or belief, and my experience is viewed as an unfortunate event that really shouldn't affect my ability to work or live. It's just something that happened; I should be able to move forward and try to go back to my normal life, the best way I can.

I displace all of my emotions of this traumatic situation, pushing everything down. No one is ready to listen or validate what I've been through or what my family is going through. My brain is scrambled by the complexity of this whole ordeal and I feel like I have no voice in any of this.

I take and make the phone calls that no one should have to do right after any sort of trauma. There should be a grace period to process and adjust, to be allowed the time to be with your family and loved ones. To learn how to cope, comprehend and understand the many layers of this harsh and horrific situation.

I try to seek help and advice. I request debriefing or counseling to help me get through this, and something to help my family get through this as well. All of it is excused, no need for debriefing or counseling, just get back to work and try to move forward and live a normal life. No one seems to see our ability to cope—or not—with this event and everything surrounding it as a problem we need help with. They treat it as something I just have to get over, like I had experienced a normal day at work. No one could understand why I may be struggling. I had been in many codes before, but nothing like this! I was the one on the stretcher and no one seems to recognize that this makes the situation completely different.

I feel lost, thrown under the bus and swept under the carpet. Fear of what I might do seems to overshadow anyone wanting to help me or take ownership of the part they played during this catastrophe.

> I just want to be heard!
> Viewed that my life matters
> I'm not just a story
> Or a fictional thing
> I am the one living through this
> All of this!

No one seems willing to hear my cry for help. I hear the same things over and over from numerous people. "I understand this happened. I could never go back to work or function, but your case is different. You came onto the unit as staff and left it as a patient; you don't fit in any category for assistance or help. It's too complicated, difficult and different."

"You should be able to deal with it—all of it—while listening and absorbing other's views, perceptions and beliefs." This is the message I was receiving loud and clear. Besides, my conscious mind can't even grasp any of this, so why do I think others can? I can't face any of this and so I hide it well, trying to fit back into the mold of my former life. It's easier that way.

I slowly walk down the stairs, conserving my physical energy and announce to my two beloved children, "My phone is turned off! Now let's go play and be free in the great outdoors."

They jump off the couch full of excitement and start their chatter about where we should go first. Their enthusiasm is intoxicating and I soak it all in, pausing from all the other shit I am dealing with. My children come first and now they have all of my attention.

Life is too precious not to stop and take these moments to be together.

>These children are my love and my light,
>As much as I am for them.
>Nothing is more glorious than experiencing
>The wondrous world of
>The great outdoors
>With the ones you love!

Taking time to breathe in the Life we are blessed to be in.

Life is too precious and too short to be locked away
In the dark
Not to be seen, heard or loved
We all matter

THE LILY NURSE

And we all want to be validated
We all want to heal

I'm starting to acknowledge that!
There's got to be more out there?

Oh wait...
There is!

Chapter 31

Back to Work

I am a bit apprehensive as I put my nursing uniform on for my first day back, just 11 days after the incident. I walk up the stairs from the locker room to my unit, pause before opening the door, close my eyes and take a breath. There is an instant flashback within my thoughts of the day that brought me here to this state of being. I am so beyond scared to enter this space again. I am terrified of what I am meant to face on the opposite side of this door. Then the door automatically opens before me; there is a patient being transferred off the unit via stretcher.

I move out of the way, watching the porter push the patient down the hall to their next destination. That was me only a few days ago after my code, after I was shocked back, saved, rebooted, re-birthed, and my world completely flipped upside-down. I take another breath. My breath is short and shaky….

"Julia," one of the nurses calls, jogging over to me from inside our unit.

THE LILY NURSE

I stand outside the unit, paralyzed in fear of entering. I do everything in my power to stuff everything I am feeling and thinking down to a deep place within myself, so I can walk in and do my job, ignoring what I do not want to face.

"Hi." is the only thing I can say; no other words want to come out of my mouth at this point.

Once I enter my unit I am greeted by several staff members. Some run over to see me and give me a hug, some are crying, and some are speechless—perhaps not knowing what to say to me—and the others don't even approach me.

As I am being embraced by some of my colleagues all I want to do is collapse in their arms, but I can't; I'm at work and I have to look professional. There's not a lot of discussion between me and the staff about what happened only a few days ago, and I'm trying my hardest to ignore their emotions or any difficulty they may be having with me being here. I stand here before them in a different state of being. No one knows how broken I really am, or what things and realms I have gone through to be here with them and no one asks. What they all see is me, here, alive in front of them; as if nothing really happened, nothing really changed. I stand before them in my old nursing uniform—with my old label on.

It appears to me that no one really wants to acknowledge what I have gone through or address the uncomfortable truth that it all happened right here, on this unit and that I was the patient which laid upon the stretcher in spot seven; being shocked back to life. No one, including myself wants to admit to the recent surreal unimaginable traumatic event that occurred right here on this unit.

I am trying so hard not to show any emotion and I deflect my hidden turmoil by using humor any chance I get. I am having an extremely hard time coping with all of this, but I don't display that reality to anyone. I don't permit myself to break down or accept the harsh reality of what happened, and is happening, to me and within me. I keep pushing through, trying everything in my power to keep up the persona of a strong, knowledgeable, caring and professional nurse.

I cautiously walk over to the nursing station, get report and force myself to mentally prepare for my day at work. I feel uneasy about being here and feel like I'm being forced to forget anything significant happened to me here on this unit. I get my assignment for the day and I freeze up at the nursing station, frozen in this space and time, as I see and then stare at spot seven—the place I died and came back only 11 days ago.

"Julia," one of the nurses says as she arrives for her shift too.

"Yes," I respond.

"I'm so happy you're back," she says, distracting me from staring at spot seven.

"Thank you." I respond, re-focusing my thoughts to what truly matters to me, putting everything back into perspective for myself. I smile at her and say, "I'm happy to be alive."

I leave the nursing station and the staff surrounding this area to carry out my day's assignment. I start walking down the hall to the procedure room I will be working in all day. This is the hallway where I was being rushed down by wheelchair only a few days ago as my code was being called overhead. Last time I was here, I was heading down the hall in a different direction, struggling to breathe, terrified and afraid for my life. I was on my last few breaths of life.

The recent memory surges through my mind, as if I am watching it unfold before me. It's like it is happening to me all over again, my mind is playing out such an active memory that it is having trouble deciphering if it is really happening or if it is only a memory. I place my hand over my throat, and whisper to myself,

"It's okay, Julia. You're breathing. It's only a memory—you lived through it. You survived!"

"I would have done the same." I hear someone blurt from one of the open procedure rooms.

"What?" I say, puzzled by this comment, not even sure if it was meant for me.

"The dose," he responds, "I would have given 0.5 too."

"What?" I say again, completely thrown by this random comment directed to me.

"0.5 is the correct dose," he continues his rant, "I am on his side."

My thoughts are so flustered and angered by this random comment. An influx of clustered comments and questions swirl around my head like an angry tornado, *You weren't even fucking there! Were you even in this hospital? How the fuck do you know what happened, and how do you know about the dose in question? What the fuck does this have to do with you?*

I walk away rattled and frazzled, without saying a word to rebut what he's saying to me. I can't be bothered putting any energy into continuing this conversation.

I approach the closed door to my procedure room, and read the assigned staff names on the door. I can't coax myself to enter; I am stopped in my tracks and frozen in an array of emotions as I read the names again. My heart drops.

"Are you fucking kidding me?!" I say out loud. I turn around, rushing over to the nursing station to discuss my assignment with the charge nurse.

I can barely breathe, and if my heart wasn't on so many medications, it would be beating out of my chest and my blood pressure would be skyrocketing. I can feel every cell in my body shaking and quivering with fear, worry, anger, shame, sadness and disbelief. I approach the charge nurse, and say, "Can I have a word with you?"

"Of course," she says, as she stops what she's doing. "What's up?"

"Can we talk in private?"

"Julia, are you okay?" she asks with a concern while getting up quickly from her chair.

"No," I remark assertively. "Can we talk in private?"

She puts her arm around me, rushes us to one of our back rooms, and closes the door. I can't hold this emotion in any longer, and I start to wail. She wraps both her arms around me and tries to comfort me.

"Oh, Julia," she says.

I take a breath, trying to gain my composure and I blurt out, "I am assigned to be in the room with the doctor who gave me the wrong dose of epinephrine."

"Oh my god, Julia," she says, just as shocked as I am.

I cry even harder and she holds me tighter in her embrace. I'm sobbing uncontrollably; I can't stop.

"You don't have to be here, Julia," she says. "This is obviously too much for you."

"Yes, I do," I respond through my tears. "I was only given a week off work."

She squeezes me even tighter, trying to comfort me further. Her embrace makes me feel so safe, loved and supported; it's so genuine and heart-warming.

"I can't even begin to imagine what you are going through, Julia," she says softly.

"It's a lot," I whisper, now starting to slow my sobbing. "I don't know what to think, what to feel, what to say or who to talk to. I feel like I'm being swept under the carpet. I feel very lost, alone, invisible and powerless."

"Why am I assigned to work in that room? Haven't I gone through enough?" I ask.

"I can put you in another room," she says, trying to fix this shitty situation. "Which room do you want to work in? What assignment would you like?"

I pause and think for a moment, and respond by asking, "Can you get Barb for me?"

"Yes, of course, I'll be right back," she says and hurries out of the room to retrieve Barb.

This leaves me alone with my thoughts in this quiet room to reflect on everything that is happening today—the ridiculous start of my shift, and how twisted and surreal all of this is. Me, back to work so soon after my traumatic incident and not having any opportunity to really deal with anything surrounding it. Even if I wanted to face it, I haven't had enough time to. *Keep pushing. Keep going. Survival Mode.* It dawns on me that I'm going to have to face this at some point, and the opportunity is presenting itself now; I might-as-well face this head on.

Face my fears,
So it doesn't control me.
I'm not going to let this hold me back from living.
I've been through enough already.

JULIA EVANS

I was brought back for a reason,
And that reason is not to be scared, quiet and fearful,
Crying in the shadows,
I need to face my new life head on.

I need to grab hold of whatever power and control I have
within this crazy situation and world.

This is my LIFE!

Barb and the charge nurse enter this little room I am quietly standing in. I explain my morning and the day's assignment with Barb. She is just as shocked as the charge nurse and I were with all of this. That's when the three of us break down in unison from the overwhelming emotion surrounding all of this. We all have one hell of a good cry. After this short explosion of pent-up emotion, I ask to have Barb with me as the second nurse in the procedure room I am assigned to; I need to do this and face what I need to face, but I want to do it with Barb by my side.

They both agree.

"Are you sure, Julia?" Barb questions, making sure I am mentally ready to face this.

"Yes, I'm sure," I respond, "I'm going have to face this at some point, might as well be now."

That's the interesting thing about challenges you are meant to face in life:

> 1) You can run away—ignore it, never deal with it, hide in the shadows and never face anything that needs to be faced.

Or...

> 2) You can face it head on so that the fear doesn't control you.

THE LILY NURSE

Barb stares at me dead in the eyes, as if she is trying to read if I am ready to actually face this. She gives my hand a squeeze and says, "I'll meet you in there. Come when you are ready. I won't leave you."

I collect my composure and all of the bravery and strength within my being before I find enough courage to enter this procedure room. I have no idea what the other side of this door will hold for me. As I approach the door, it swings open before me; the team has just finished up with the last patient's procedure and is heading to the recovery area. As the stable patient is being wheeled out on the stretcher, I approach the threshold of this room and freeze. There's an eerie stillness as I stand here looking into this room. The two doctors and Barb turn their attention to me and the four of us stand in an awkward silence.

My brain is racing and flashing back to the last time this door swung open before me—I was struggling to breathe, drowning in air as my throat closed. A code blue had just been announced and Barb had opened this door to see me on the other side of it, dying for help.

> Only a few days ago,
> I was just outside of this room
> Struggling to live,
> Struggling to continue.
> Scared beyond belief and losing my fight to survive.
> I sat before these people in a wheelchair, blue in colour;
> Silently pleading for their help -
> By clenching my throat with both hands and
> Staring at them in desperation through my piercing frightened eyes.

Barb and I lock eyes again. This time my throat isn't closing up and I am not blue in colour, but I feel like I can't breathe again, as though my breath is stuck between my heart and my throat—no breath wants to enter or exit my body. Everyone in this room seems to be holding their breath too and everything pauses in time. The silence is eerie and the energy seems thick and unsettling. There is a heaviness within me and within this space, time and environment. The tension in this room could be cut with a butter knife. I finally am able to get a breath in and then let out an exaggerated exhale. I have my eyes fully open to all of this, addressing the first thing I am needing to face and I smile the biggest smile. Letting all the people in this room see me and the light I am blessed to maintain within my being as it is presented to them through my beaming smile.

> I am so blessed to be here,
> Alive.
> I am thankful for the work from the team
> for doing what they did for me
> In my time of need.
>
> Despite all the other pieces to this puzzle,
> I stand before them
> Alive!

I am Alive!

"Morning," I say. "I'm working in here today."

Barb lets out a large exhale as well and gives me a reassuring and loving smile. She smiles and looks at me with such maternal pride in her gaze. I am trying to take my power back and standing up for what is rightfully mine—my life, my world and my self-preservation. I have lived through enough the last few days. I'm not going to let fear take over my life and prevent me from living.

> I want to show the world
> I'm not invisible
> I am here.
> I am alive and am ready to live.
> I am starting to wake up from having my eyes closed to everything.

"Good morning, Julia." Barb says. Her words act like a radiant magical force that puts a spotlight on me, opening and permitting the observance that I am standing before them all.

"Julia," one of the doctors says, "you're here! You're back!"

"Yes, I am!" I proudly say.

"Can I have a word with you?" he sheepishly asks. I nod and we step outside the procedure room into the open space of the hallway.

He gives me a hug. I don't reciprocate; I stand rigid and cold with my arms by my side. He appears to be quite emotional. He's having a hard time getting out his words and he's welling up. As I glance at him, he appears to be struggling with this far more than I had anticipated, but seeing this doesn't help me with how I am feeling. I still feel completely broken inside and I need him to validate what I went through.

I'm not sure of how to react to this, so I wait to hear what he has to say. I don't want to show off how broken I really am; I display a flat expression upon my face and wait for him to speak, to say what I so desperately need to hear—it wasn't the lilies that caused my heart to break.

"You're alive!" he says. "You were blue!"

"Yes, I'm alive and I'm a better colour now." I say.

"I…I'm…I did what I could," he says to me with his words and voice broken and shaky. "It was so scary watching you like that. You're one of us…" he continues, as he appears to flash back to that day. "The look on your face…you looked so scared, begging me to help you with your piercing eyes. You were blue…"

"I know," I say, now letting the tears roll down my cheeks.

Barb steps out of the procedure room and asks, "Julia, are you okay?"

"Yeah, I am," I say to her, but I'm not really sure if that's the truth. I feel broken and numb and I don't really want to face any of this right now.

The next patient is heading towards us, so I wipe away my tears. We all gather our composure and professionalism, setting aside everything else and putting on our medical masks—literally and figuratively. We don't talk about this any further, or anything else that happened that day or since; we just converse about what is needed for the patients who come into our care.

I finished my shift,
but with great difficulty.
It wasn't only emotionally draining
but physically too.
I had to rest and pause numerous times throughout the day.
My heart could barely withstand the additional pressure placed
upon it.
My heart struggled in more ways than one.
My breath was labored:
I was short of breath and physically fatigued,
I would have to supply my body with additional spurts of oxygen
between
my patients' procedures.

But I did it!
I did what I had to do
to get through and complete my day at work.

Why?
Why did I push through, like nothing happened?
Because that is what I led myself to believe that I had to do.
I wasn't granted time to heal from this,
any of this.
And since I'm not able to fully accept or face what I need

THE LILY NURSE

to heal from,
I keep pushing through the best way I know how.
Facing things one piece
and one step at a time.
I still have my eyes closed to the bigger picture,
I haven't found all the missing pieces or links
I am still lost on this journey
Trying to heal.

I arrive home after this completely draining day and I am greeted by my loving family. We were all fearful of what would transpire today, unsure if my heart could withstand the additional pressure or if I could get through the emotional toll of going back so soon after my horrific incident. The last time I went to work, I came back to my family completely changed. I had died and came back within minutes of being at work, rebooted and re-birthed, broken and saved. My family only sees the aftermath of it all. They get to struggle through this too. Our lives have completely flipped, and we are forced to face, deal and heal with everything all on our own.

At least we have each other
And the love between us will help us heal.

And now, as I arrive home the same as I left for work, we are able to breathe and set aside our anguish and fear. We are able to focus on what matters to us most—the power of our love to get us through this. We don't talk about what happened during our day.

We go outside to our backyard,
and lay in the grass together.
I don't have enough energy to do anything more.
I look towards the endless blue sky,
And with my family by my side,
I am able to finally pause
and breathe.
Letting go of everything that occurred today.

I know I have far more healing to do,
but there's so many layers and levels to this;
I just need more time to process it all.

I don't even bring up how my workday was.
Right now that doesn't matter.
I am able to absorb and concentrate on what really matters to me,
all the love my family gifts me.
I came back for them,
I show them love and light
And in turn their love will help me get through this.

Tomorrow is another day to face, another challenge which lays before me,
So right now,
I'm going to forget about the things that don't serve me,
and concentrate on what matters most -
My family and me time.

Breathe,
Pause,
Repeat.
Heal from the day...

As I start healing from the little things—big shifts will eventually follow.

Chapter 32

Everything Happens for a Reason

~  ~

Nothing was malicious.
That thought never entered my brain.

There is no one to blame.
For everything I have been through had to happen the way it happened.
Everything I have gone through has a reason and a purpose,
for me to live through it.

It's meant for me as a message
from something bigger than us.
To help me face and heal from what has always been right in front of me.
A message to either learn or to heal from.
Leading me to a path I have always meant to be on.

I came out of this chaotic and horrific situation
with a new knowledge, belief and insight.
I am alive
Rebooted/Re-birthed

Supercharged to another level of awareness.
I am learning every day what to do with this new existence of mine.
I am so very blessed to be here,
Alive.

Despite all the turmoil, struggles and pieces that I am dealing with,
I am so very thankful to have been given a second chance at life.

Yes, I have flashbacks,
I try not to be consumed by them,
or from the emotions that are tied tight to them.
But it is hard not to ignore all the pieces to this crazy and surreal puzzle,
I wish I could see the full image of this.

This is my life.
Not some made-up story
I fabricated to tell a tale for people to be shocked by,
But I share this so I can learn and heal from it too.
To see it in a different light.

All I want from this, is to learn how to live the life I was always meant to live;
Happy, joyful and free.
Free to be heard
and seen.
Free to be me!

I realize with each flashback and each interesting piece to this story,
There is a message for me to receive.
I am yet to be fully aware of the bigger picture I am meant to see
What is it that I need to fully heal from?
Why am I not computing these messages?

I realize that I am still picking up all of my broken pieces,
I am desperately wanting to become whole again.

I am trying to become aware and analyze all the pieces

And as I do so, I find that
Some fit in this puzzle,
while others don't seem to have a place.
Making it hard to see the full picture,
It confuses me and distracts me on how to truly heal from this.

I am not quite sure what to do with everything,
I'm trying my best to figure everything out.
There has been so much that has happened in such a short period of time,
I need more time to be able to process and address
what I am needing to face.
I'm not quite sure if I understand the bigger picture in this.
I need more signs to help me on my way
to the path I am meant to be on.

Everything I have and am going through
has happened the way it was intended to happen.
~ Everything happens for a Reason ~

CHAPTER 33

ONE MONTH LATER

~  ~

Before heading off to work, I take a moment for myself and lay in the grass, as part of my new morning routine. This little ritual is for me, so I can have a quiet moment to pause before I start my day. I meditate on the blessings and good I have in my life and let go of the rest. I soak up the warmth from the sun's rays and I look towards the endless blue sky, trying to get a new insight to why this all happened. Why am I so connected to and yet still so disconnected from what I need to see? Why am I gifted with this broken heart but none of my previous MS symptoms? What am I missing? Why am I here—what is the reason? Am I fulfilling my purpose? Or better yet: What is my purpose, my path? Who am I?

It's as though everything is still continuing to be rewired and rerouted
within my being:
My body, mind, spirit and now soul.
As if I need this time and perhaps more
to process and download everything I went through.
I find the more connected I become with my environment,

and the more centered and grounded I become with the earth -
The more aware I am to the messages from the Universe.
Every day I become more aware and enlightened
But I'm not sure if I am getting the full message from something greater than me.
And the messages I am acknowledging and am aware of,
I don't know what I do with them.
I'm overwhelmed by everything.
And even though I am keeping my eyes wide open to everything
I feel like I'm still not getting it,
not comprehending,
still in the dark.
I want my light to shine
And I want to share that light with the world,
but how?
Why?

Is that my purpose?

Am I really awake to all of this?
Or are my eyes still blinded by what my conscious mind does not want me to face?
Perhaps it's still protecting me from further agony
of dealing with the truth of the situation?

So, as I lay in the grass and breathe in the fresh air of the great outdoors, I ask the Universe to further guide me to where I am meant to be in this world, to the path I am intended for, and to continue highlighting and sending messages to me—I will know when the time is right. I will receive the full message loud and clear.

When I do become aware of what I am missing right now,
that will be the time to address it,
To heal from whatever it is I need to heal from.

***

As I start my shift on my unit—history slightly repeats itself.
Giving me yet another message from the Universe.

Exactly a month after my incident—to the day, to the hour, to nearly the minute—a code blue is called overhead on my unit. I rush over to respond to the medical emergency, to provide assistance to my colleagues. As I approach, I stop in my tracks. There is an array of staff taking charge of this situation, and I don't need to step in. I take a step out of the way, but stay close if they require a runner for supplies or anything else to save this person. To bring them back to this world, this realm, this life. I am not needed at this point to assist them in any way. So, I take a few more steps back.

As I assess this situation from afar, my awareness is brought to the area that this is occurring in: spot seven. I take a few more steps back as I realize this where I died exactly a month ago. I look to the clock and the time registers in my thoughts. I look back to the scene and my heart skips a beat.

I am standing before this patient,
Watching
Gaining another perspective of my own code

The code team rushes in and takes charge. It is the same team that worked on me! I start to get flashes of my code and what it would have looked like as a nurse being on this side of the trauma. A colleague walks over to me and puts her hand upon my back. She recognizes the significance of this and what it represents for me.

"Are you sure you should be watching this?" she asks, concerned and acknowledging how difficult this would be for me.

I stand there, paralyzed by this sight but still on guard to activate my nursing role if required. I can push my emotion and pain down in a split second, hide all my personal garbage instantly and activate auto-nurse, as I have trained myself to do over the years. I am at work and my attention is always for the patient and their needs; mine can always be moved to the side. Nurses are notorious for that strength/weakness.

"Yes," I abruptly respond. "Are you sure you should be watching this?"

My tone is concerned, yet slightly cold; I am lost for how I should be feeling or thinking. The sight of this trauma would have an effect on her too, but her comment also frustrates and angers me. Now someone is finally showing me compassion?

The slightly passive-aggressive response is a small emotional explosion misdirected at her, similar to what my father did to that nice lady in the grocery store. My internal voice yells: *Let me do my job and let me process this the best way I know how. Get the fuck away from me and let me deal with this on my own by jumping right in and facing my fear head on!*

I'm not sure how she took my comment or tone, but she stood by my side, her hand on the small of my back, without saying another word. We are observing, watching and waiting to help the team if needed. This is difficult for both of us and we stand here together, having a personal moment of reflection — supporting each other silently. I remember seeing her there the day I coded, standing and watching from this side as we are doing together now. While similar actions are being done with this patient, I stand frozen beside my colleague. How do you not be affected by this?

> That was me exactly one month ago
> in the same spot.
> With the same people working on me.
>
> This is not a flashback
> but an actual repeat in history.
> Not all the pieces are repeated -
> like the lilies, anaphylactic reaction or epinephrine.
> But I stand here watching a very similar case.

I have already seen this unfold before my eyes from this angle or
side of the code
I watched myself upon that stretcher
As I was looking down on myself
while the team worked on me.
I also know what is happening to him as he is going through this;
I know where he is
and what he is going through.

A place that there are not enough words to describe.

The patient gets shocked back twice after compressions had been initiated, and sits straight up on the stretcher, just as I did. He looks directly at me, as if he can sense that I too have been where he just was. In that moment, it seems like it is only the two of us in this unit, and time doesn't exist. It's paused and this area is illuminated with the most brilliant infinite light. As he stares at me with inquisitive eyes, I smile and nod at him, and he does the same to me. It's as though we are acknowledging for each other what just happened; that it was real.

He lies back down on the stretcher, talking at a rapid speed and in awe of what just happened, what the staff are telling him—that he coded and he was saved. I remember that exhilarating feeling: supercharged, rebooted, re-birthed. I remember the feeling of disbelief that I was alive one moment, dead the next, then back again. So much happens to a person, not just to their body, but to their mind, spirit and soul.

As the stable patient is wheeled away off our unit via stretcher, as I had been wheeled away one month prior, we are left with the aftermath of the code. The ICU nurse who did my compressions too turns around and faces me in disbelief.

"That was you a month ago! That was you!" she blurts out.

"Hi," is all I can say.

THE LILY NURSE

"What are you doing here?" she questions me.

"I only got a week off," I sheepishly say.

She walks over to me and gives me a loving embrace. The rest of the code team turns their attention to us as we are hugging, and several of them say in unison, while pointing to spot seven, "That was you a month ago."

"I know," I say through tears. "Thank you for saving me."

***

A few days later, I am taking my turn working in the procedure room and conversation turns to his code. The three of us were in his circle of care and we are in the procedure room alone. I am standing at my station, listening to my colleagues debrief.

"I can't believe we had a code here," one says.

"It's rare for us to have a code blue here," the other adds.

"I wonder what it is like?" the first one ponders.

"What?" the second inquires.

"I wonder what it is like to die and come back?"

I pipe up and say, "Why don't you ask?"

"What?" they both say.

"If you are curious," I say, "why don't you just ask me?"

"What would you know about that?" one harshly responds.

"That was me in the same position, exactly one month before, to the date, to nearly the minute."

"Yeah, but yours was different."

"Why?" I question.

That's the golden question I always hold inside my thoughts. *Why is my case so different? Why can no one acknowledge that I had a life-changing incident here on this unit? Why can't anyone admit and validate what I have gone through?*

> **I need to find my voice**
> **Step out of the shadows and into the light**
> **so I can shine and gain my power back**

> Perhaps this is another missing piece to my obscure surreal experience that I have to heal from?

Chapter 34

Aha Revelation

This story is hard to wrap your head around. It's hard to breathe it all in. It's easy to turn a blind eye to the truth of it and what it does to a person at every level. But several people finally have an aha moment, a revelation in their minds about what actually happened. As they begin to process their take, perceptions and perspectives of this event, some suddenly become aware and tuned into the effects and turmoil it had and is having on not only me, but my immediate family too.

My Family...
Greg (my husband, my love, my light, my Everything),
Titus (our little boy),
and **Jayda** (our delicate little girl)

These three tend to be overlooked, just as I am. People seldom look at this situation through their eyes, their perspective. The fact is, they all experienced something extremely traumatic. Even though none of them were physically there, they were all traumatized by it. They had to process this very quickly. All three of them having a rapid flood of emotions, a vast influx of feelings and thoughts: up/down, dark/light, loss/gain, grief/worry, happy/sad. Their world was completely flipped upside-down. My immediate family all experienced this traumatic and life changing ordeal as well.

Some will comment in an aha revelation, "I can't imagine what your family went through. It must have been so hard for them!"

All I can say in return is, "I can only understand and see what they are going through, through my perspective. I get glimpses of the trauma, turmoil and chaos they all face, and do face on a daily basis. It's a steady wave of emotions for them. This mind-boggling, heart-wrenching situation continuously and subsequently affects them. I can only touch the surface of what they truly went through. I believe that they all went through something far more traumatic than anyone who was standing there before me."

What they experienced is actually so much harder to understand. They lost and gained me back, and had to come to terms with that knowledge instantly. They had to conceptualize the actual turn of events and then having me back as a changed woman—a change that they could see, and can't understand. There was no time to process, no time to think, no time to be happy, sad, or in between. What they experienced is far harder to understand and so beyond anything we could imagine. It is extremely hard for them. All three of them.

> And I have to watch them struggle just as much as me,
> if not more.
> And I hold what they are going through in my heart as well.
>
> I can't protect them from this,
> and since I'm struggling with all of my own pieces and my own journey,
> I don't have enough energy to help them with theirs.

THE LILY NURSE

So the best thing I can do for them is—show them light in the darkness.
Show them unconditional love.
For that is what I have an abundance of.

Light and Love

CHAPTER 35

TILL DEATH DO US PART

~  ~

It's June 28, 2018—the day of our 15th wedding anniversary. The traditional gift is crystal, representing clear and sparkling love—but in our case, we give each other our crystal clear insight.

"Greg, what would you like to do for our 15th wedding anniversary?" I question my loving husband.

"I'm not sure," he admits. "Everything has been flipped upside down for us. I haven't even thought about our anniversary."

Our world *has* been completely flipped and torn apart, but we as a family unit have been doing the best we can to view our world differently. We change our perceptions to view this precious life with love, believing that this life we share is sacred and shouldn't be taken for granted. Now more than ever we truly cherish every little moment within our lives. We spend most of our time outdoors together as a family unit, and we do what we can to find the moments that make our hearts sing, and our souls fill with love.

"Will you marry me?" I blurt out to Greg.

"We're already married," he responds, puzzled (and correct).

"I know we are on paper," I say. "but till death do us part…and I died."

"Yes, you did," he says, realizing what I am saying.

"I know a lot has changed—I've changed—but the love I have for you has never left my being. Will you marry me?" I ask him again.

Throughout the day, I continue to pose this question to him—13 times to be precise, the same number of times I made him ask me before the first time we were wed. I attempt to woo him all day, sending him lyrics and audio from songs that we hold dear to our hearts: "Marry Me" by Amanda Marshall, and our original wedding songs by Elton John, "Your Song" and "Can You Feel the Love Tonight."

Finally, I get him on the phone and say, "Gregory Neal Evans, you are my light, my love, my everything. I love you from all of the depths of my heart and beyond. Please give me the honor to realign our souls as one. The love I have for you has never changed. You are my biggest support, my anchor and with your love, I am able to find happiness, joy and peace." I pause and take a breath, taking in this significant moment between us and asking one more time, lucky number 13. "Greg, will you marry me?"

"Of course I'll marry you!" He accepts my proposal.

That night, on our 15th wedding anniversary, Greg and I have a private backyard ceremony, just for the two of us. We dressed in simple wedding attire, him wearing his original boutonniere and I holding my original wedding bouquet. I finish getting dressed at a friend's house, across the golf course between our houses, waiting for him to get home from work, get dressed, and meet me in the center of the field that is separating us.

We are to meet in this field; our field of endless possibilities.

I get his text:

I'm ready.

> Meet you on the golf course.
> Your bride will be waiting.

I have butterflies fluttering in my stomach. I'm excited and nervous from the anticipation of remarrying the man I love, my light, my soulmate, Greg. My girlfriend gives me a hug and watches me walk towards the center of the field, where I am to meet the love of my life. As we walk across the plains of this field to join together, it's like walking down the aisle of the church at our wedding, the original day we promised our love for each other in the presence of our friends and family. This time, is just for us and no one else.

We finally reach each other and it's like seeing each other for the very first time—love at first sight. We embrace each other like we have never embraced before, as though there is a new energy, light and force driving us together. After sharing the most incredible kiss of my lifetime, we grab hold of each other's hand and walk to a new journey and destination together. Our children greet us as we enter our backyard, showing them that the power of love brightens even the darkest moments.

Jayda takes a few beautiful pictures of Greg and me to commemorate this moment. We then begin our evening together, going out for dinner in our wedding attire, being congratulated by strangers on our blissful union, then driving around in the open prairies with the top down in our convertible. We are waiting for the perfect moment to commence this ceremony and to realign our souls.

We finally arrive back at our house, our home, and realize this is the perfect spot. We create a little area in the center of our yard and partake in the most beautiful ceremony that is only for us, saying new vows to each other, cleansing our rings and saying our *I dos*, all under the light of the full moon. We spend the remaining portion of our evening and into the depths of the night, consummating this new union we share.

The power of love
Can get us through our darkest times
Shining light on what we need
To become Whole
To heal
To be present in this beautiful life we live.

CHAPTER 36

WHAT HAPPENED TO YOUR HEART?

I'm at the Congestive Heart Failure clinic again, getting more tests done and seeing how I am doing physically. I'm back at this place, right above my home unit. I popped up for bit to get assessed, tested, and gawked at. Most of the people here are aware of my story, both the staff and some of the patients.

"You're the nurse who came back. You're the Lily Nurse!"

It always astonishes me how people know very specific details of my story—the details of the incident which happened to me—without me even sharing it. It's a horrific and miraculous story that spreads like wildfire through an open field. It destroys small portions of me, for I am not ready to face it all. I am just trying to live life the best way I know how, within this new world that I am forced into. No one really sees me for me: the nurse, the woman, the girl who had laid upon that stretcher and had an experience like no other. They often see it through their perceptions of the story, not willing or wanting to hear what I have to say.

I just keep smiling and burying it all down, for that is the coping

THE LILY NURSE

I have always known. That is a core belief instilled into me at such a young age: Survivor Mode. I squeeze and try to force myself back to a former life that I knew, the life of the strong, knowledgeable, caring nurse—the fixer, what I believed to be a healer. I keep going, letting all of these comments, beliefs, perceptions and points of view run off me like water off a duck's back. I'm the duck that seems calm and going with the flow on the top, but underneath the water, the action is frantic, trying to keep me afloat. I'm not ready to face that portion of myself, not completely, not yet.

My cardiologist enters the room and still he won't look at me, really see me for me, a person who sits before him searching for someone to listen, someone to help. He talks to me in this robotic, non-nurturing voice, speaking of levels, tests and the measures that provide information only about my physical being and nothing else.

Can you even see me?
This person sitting before you,
Who has been through an immense amount of
Trauma, pain and suffering.

I am mirroring his response to me, not saying much and not even listening to what he has to say. I can't allow this to be put into my brain. I can't absorb I am just an object that sits before him to run tests on, something with no feelings and no recollection of anything that has happened in the last few months. I am a person—a human being who needs love and support, not to be pushed under the bus and swept under the carpet. I need to be seen; I need to be heard! I won't allow him or anyone else to take any more power away from me. I can't! This all makes me feel powerless! Just treat me how you would want to be treated; put yourself in my situation. Look at it from my point of view; for once, look up and see *me*!

He flips through the papers of my chart in a slightly hurried and confused manner, as if he came across something that made him look again, something that made him pause and see what is right in front of him.

"How is this possible?" he says out loud—but mainly to himself.

"What?" I ask, reminding that I am here in front of him.

He finally looks up past the notes in his hands and looks at me. He seems puzzled, confused and a bit uneasy—on edge. It's as though he doesn't want to know but has to find out for his own peace of mind. I sit here hunched over, staring at him, waiting for him to ask.

"Your heart function…" he begins. It's as though I can see the wheels turning in his head. He looks confused, uncomfortable and a bit curious about the results that appear on the papers. It's as though an unexplainable, magical result is staring right at him. It looks like he is trying to formulate a conclusion, a reason to his findings.

I nod, almost knowing what he has found.

"Your heart is healing?!" he says to me, bewildered.

"Yes, I know," I respond.

"What do *you* mean, you know?" he questions me.

"I've been healing my heart?" I respond in a very casual tone to my voice.

"What do you mean, *you* have been healing your heart?" he asks angrily, as though his ego is against the wall.

"I'm tapping into something that is bigger than us. I've been doing a more holistic approach to my healing. I have been listening to my body for what it needs to heal from." I respond, beautifully smiling. "I am healing from a place of love—I did go to the other side."

He doesn't seem pleased with what I am telling him. He's agitated and uncomfortable with me being in his presence.

"I'm discharging you from my care," he promptly says.

"So, my heart is fine?" I question, using my most-hated word, for it doesn't describe anything. It just puts a label on an emotion we don't want to admit to or face.

"It's fine; your ejection fraction is good enough," he retorts. "You can stop taking your medication when *you* want. I don't need to see you anymore."

I am a bit shocked, but not surprised by the way he is treating me and this situation. Not many more words are exchanged between us. Both of us know where we stand, and I have to be at peace with that.

I'll find my way to heal from all of this, on my own time, when I am ready and willing to face it all. I have been instilling a lot of my trust into the physicians to help me, fix me, but it is going to take a lot more time to really heal from all of this. There are too many layers that I have to strip away before I am able to truly heal from this fucked up situation that I am living, or trying to live with.

I know I can and will heal from all of this; it will be some day when I am ready to address what is right in front of me. I know I have to step away from what doesn't serve me anymore, the place that hides me in the shadows and in the dark. I need to step into the light to see and become aware of where my power is—it resides within me, an internal wisdom I am just tapping into. My power will not be taken away; I can't be boxed up and shoved away into the corners of people's minds, never to be looked at again. There's no label I can be named with, no suitable box I can fit into, for what I have experienced is different from the norm

JULIA EVANS

and no one knows what or how to deal with me or this situation.

I am a human being
Who has been through a horrific and tragic series of events.
And yet, have been to a place that radiates love
I am just looking for love and support.
So I can live the life,
I am meant to live.

Not to be made invisible
But to be acknowledged, and heard.
I am trying to preserve
The beauty
of my precious life that I am blessed to get back.

I am trying to process and see what it is I need to heal from
And I search for help from others along the way
but what I need to listen to
is the voice inside

Listen closely
There are a lot of layers to this story.

Chapter 37

The Quest to Finding My Path

"Greg, I don't know who I am anymore," I say to Greg as we sit nuzzled up together in the sand, watching the waves roll in from the lake. "I feel like I'm just going through the motions of life and not fulfilling the path I should be on. I came back for a reason. I feel like I'm still missing something, but I can't figure it out."

"You're still you," he responds. "You're right though; there is something different about you and I can't explain it."

"I feel like I have all this power, energy and light inside of me and it's wanting to be shared with the world. I don't know what to do with it. I feel like I want to explore it further. I want to understand it, be enlightened to it, but I still feel like I'm missing a part of myself. I want to find that missing piece, and when I find it, I know it will help me see me and the path that I am meant to be on."

"Why don't you take some time for yourself?" he encourages.

"Go visit your friend Shannon in Saskatoon; take time for you. Have an adventure and find what you need to find."

"Really?" I question.

"You did come back for a reason," he emphasizes. "You'll find your path. You haven't had the opportunity to pause and think of everything that has happened since you died and came back. A lot happened, and I can't begin to imagine everything that you have gone through. Take this time for you. Call your friend, go for a visit, have fun and find yourself."

I listen to Greg's advice and go to Saskatoon to visit my friend for one hell of an adventure. Shannon allows me to grieve my old existence and embrace the new. She lets me say goodbye to the things that don't serve me anymore. She helps me see the beauty of pausing from the world and my chaotic thoughts—allowing me to see all the wondrous beauty that we often skip by without acknowledging. Together we learn what it is like to be fully connected and grounded in this world.

She is exactly what I need. She allows me to talk about everything and anything; we cry and laugh, and I can pause and be present in the moment. She allows me to start taking off my Survival Mode mask. She supports me by being by my side, there for whatever I need. She supplies a place for me to feel protected and safe, a place in her heart and home, which helps me start figuring out who and what I need to be in this world. She is the first and only person I confide in about everything I went through. She shows no judgment and doesn't impose her own personal views. She only gives me love and support, and holds space for me. She does this so I can process things, so I can come to terms with what I need to be aware of—to help me find myself.

I need that female sisterhood energy beside me to help me further my quest for enlightenment—to find myself and the path I need to follow. Greg was right: I needed time for myself and the help from my friend to guide me further on my path.

After our little adventure, I feel like I was able to start healing from different segments of my past. I am led to many areas of my life that had great significance and meaning to me. It's as though my past and my life is being played out for me to see, the Universe highlighting all the happy memories I need to hold on to and the ones that caused me pain and suffering I need to release. But as Shannon and I physically walk and talk through the path of my previous life, there is something I'm still not ready to face.

My logical brain put me on this quest to find a purpose, but the more I search for it the more I feel lost and confused. My conscious mind is trying to force me on this quest to find myself and my path. But I am already on the path that has been laid out for me. The Universe had always been giving me messages like a little bread crumb trail, permitting me to see what has always been right in front of me.

I need more time to process and digest these new understandings and findings. I need more time to pause and be with my thoughts. As the months go by, I strip away other layers and pieces of this puzzle, until the day I was finally open to a new level of awareness, the time I was finally able to face and address the root cause I hadn't been able to heal from.

My first step had been to ground myself,
pause and breathe.
Go with the flow of the Universe and trust the process.
Then I would be ready to acknowledge there really is more to this world,
more to this picture and my unique story;
I don't have to hide from it,
or be in the dark.
I don't have to make myself believe that I'm not on the right path.
I am on the right path,
I am being guided to something better,
to being a whole and complete version of ME.

I can start to shine a light on it,

JULIA EVANS

shine a light on me.

I don't have to be invisible anymore,
I can speak my truth,
people are willing to listen.

I am on the path I need to be on.
The Universe and something bigger than us,
is guiding me.
It is lighting the way with many messages
Each and every step of the way, of this enlightening journey
It leads me to where I am meant to be,
and helps me see what it is to be ME.

The quest for finding my path…

Putting myself into that mindset spins me into a chaotic tizzy.
It's like searching for my car keys: the more I search, the more
frustrated, scrambled, aggravated and lost I feel—and it was right
in front of me the whole time!

I didn't have to be on a Quest...
I just had to be willing to open my eyes and focus on what I
already had already known:
the insight and knowledge that has always been right in front of me
and right inside of me!

The piece missing from my mind, body, spirit and soul.

It has been pushed to the back of my mind,
for far too long,
Patiently waiting to be acknowledged.

CHAPTER 38

SIX MONTHS LATER

I'm at work, on my home unit, working in the admitting area. I am doing my nursing duty, taking a health history of my patient prior to their procedure, assessing, educating, taking vitals, starting an IV. This is our job, our duty to the patient: make them comfortable, be attentive, and advocate for their well-being. I love this part of my job. Actually, I love every aspect of my job, my career; that's why I chose this profession.

I love being a nurse!
I like to help people, when they are in need.
Help with their healing process
While providing them comfort, and support!

That's who I am
A Healer!

As I am in the middle of my assessment and admission of my patient, I write down the date on their paperwork. It's the six-month anniversary of my death, my reboot, my re-birth, my traumatic code, here on this unit. I lean over to my left, unblocking the sight of spot seven without stepping out of the admitting area. All I have to do is lean slightly to the left, and there is the spot: highlighted and unveiled, presented, right before me.

I stop what I am doing for a moment as I look to this area—the spot, the stretcher where it all happened. The reenactment is rapidly playing out within my thoughts. In one split second, the whole event plays out in my mind, as if my conscious mind was ready to finally see it, address it and face it.

That's where it all happened!

As I stare in the direction of this area, I am mesmerized by this spot. I pause everything that I am doing, pen in hand, patient, chart and computer right in front of me. Everything stops in time, breaking me from the normal pace of the everyday.

I feel a soft breeze to my left. Someone is walking by me and they greet me. "Good morning, Julia!"

I instinctively start turning to face and greet the person with a familiar voice. It's the sound of a colleague, someone on my team, my work family; it's the sound of someone I trust.

"Good morn.—" as I start to respond, there's a call overhead.

"Code Blue..."

I speed up my turn towards this familiar voice, and I am face to face with the physician who inserted my intravenous. The one who pushed the epinephrine into my vein, to my blood, to my heart.

My heart sinks.

We stare at each other as the code is called overhead. It's not for this unit; it's being called across the entire hospital. We are both aware of the significance of this call being announced. We both glance over to spot seven and then back to each other.

My breath is still, and my heart stops for a brief moment, waiting for him to say something else, anything.

He looks directly in my eyes, and I into his. It's as if we are looking into each other's souls. We both pause for a moment.

We both know what happened. We both are aware, but we both have our own experience and version of what happened that day. Our own unique story, experience, and interpretation of that day, of that event. We were on different sides of the vitals machine, neither knowing the other side. We never ask and we never talk about it—no communication or debriefing. We are both stuck with our own memory of what we had experienced in all its horrific detail.

He changes his posture, and lovingly remarks with such intense eyes, "I'm happy you're here. Thank you for coming back." Then he walks away, carrying on with his day like nothing ever happened.

I look down towards my patient to continue on with her admission. I go right back into my nurse role. This time is different, though; this time, I can't shove my thoughts and feelings down. They come right back up to the surface to be faced and addressed. But I am still at work and I have a duty to my patient. I am not able to address this here, in this space. So, I carry on with my task at hand.

"Sorry about that," I say. "I had to hear where the code was taking place, just in case I had to run to it."

"That's fine." She responds, shrugging off my need to explain myself. "Hey, weren't you the nurse who died here?"

"Yes, but I came back," I confidently reply, with a slight chuckle, nod and smile.

"Oh my God, you're the Lily Nurse," she blurts out.

"Yeah, I guess I am," I respond. "How do you know about me?"

"Everybody knows about you," she says. "Your story is incredible, surreal and out of this world. You should write a book about it!"

"Maybe someday I will," I say. "I just haven't wanted to talk about it yet."

CHAPTER 39

LEAVING IT ALL BEHIND

A few days after the sixth month anniversary of my reboot, my re-birth, my traumatic code here on this unit, I still feel a little rattled, like something inside of me was shaken up. Now I feel quite uncomfortable at work. I feel sad and bitter that everyone here got to heal and move forward from this incident, leaving me to deal with it all on my own. Everyone got to debrief and tell their side of the story, not acknowledging mine. As I watch everyone around me carrying on like nothing happened, I feel broken, alone and incomplete. I feel like I am sinking into the depths of a dark abyss again, and I know damn well that I didn't come back to feel like this.

I enter the procedure room where I am assigned to work today, and I start my day like any other. I say good morning to the staff in the room. There's an unfamiliar face and I start to introduce myself, but get interrupted by the physician introducing me.

"Oh, she's The Lily Nurse," he blurts out, not even considering the impact of what that name does for me.

"Wow, you're The Lily Nurse," the resident says. "I've heard all about you and the code. You're the nurse who died here and came back."

"Yeah," I respond. "But that's not my name. My name is Julia, and I am the registered nurse that will be working in the procedure room with you."

I am taken aback and angry at this introduction, his label for me, and the resident's comment. This name I have been given sticks to me like glue. Three little words to define and label my traumatic near-death experience. Everyone seems to know about "the story," "the incident," and yet no one has heard my side of it, no one knows my experience of the whole ordeal. *What does this have to do with anything we are doing in this room? It's hard enough not show any emotion regarding this incident when I'm working, which actually happened here, at work, only six months ago.*

I don't respond any further to the comment or name, sweeping away my feelings under the carpet—just like how I feel everyone has done to me. I gain back my composure to just do my job. I try to teach and explain to the resident what is happening during the procedure. As the lights are turned out and the doctor's and the other nurse's backs are turned away from us, the resident leans in close and asks me, "What was it like? Did you see the other side?"

I stop what I am doing, pause, and look deep into his eyes. He looks into mine.

"Yes, I saw the other side." I whisper. "It was pure love and light."

"Why do you remain here on this unit?" he questions using a very light whisper.

"I don't know," I respond.

"There's a reason you came back," he tells me. "Tell your story. Find your path. Find you."

> I do have a story,
> and a name to put to it too.
> Maybe it's time to share my version.

Many things have happened over the course of six months—I am more inquisitive and learn about holistic healing and energy work. I have seen a drastic change in myself, as I find myself more in tune with the Universe. I have learned to ground myself, quiet my mind and breathe. I can feel the energies around me and within me. I am waking to the knowledge and understanding that there is more to this world—more to this life I have boxed myself into. I am ready to let go of that box.

This whole time I've been trying to fall back into my old life the best way I know how, trying to conform myself to be the same person, in the same shell of my body. But I never really could do that. I've changed. How do you not, when you have been given a second chance? Especially when you have gone to a place of bliss, to "the other side," a place full of love and light, and to have gained a new perspective on life, a new knowledge and a new awareness. This is something I don't often speak about, but it is a huge weight that still holds me down, wanting and waiting to be looked at.

The people I'm surrounded by at work all got to heal from this and I still haven't. They all got to debrief and move on, while I just displaced my experience and all the components around the incident to the side, not to be looked at again. When I was reminded this week of what happened to me only six months ago, I'm surprised to realize that I am not where I need to be. I need to step away and figure out what I need to learn from all of this.

I arrive home after work and have a life-changing talk with Greg. I tell him that it is time for me to step away from western medicine, from nursing, and find what will help me heal. He agrees with my plan to step away, neither of us knowing for how long, but both knowing it is the right thing for me to do.

"When are you going to leave work?" Greg questions me.

"I'm not sure," I reply. "I will know when the time is right. I do know it will be sooner than later. My time to heal is upon me and I'm ready and willing to let the Universe guide me."

The next day, I wake up like any other day, but it immediately feels different. Today I feel weak, tired, dragged down and without a voice. I get out of bed and look at myself in the mirror, shocked by my appearance. I look like death but I can't be bothered to fix my appearance. I head off to work after croaking my I love yous to my family. As I arrive on my unit, everyone is commenting on how sickly I look. I find it amusing, for they are finally seeing what I feel like under the mask I put on for them each and every single day. This is the look of a person's spirit dying.

I look to the assignment board and my name is missing. My first thought is that I put in for holidays and I shouldn't be here. I check the scheduling book and see my name as having to work today. As we get the morning report, it's a shock to all of us that we have more staff than we know what to do with, because some procedure rooms aren't running.

As we are getting this information, our manager walks by, and my voice suddenly comes back to life. I can speak again, and I say to my manager, "I'm not on the board; we have too much staff. Can I go home?"

"Sure," she responds.

"Do you have a minute to talk in your office?" I ask her.

"Yes, of course," she says with a concerned tone.

THE LILY NURSE

We enter her office and before she has the door fully closed, she can sense what I am about to say.

"I think I'm done here."

She closes the door completely and sits at her desk.

"I can't work here anymore," I continue. "It's too hard for me to face being here."

"You're one of our best nurses," she boasts. "I was dreading this day."

"It's too hard for me to be here. I died here!"

"I know," she responds. "I was there; it was one of the hardest things to watch."

I start crying. "There are too many things that haven't been addressed," I say through my tears. "I've helped heal everyone here, and now it's my time to heal."

"I understand," she says. "But don't throw it all away; you are an amazing nurse. But you're right, you have to heal from this. Take time for you and when you are ready, we will be here waiting for your return."

"Do you listen to the Universe?" I question.

"I know you do," she deflects the question.

"I can't get better in a place I got sick in," I tell her. "I shouldn't be here; I need to follow what the Universe has in store for me, but I don't know what that is. I love being a nurse, but I have to step away."

The two of us talk and cry in her office for nearly 45 minutes. We talk about perhaps me having PTSD (post traumatic stress disorder), other nurses who struggle with it and how they got help to heal from it. We talk about the day when everything changed and the many things that transpired for me after it. We discuss me doing what I need to do to heal from this, and she says she will support my decision. We talk about all aspects of the incident, and I feel heard, validated and acknowledged by her.

She gives me a warm heartfelt hug and asks me one more question, "Is there anything I can do for you?"

"Yes," I respond. "Let me walk gracefully off the unit and don't allow people to talk about me anymore."

She gives me another hug, and bids me farewell on my journey to heal.

I walk past the nursing station, not acknowledging the charge nurse. In my head I say, *You bought the lilies that changed my life forever, and I don't know how I feel about that!*

I walk into the lunch room and say goodbye to the person who heard my last words of my previous life.

"Thank you for all that you do," I say to her, while looking deep into her eyes, ignoring everything and everyone else around me. "You made my spirit come alive. I am blessed to have worked with you; I wish you all the best on your journey in this life."

I quietly and gracefully walk off the unit to the locker room, change my clothes, lock my old life away into my locker, walk up the stairs and through the staff entrance, pause and take my first breath of my new life. I could finally smell the sweetness of this precious life I have been granted back.

Now let's see where the Universe will guide me next...

Chapter 40

One Year Later

It is exactly one year since my re-birth. It has been 365 calendar days since my traumatic event, the code, the incident, the unfathomable and surreal occurrence of my reboot. Now, one year later I am at home reflecting and reliving it all over again.

I am curled up in my favorite chair beside the beautiful bay window facing the backyard. I have no idea how I am going to react to this day. No idea what feelings, emotions or thoughts will transpire for me. As the clock strikes nine o'clock, I am brought right back to that day and the minute, the moment, it all changed for me. I need to review it, to look at it again from a different perspective. I need to share it and say it out loud, to look at it in another light. I need to truly see and hear all of what I went through and not shy away from it anymore.

So, I turn on my iPad and start videoing what I need to get off my chest, recording on camera what I need to hear and say to really start healing from all of this. I start sharing my story from the beginning of that day. I need to live through this to emerge from the depths of the abyss my conscious mind put me in.

As I submerge myself into the depths of my subconscious, I am becoming aware. I am becoming enlightened. I am healing! I am not doing this for anyone else, but for me. It is so I can see and hear all of it, so I can lift the burden of what I hold inside and be able to finally come to terms with all I experienced that day. The time has finally arrived. I am aware and I am ready to finally face it!

Everyone experiences anniversaries. Some are good, like wedding anniversaries. Some mark something incredible or traumatic. Then there are the anniversaries of the death of a loved one. These anniversaries make us sad and hurt all over again. And if there was no closure, it's like ripping open the wound again, having it raw and exposed, wanting to heal. These anniversaries are also the ones that make us remember and reflect on the event and on our emotions surrounding it. We get transported back to that very instant when our world collapsed or ignited.

> Today I reflect on the whole picture!
> The anniversary of something incredible,
> something traumatic,
> and not just one remembrance anniversary,
> but several I need to heal from.
> This is the significant moment that puts it all together!

Chapter 41

Cheryl

It took me a full year to see this layer, this portion of my story, the piece of my experience that I was not ready to face, not ready to share.

I hadn't allowed my conscious mind to face this part of my experience. I wanted to keep it locked away, not to be looked at or addressed, for it seemed too painful to really acknowledge. I had a near-death or death experience!

Only after telling my story on video did I finally become awakened to the magnitude of all of this. I was finally able to see the bigger picture of yet another element to this whole experience. I finally was able to comprehend and accept that this portion of my experience actually happened. I did go to a place like no other, a place that we all wish to see and experience, a place of love, light and bliss. I was rebooted then re-birthed from a loving light and was pushed back by something or someone entirely.

As I review the footage of my video, my attention is on the areas of the recording when the iPad popped up a "Storage Full" message. It's interesting because my iPad had plenty of storage on it, but it's most interesting because of *when* the message popped up. It happened every time I was sharing some of the hardest moments that I had to endure.

The most fascinating moment is when I am talking about the ICU nurse, Cheryl; I actually caught a glimpse of the light I am describing on camera. Out of nowhere, an incredible light illuminates the area I am in. It's so bright! It looks like the exposure of the film being overexposed, right before my eyes. I can see and prove the light is there with me; it's not just a feeling or my imagination—it's lighting up my world around me. It's breathtaking!

This is when my conscious mind becomes ready to believe the details of what I saw that day and where I had been, gone and come back to. My mind is finally willing and able to comprehend it, instead of passing my own judgment or previous unhealed, unaddressed belief systems. I had to go through an incredible journey of healing to finally be able to understand and know in my heart that this was, in fact, true. True to my story, my perception, and my understanding.

Opening my Heart
To further heal
and to understand what the underlying
root cause of all of initial pain and suffering was from.

I am becoming more and more aware of the many layers to this and the sagas of my life, both new and old. I have been on a journey of unraveling all the tangled up pieces that I always shoved into a box and pushed to the dark corners of my mind, never to be seen or addressed. I have learned that even that itself was a core belief: Don't let anyone see your true hidden self - only be in Survival Mode. Just put on some extra lipstick and hide behind a mask.

It took a full year to finally realize the significance and role Cheryl had in this whole ordeal, this life-changing reboot and re-birth. It took a whole year for my brain, my conscious mind, to actually come to terms, accept, and acknowledge what truly happened when I was in a place where time stood still, a place of bliss, light and love.

I was pushed back—brought back by the hands of **Cheryl**.

Up until this point, I hadn't even told or acknowledged the complete story of what happened to me exactly one year ago, on May 10, 2018. As I reminisce and share the complete version of my story on camera, my attention is brought to the portion where I am talking about Cheryl, and I feel like I am transported back to that very moment in time.

As I say these words on camera, the story starts unfolding for me.

***

"I brought you back. I... brought you back." Cheryl said.

"Back from what?" I responded.

What is this she speaks of? What is she trying to say to me? I'm trying to comprehend and lock in my brain what she is saying to me. The words "brought back" echo throughout my mind, ricocheting between both sides of my brain—but what does that mean?

All I remember is being slammed, thrown, pushed and pulled right back into my body. There was this light, this angelic radiating light. It was within me and surrounding me, radiating from both sides of the spectrum. This light, this beautiful radiant light! It was as though I had been born from this exquisite, infinite, loving light. It was the only thing I saw when I came back, this incredible, infinite, blinding light! It was so beautiful, so still, so loving, so pure and peaceful. Beyond the opposite of darkness beyond any light I have ever known. Brighter than the sun and the moon combined.

As I was brought back into my body, I was propelled straight up to a seated position and I gasped. Gasped as though it was my first breath of my new life, just like a newborn baby, having this new-found breath within its new environment. That breath inflated my lungs, as if it was the very first time doing it. From in this breath, my central nervous system was reacting to a sudden change in my environment, a new place of being. I have never knowingly taken a breath like that before. Perhaps when I was actually born from my mother's womb, 38 years ago. So, first when I was actually born into the world, and now again, rebooted, and re-birthed from a light, a place of being, a place of love!

"I brought you back. I did compressions. We shocked you twice. I brought you back," Cheryl states.

At that point, I remember seeing Cheryl, this beautiful little short-haired ICU nurse. And yet at the same time, seeing my biological mother, Cheryl. Both are standing before me, at my right side. I feel an array of emotions: puzzled, confused, dazed, angry, betrayed, and abandoned.

You left once before! You abandoned me when I was three. You left me behind, I said within my head to my mother. You weren't there to protect me, to make me feel safe and loved! You left me alone in this world!

I was puzzled and confused by this whole situation, this environment, this world, this realm. Being with her in that pure radiant loving light, then having her tell me she brought me back…I am broken again. I want to be with her, not in this realm without her. I want her to be by my side, always and forever! I want to see her, hear her, smell her, touch her; I want to be able to do this with all of my being, knowingly, consciously! I want and need my mind to compute this. I cannot lose her again.

THE LILY NURSE

Without Her....
I AM NOTHING!

"Back from what?" I am completely flabbergasted by what I am hearing.

The ICU nurse put her hand on me, upon my shoulder. I can see her; I am aware of her! I am mesmerized by her; I can't take my eyes off of her. I'm staring right at her, but who I see standing before me is my mother.

> As I am reflecting this potion of my story
> Viewing it through my iPad
> The room of the video
> Lights up...
>
> It looks as though it is overexposed!
>
> The moment when I say,
> "Put her hand on me...."
>
> That's when the exposure changes!
> And this Light appears.
>
> Once I change my view of what I was seeing back during that moment,
> The actual ICU nurse
> The light fades, and goes back to normal.
> It brightens up again when I am becoming aware of
> what I saw, and experienced in that moment.
> I am seeing and experiencing....
> My mom...
> The light and the love.
> **My Mommy!**
>
> When I finally allow my conscious mind to believe it
> You can see it!
> I can actually see it;
> Right there on the footage.

JULIA EVANS

You can physically see the Light.
Then the iPad shuts down…

Full Storage.
Too Much to compute.

It is absolutely fascinating
This actually occurs.
Right in front of my eyes!

It's ironic;
This all happens when I am telling the most significant things
It's ironic that the Light appears
And when the iPad spontaneously disconnects from the story.

I go back and review it more.

"I brought you back!" echoes through my ears.

Her name is Cheryl. That's my mother's name.

I remember putting my left hand on top of hers and saying, "Back from what?"

The left side often represents the past and also feminine energy. The hand represents the minor hand chakra: Healing Energy! The minor hand chakra is a small reflection of the heart chakra. When balanced, it is able to communicate love and harmony. Opening your heart and permitting loving touch, allows healing to happen. Opening your heart lets the love and the light in.

The hand placement sparks an active memory of when I was three, right after my mother died.

The memory is of me standing in the middle of the kitchen that morning, my head just peeking over the kitchen counter, but my eye level not quite high enough to see over it. All I remember is a white light. I was standing in the center of this white space, a white luster surrounding me. I was alone in the center of it, looking for my mother, oblivious to what was happening in our house, our home. I just stood there in this white space, not realizing the significance of this moment, nor the heartbreak I was about to endure, from the words that were about to be spoken to me. The words that would stick to me forever.

"Where's my mommy?" I questioned anyone who would listen.

My dad was not even functional nor aware of how he was supposed to address this question. He blurts out, "She left us. She died. She's gone."

I was so angry, hurt, scared, lost, and all I wanted was to have my mommy back, beside me in this space. I wanted her to hold me, protect me, make me feel safe and loved. I couldn't accept this reality. *Why? Why was she gone? Why can't anyone see that she is still here?*

I remember talking with her as if she was right there with me, always with me! But how can a child be happy and joyful with that kind of connection where I knew that my mother is always there, always with me, even if she is not in this realm. How can a child continue on with that form of healing and insight, when there is so much pain and suffering around her? By obscuring that sense, belief or knowledge.

I was ostracized for that belief, that knowledge, that healing, that power and insight. So, I displaced those memories, emotions and knowledge deep down to a dark abyss of nothing. Never to be seen, felt, or thought of again. As I became emotionally and spirituality separated from her and her energy, my world became dark, cold and ripped in two. I saw and sensed the turmoil within my environment from this tragedy of losing her, and it consisted of far too much pain and suffering.

I took it upon myself to deflect the pain I was feeling, and I pledged to help everyone around me heal. I took on a new role:

her role, the mothering role, and what I perceived as the nursing role! Nurse them all back to health, heal them all, so I won't have to face how I feel inside. At that point in my young life, that was what I knew: Fix them all. Heal them from the tragedy they all faced, from the pain and suffering of all of it. I wanted to let them see and know that there is a new world of hope, dreams, love and light, but as I tried to save them, I put what I needed behind me. I forgot about me. I made myself invisible, unheard and unworthy to heal from this part of my past.

I was utterly convinced, that this was my purpose in life
I fully believed,
it was...
What I needed to be.
What I was meant to be.

The Fixer!

At that young age, the only way I understood to fulfill this need was based on my experience; I didn't have anyone to guide me otherwise. Western medicine! That's how you heal!

Become a Nurse!
Heal those around you
Help with their pain and suffering.

It was as though there was too much pain and sorrow for my little body, mind and spirit to hang on to. I needed to prove to the world that there is light in the darkness; you just have to open your mind to both sides of the spectrum. What I actually needed was to see that love and that light for myself. I led myself to believe other people's healing had to take place above my own. I thought the light and the love were for someone else; this was a facade and a trickery that my conscious mind played on me. I couldn't allow myself to heal, for it was too hard and too difficult to face on my own.

I truly believed that I had to heal everyone first. I didn't want to look at myself, what I needed, what I needed to heal from. I needed those around me to heal first, so they may be able to understand me, accept me, hear me, see me, believe what I sensed, saw and heard. Remember that I have a story too, an experience like no other. I was just a little girl who lost her mommy. I put myself, my feelings, emotions, and thoughts into the shadows, while I tried to figure out how to heal everyone else. I put myself out of the equation, out of the need to be heard.

> My memory from that point is black and dark.
> Always blinded or closed off from
> My inner Light
> The area I needed to heal.
>
> I lost my spark and my shine.
> My joy
> I lost part of me after my mother died.
> That part was the thing I needed to make me whole again.

***

Now, sitting in my chair in the comfort of my living room, telling the story of what happened, the memory of me lying in the hospital on the stretcher is further activated, and I realize I am on the other side of everything. Everything has finally come up to the surface for me to look at and face. The world that I knew, the realm and my feelings that I didn't want face, is ready to be addressed. I had blocked the memory when I was three and tried to block it again after my near-death experience.

Now I'm questioning everything once again. Oh, how I long to be back to being the fixer. The one in control, the one taking care of people, not having to look at myself or heal from what I shoved deep down! I shouldn't be on the stretcher. I should be working on the unit, taking care of others who need my help, not in desperate need of healing and being saved. I didn't even know I had to be saved, but now here I am saved and healing on so many levels.

JULIA EVANS

How did I get here?

I've taken on another role, as I lie on the hospital stretcher, the place I am bound to. I'm bound to the salvation of a higher power. Bound to the help of others, requiring all the powers and components to help me heal, at all levels that I could never face. I have to admit to it; I have to face it.

I never saw this coming. I never anticipated that this would be where I'd end up; that this would be my world. Me lying here vulnerable and weak, drastically stopped in my tracks to view my world in a different light.

> I have been gifted another chance at life!
> To Live
> I am Alive!
> I am Awakening!

I look around my environment and watch everyone around me. No one knows what I had to endure to be here, to start my healing process. Everyone carries on with their duties and routines, their own perception of their world. No one is aware of what actually has or is happening to me right in front of them. I am having this miraculous moment in the light of love and find myself not able to talk about it, again.

> It's my turn to finally be heard
> Tell my story
> My turn to finally heal
> Open your eyes Julia
> Become aware of it
> The time is now

I remain quiet in my bed, unsure of my new role, the role of the patient. As I am transferred to the emergency department via stretcher, I watch the ICU nurse, Cheryl, walk away. I feel as though I missed my chance to say all I needed to say to her, to my mother. I didn't get a chance to be heard, or to hear her.

THE LILY NURSE

> That's too difficult to accept
> and too absurd to believe
> That she was right in front of me
> Helping me come back to this life that I am in right now.

My mind spins in a tizzy as I start thinking about how and why I got here. In this space, in this time— in this hospital bed.

I needed to see this and reflect on it on my anniversary or my re-birthday, celebrating the first year of my new life. That's when I start taking those baby steps; cruising on a new path and destination, and my path is to heal. It's time to turn those baby steps into bigger steps to heal and view the world in a different light.

> I'm starting to see the bigger picture.
> **It's my time to heal**

I look back, and think of me staring at the ICU nurse as she stands at my bedside, and remember asking her, "Did this really happen?" She wouldn't have the foggiest idea who and what I saw; it was for me to experience and no one else. So, at that moment, I thought I had to block from my mind that experience of my mother being beside me and her pushing me back.

Once again I blankly stare at the nurse in front of me, and I wish I could be back on the other side of that vitals machine, back in the role as the nurse, not where I lay, as a patient in this hospital bed, trying to accept her help when I don't even know what I need. I just want to shut it all away. I was so lost without my mother by my side. She was my everything, my light and my love. Her passing changed me forever; it scarred me beyond belief when I had to let go of her and my light and hide in the shadows. It really wasn't others who needed the light; it was me. I closed myself off from ever healing from this moment, and the moment when I originally lost my mother.

I didn't have the knowledge or the tools to listen to my inner voice, to speak up and say what my body, mind and spirit really needed. I was burdened by the notion that no one could fix this situation, no one could see this happening. No one could save her or me. I decided at the age of three to fix, help, make things better for those around me. I recall vague whispers in the shadows of people discussing and saying, "If only..."

If only what? I think to myself. Western medicine is not the be all, end all! It is just one of the things that help us break, repair, fix, or mend the body. It's up to us to become aware of the other components we need to communicate within ourselves to actually heal. We need to address the underlining cause—the whole picture.

As I come into the realization and that aha moment as I watch the video, I can finally see the bigger picture. The blinders are off, I am aware, and the time is now. As I sit on my chair in my living room, I reflect and digress back to what I was actually experiencing, as I came back to this realm.

I remember that all I had seen was me, naked, completely naked from the waist up, and there was this light, this unimaginable light. I slowly started waking up all of my senses, like a baby being born and learning their five senses all at once. I started seeing people like tiny little spotlights were being shown only on particular things. Out of the darkness and having the light shine on what is and has been right in front of me, ready to finally face it. Awakening!

Then the blinders finally came off and I could see. I could start seeing people crying around my stretcher. Then, I became aware of the smells of the alcohol swabs, and the hospital (I still fear those smells). I could see every single person; it was like tiny little lights of awareness. I look down again and I can see the leads and garbage, and the people in this frantic and horrific situation.

I died...oh my heavens...I died and came back.

Then another layer starts opening up for me. I go from only seeing and feeling the light to hearing and only seeing Cheryl, the nurse, and Cheryl, my mother. Behind them, are all the ones who have left and passed before me, the ones who remain in the light, the place of bliss! Amanda, and other friends who died before me, my family that I have lost, my ancestors, and my dog! All of them are standing in the light of love, here with me.

I never did initially thank my mother for pushing me back, for loving me enough to give me a new beginning, a new start. She forced me to let go of what doesn't serve me, the anguish, pain and suffering that I allowed to consume me. I am grateful she sent me back for my children, that she reminded me that I am—and always have been—safe, loved, protected, and wanted.

My children need me, and I need to be here for them. I need not be consumed with all of this suppressed hurt, pain, and anguish that has resided within me for far too long, the pain and unresolved emotions from losing my mother back when I was only three years old. I finally have the power to heal from the burden of life I pushed down.

I am starting to face my past and heal from the areas that cause me pain and suffering. I am my own person and I wish to be heard! No more crying in the shower to wash away the pain, trying to displace it to the depths of an abyss. That abyss is not down the drain, but in my core, my being and I need to hear myself to heal from all levels, body, mind and spirit!

I am starting to acknowledge that I do in fact, have a gift; I am a healer, always have been. I had just forgotten how to do it. I pushed it down and never wanted to address it, never wanted to know my true self, my true form. The fact is, we all have this power within each and every one of us. The power, the knowledge and insight to heal from within. Sometimes those lines of communication are lost and forgotten; pushed down and not to be seen, heard or addressed. Once these are finally brought to the surface of our conscious minds to be seen, accepted and faced, we are able to see it from a different perspective, view and different light—a light for love. To love oneself is enough to heal from whatever ails you, accept the love that surrounds you and to know you are worthy, and you are heard!

I am letting go of that blame I put onto myself; it wasn't my fault! None of it was my fault: my mother's death, or my own. I let go of the resentment towards the medical field, western medicine. I don't have to become a fixer to try to heal people; healing comes from within a person. I can help ease the pain and suffering they are facing by listening and doing my job, but by no means am I here to decide what path someone is supposed to take, what is meant for them in their journey of life.

***

After my mother died when I was three years of age, what I didn't do was let anyone—including myself—in to see the real Julia, the scared, lost girl full of pain and suffering. I did not let people see her, that little girl, which brought on the….

> Depression, pain and the reality of my MS
> I wasn't about to repeat history
> it's real and it's raw
> but finally, it had to be said for all to hear.
> A glimpse at the depths of my Abyss.
> And how I am no longer bound to it.

Chapter 42

I Have Been Heard

~  ~

As I share my story and reflect on what really did happen, I begin to illuminate some of the key components of this incredible journey to my new path. I replay the memories over and over within my thoughts. I am fascinated with the series of surreal events that transpired for me during all of this. This has been truly enlightening for me. The sheer magnitude of everything that happened, and the knowledge, acceptance, awareness and enlightenment I have gained from it all…it is beyond anything that words can actually describe.

While writing my book, I tried to find the right words to represent what I went through, but it only shows a fraction of everything I have experienced. I gave you, the reader, just a glimpse of the various layers that are associated with all of these significant moments throughout my life's journey. I would like to thank you, for holding space for me. I recognize that all of us, as individuals, have gone through an array of wild experiences.

JULIA EVANS

**We all need to go through, what we go through,
for that is the path of our life.**

To live a life the best we know how
Accepting and acknowledging that everything happens for a reason.
We all have a story
A unique story of our own unique experiences,
This is all part of our own existence.
Our own personal path and journey,
To enlightenment
And Bliss!

Finding your Voice
And having someone kind enough to listen
Is true Empowerment!

Trust the process
Live life to the absolute fullest!
You may not always get a second chance.
Find your joy and happiness in life,
For Happiness is…

Having a Voice

***

As old doors close,
New doors are opening to endless fields of possibilities.
This is only the beginning…

The Universe or a higher power has a bigger picture in store for me!
My story does not stop here;
Now that I have found my voice
I hope to help others find theirs through sharing my story,
Sharing my journey and my path to enlightenment of
Love & Light.

~ Blessed Be. We are all here for a Reason ~

About the Author

Julia Evan's background is in western medicine; she has a Bachelor of Science in Nursing and was a Registered Nurse for more than a decade. Only after years of suffering with Multiple Sclerosis and being faced with a traumatic near-death experience did she finally and truly open her heart and mind towards the notion of holistic healing and energy medicine.

As Julia immersed herself into learning about what she believed to be a new age form of healing, she began searching for an understanding of what it is and what she is actually capable of. She found a modality that really spoke to her and through that became a Certified BodyTalk Practitioner. This modality fuelled her passion and interest towards a journey of self healing and the ability to help others find their missing voice within themselves—to help find the root cause and underlying components that hold people back from truly healing. It has given her a new perspective on what "healing" is.

As she continues to broaden her knowledge and develop an even better understanding of the essence of BodyTalk, she now is able to view a person as a whole and focus on the priorities of what each individual needs to heal instead of defining them by their illness or disease.

Julia Evans is the loving mother of two, and is happily married to the love of her life and soulmate. Julia lives in the Land of the Living Skies and always has her eyes on the horizon, to endless possibilities.

Website: www.thelilynurse.com
Instagram: www.instagram.com/thelilynurse
Facebook: www.facebook.com/thelilynurse

www.ingramcontent.com/pod-product-compliance
Lightning Source LLC
Chambersburg PA
CBHW071953070526
44583CB00015B/1178